School and college

£3

gc

18/30

By the same author:

Values and Involvement in a Grammar School (1969)
School Organisation and Pupil Involvement (1973)

School and college
Studies of post-sixteen education

Ronald King
School of Education
University of Exeter

Routledge & Kegan Paul
London, Henley and Boston

First published in 1976
by Routledge & Kegan Paul Ltd
39 Store Street,
London WC1E 7DD,
Broadway House,
Newtown Road,
Henley-on-Thames,
Oxon RG9 1EN and
9 Park Street,
Boston, Mass. 02108, USA
Set in 10/11 Linotype Caledonia
and printed in Great Britain by
Willmer Brothers Limited, Birkenhead
© Ronald King 1976
ISBN 0 7100 8359 9 (c)
ISBN 0 7100 8360 2 (p)

Contents

Acknowledgments   *page* 7

Introduction   9

1 The expansion of post-sixteen education   12
2 The traditional sixth form   24
3 The changing sixth form   40
4 The sixth form centre   55
5 Sixth form colleges   63
6 Short-course comprehensives   81
7 Technical colleges   98
8 School-college cooperation   115
9 The tertiary college   126
10 Ideologies, identity and interest groups   150
11 Organisation and experience   173
12 Policy and practice   188

   Bibliography   204

   Index   217

Acknowledgments

The original research reported in this book was financed by the Social Science Research Council over the period 1970–3. For some of that time I was assisted by Bonnie Lucas and Gary Easthope. Joan Fry was a research associate over the whole period. I should like to thank her for the way she kept the research going during a long period of convalescence I was obliged to take, and for moving it in a new direction when our original plans were obviously not going to be fulfilled. My thanks also go to my secretary Karen Brewer and to my wife Rita, who between them prepared the typescript.

I also thank the many teachers, headteachers, lecturers, heads of department, principals, administrators, sixth formers and students, who gave their time for interviews and the completion of questionnaires, allowed us to be present at meetings and to observe them at work.

Introduction

There are two major issues concerning the education of the 16–19 age group: what they should learn and where they should learn it. It is the second of these, the form of post-sixteen education, that is dealt with in this book. However, the two issues are not independent, and some of their connections are explored. The recent expansion of education for this age group, outlined in chapter 1, has been accompanied by an increase in the number of forms of educational organisation they may attend, which now include integral sixth forms, sixth form units, sixth form centres, sixth form colleges, school-college consortia, technical colleges and tertiary colleges. The issue concerns their relative educational, economic and social merits.

Michael F. D. Young (1971) has suggested that sociologists of education should concentrate on sociological rather than educational problems. In contrast, Julienne Ford (1969) has echoed Alvin Gouldner's (1963) view that sociology should be concerned with human problems. These two views are not necessarily incompatible if the sociological perspective is one that regards the subject as being concerned with the study of human social action, where, following Weber (1948), this refers not only to social behaviour but also to its meaning to those carrying it out. Part of the sociologist's contribution to the study of social, or, more particularly, educational problems, is to consider who defines the situation as a problem and why they do so.

This study attempts to answer these questions in relation to what is defined by some as the problem of the form of post-

9

sixteen education. The groups who see a problem include teachers' and lecturers' associations, officials of local education authorities, as well as individual educationalists. Each interest group makes statements about the different forms of education, usually based upon what is supposed to happen in them, particularly in relation to the pupils' or students' experience. Existing and original research is used to get closer to what actually happens. The results, reported for each kind of organisation in chapters 2–9, provide several examples of the way in which social actions have unintended, and even unrecognised, consequences, in that what is supposed to happen sometimes does not.

The existing literature in this field mainly consists of the cases made for and against each of the organisational forms by those urging particular courses of action or sometimes justifying actions already taken. In addition there have been a number of large-scale surveys of student opinion. For reasons dealt with in chapter 11 these have a limited value in the discussion of the issue. The original research was an attempt to overcome some of their limitations, and was based upon twelve different schools and colleges. In doing this the usual considerations of sampling were not altogether applicable, in that some of the types of organisation existed in very small numbers. At the time there were twelve sixth form colleges in the whole of England and Wales, of which two contrasted examples were the subject of research. There were two so-called tertiary colleges, one of which was studied. In effect twelve case-studies were made, the results of which should be taken to indicate the possibility of particular methods of organisation and of student experience, rather than an indication of their frequency or distribution. These studies are collated in chapter 11.

The sets of ideas, or ideologies, used to defend and justify the different forms of organisation are compared in chapter 10. In an attempt to understand why particular groups feel there is a problem, their ideologies are considered in relation to the interests of the group and the social identities of its members. The two principal ideologies involved are those of the sixth form as part of the school as a community, and that of the technical college as an association. These concern not only the form of educational organisations but also the relationships between teacher and taught, and the nature of education itself.

This book was not written to advocate a particular form of

post-sixteen education. It is an attempt to illuminate and understand the issues. However, as a result of that attempt some suggestions are made about possible future policy in chapter 12. It should be stressed that these arise from the studies reported, and did not precede or guide them. The value judgments and choices, which underlie any policy, are those made by the interest groups in this area of education.

Chapter 1

The expansion of post-sixteen education

There are more young people over sixteen receiving full-time education in Britain than ever before. This is part of the general expansion of British education which has taken place since the end of the Second World War, and is related to two factors which in educational jargon have come to be known as the 'bulge' and the 'trend'. The first refers to an increase in the birth rate, the second to the increasing tendency for young people to choose to stay in full-time education.

This expansion of education for the 16–19 age group has been accompanied by an increase in the number of forms of educational organisation catering for them. In the early 1960s most of these students were members of sixth forms in maintained grammar, direct grant and independent schools. Ten years later less than half of the seventeen year olds in full-time education attended such schools. The rest went to technical colleges or colleges of further education, and comprehensive schools of several different kinds. These include the all-through 11–18 school with an integral sixth form, sixth forms in upper schools with recruitment at twelve, thirteen or even fourteen, sixth form colleges catering for post-sixteen students only, and sixth form centres where the sixth form not only recruits from its own fifth year but also from those of other schools.

The bulge

When birth rates are plotted as a graph an increase over several years appears as a bulge. There have been two bulges in the birth rate in the post-war period. The first occurred immediately after the war and was at its peak in 1947 when 19 per cent more live births occurred than in 1945. The children of this first bulge entered the primary schools in the early 1950s, the secondary schools in the later 1950s and higher education in the mid-1960s.

The birth rate fell in the 1950s until an upward trend in 1956 led to the second bulge which reached its peak in 1964 when the number of live births (875,000) almost reached that of 1947 (881,000). The children of this second bulge were passing through the primary schools in the 1960s and are now in the secondary schools, where the peak will pass in the early 1980s.

It is outside the scope of this discussion to deal in detail with the cause of these bulges. Because of the delicacy of the subject even the specialist research gives only tentative answers. Demobilisation and the resumption of married life were likely factors relating to the first bulge. More speculatively, the affluence of the early 1960s has been suggested to account for the second. However, the relevant educational point about these fluctuations in the birth rate is that the number of 16–19 year olds in full-time education is related to the greater number of people in that age range.

The trend

The bulge does not, however, completely account for this increase; it is also due to a rise in the proportion of young people choosing to remain in full-time education. There was a 5 per cent increase in the number of seventeen year olds between 1961 and 1973 (see Table 1.1), but the number of them in full-time education increased by 115 per cent over the same period. The trend is therefore a more important factor than the bulge. In 1961 14.1 per cent of seventeen year olds were in full-time education; by 1973 this had risen to 28.8 per cent (see Table 1.1). Explanations of the trend are more relevant than those for the bulge but are just as speculative.

In the early 1950s there was some concern about the low rate at which pupils remained at school after sixteen, which lead to the Central Advisory Committee's report 'Early Leaving' in 1954. The Committee's survey of a sample of the 1946 intake into

Table 1.1 *Seventeen year olds in full-time education, 1961 and 1973, England and Wales*

	Percentage of age group attending	
	1961	1973
Modern	0.2	0.7
Grammar	7.1	7.1
Technical schools	0.4	0.3
Comprehensive	0.3	7.8
All maintained schools	8.1	16.6
Direct grant	1.2	1.7
Independent efficient	2.1	2.4
Other independent	0.2	0.1
All independent schools	3.5	4.2
All schools	11.7	20.8
Technical colleges	2.4	8.0
All full-time students and pupils	14.1	28.8
All seventeen year olds	635,000	669,000

Derived from 'Statistics of Education', DES, 1961–73.

grammar schools (then virtually the only maintained schools providing post-sixteen education) established the extent of early leaving and suggested some of the conditions associated with it.

A first set of conditions concerned the homes of early leavers. They tended to be overcrowded, with inadequate provision for doing homework. Perhaps more important, early leavers were often the children of low wage earners.

The second set of conditions suggested by the report concerned the occupational market. Many leavers left because a job was made available to them. This factor was confirmed by the Social Survey of the Crowther report in 1970 which linked it with the level of family incomes. Where this was low the chance of a pupil taking a job that became available was very high.

A third set of conditions concerned the early leavers' experience of school, which was one of dissatisfaction with having to conform, with having to wear a uniform and do as they were told by the teachers. The later survey of the Crowther report confirmed this picture as did that reported by Case and Ross

(1965), which found that early leavers were less punctual and rated less obedient and amenable to discipline by their teachers, compared with those who stayed on. A case study (King, 1969) of a single grammar school showed that early leavers were only to a small degree involved in many aspects of school life. However, this experience of school was not necessarily due to their level of ability. The 'Early Leaving' report showed that a large proportion of early leavers were in the top third of eleven-plus successes. Both the Crowther report and Case and Ross found that many early leavers expressed some regret at not having stayed on.

A fourth and less important element suggested by all three surveys was that of the influence of friends. Early leavers often had friends who themselves left school early and were in employment with money to spend on themselves. This was the 'pull of the peer group'.

The trend towards more staying on in education after sixteen may be explained by examining the changes in the three more important conditions since the early 1950s. Despite the continued existence of many poor families the general standard of living has improved. There has been a decline in the traditional apprenticeship system and less opportunities for young people to take up low-skill jobs. The proportion of unskilled occupations fell from 12 per cent in 1951 to 6.6 per cent in 1971.

There are no surveys which enable a comparison to be made of changes in the internal organisation of schools since the 1950s but it is commonly assumed that some of the 'reforms' advocated and implemented by headteachers such as Harry Davies (1965) have been carried out in many schools. These include the relaxation of school uniform and school rules. An additional factor has been the blurring of the distinction between fifth and sixth form studies. Before the introduction of the General Certificate of Education in 1951 entry into the sixth form was generally confined to those who had at least the General Schools Certificate and who wished to proceed to the Higher Schools Certificate. It is now common for pupils over sixteen and defined as sixth formers to be retaking O levels they have failed or wish to improve on, to be taking new O levels, and in some cases not be following an A level course (about 11 per cent of seventeen year olds in 1974) (DES, 1961–74).

These explanations of the trend can be slightly refined by an examination of the social origins of early leavers. The 'Early

Leaving' report showed that they were often from working class homes, particularly where the father had a semi- or unskilled manual occupation. A comparison of the social class origins of the early leavers of the report with those leaving in the early 1960s was made by Kelsall (1963). This showed that although the early leavers were still characteristically working class the rate at which they left had been greatly reduced, particularly among the more able, so that the gap between the social classes had been narrowed.

The late 1950s saw the emergence of what were called, originally by Ferdinand Zweig (1961), the 'newly affluent' workers. These were the skilled and semi-skilled manual workers who began to earn high wages in the manufacturing industries, especially those of consumer goods. The studies carried out by Goldthorpe et al. (1967) of a sample of such workers in the car industry in Luton showed that although they had not become middle class in their life styles, they had become more home-centred. Toomey (1970), in a study of workers in a Medway town, found that the children of the more affluent, home-centred workers' families had a longer educational life than those from less affluent, traditional working class families.

A number of surveys have shown that both older pupils and their parents have a very strong calculative orientation towards education. They see school as the avenue to the occupational structure. The young school leavers in the survey commissioned by the Schools Council (Morton-Williams and Finch, 1968) placed, 'Teach you things which will be of direct use to you in a job' as the most important school objective. Another survey (King, 1973a), of over 7,000 pupils in different kinds of secondary school, found that 94 per cent agreed that 'The main reason for working hard is to get a good job', and 88 per cent agreed that 'Passing exams is the way to get on.' The reward for doing well in school and for staying on is a better, more desirable job.

Several surveys, including those directed by Glass (1954) in the early 1950s, have suggested that educational success is an important element in the upward social mobility of children from working class homes to middle class occupations. An effect of greater affluence on some working class parents may have been to make the holding of such ambitions for their children more acceptable. Young and Willmott (1957) in their study in the 1950s of Bethnal Green, a working class area of London, found that some adults had not taken up the grammar school places they had been offered for fear of their 'going above their station'. But Douglas (1964), in his longitudinal study of children born in 1946, found the refusal of a grammar school place to be very rare.

The trend towards a longer educational life has continued steadily since the end of the Second World War, although the rate of increase has slowed a little in the last few years. It is usually assumed that this trend will continue, and a great deal of educational planning is based upon this assumption. However, there have been times when the rate of staying on after sixteen has declined. The national study of Olive Banks (1955) and a case study of a single school (King, 1969) showed high rates of early leaving in both world wars to be associated with the high demand for youth labour and a relaxation of the tied-grant system which kept the grant holder in school with a commitment to train for teaching. The economic crisis of the early 1930s was also associated with high rates of early leaving. With lowered family incomes some pupils left school to try to get jobs and because their parents could not afford to keep them there.

These unpleasant possibilities are left aside in the forecasts of the level of the trend. Those made in 'Social Trends' (Nissel, 1974) were of 30.3 per cent of seventeen year olds attending school by 1980, and 35.7 per cent by 1985. If the expansion of numbers in colleges of further education were at the same rate the figures for all forms of education would be 41.5 per cent and 48.8 per cent respectively. This presents the prospect of a doubling of the number of 16–19 year olds in full-time education in the next ten years.

Comprehensive schools

The early arguments for comprehensive secondary education concentrated as much upon what were thought to be the defects of the selective system of grammar and modern schools as upon the supposed merits of comprehensive schools. Drawing on the surveys of the 'Early Leaving', Crowther and, later, Robbins reports, a large wastage of educational talent had been shown to occur, particularly among working class children. This wastage has been attributed to the operation of the secondary selection procedure, shown by Douglas (1964), Floud and Halsey (1957) and others to contain a social selection element favouring middle class children, particularly at the borderline level, and to the middle class value system of the grammar school, which Jackson and Marsden (1962) and a previous case study (King, 1969) have shown to be unacceptable to some working class pupils. A major ideological justification of the comprehensive system is that it will widen educational opportunities and reduce the class gap in educational attainment.

The move towards a national system of comprehensive schools is slow. There were 10 such schools in 1950, 130 in 1960 and 2,273 in 1974, with an attendance of 60 per cent of all children in maintained schools. Pupils over sixteen may be educated in a number of different forms of comprehensive school. The Department of Education and Science's Circular 10/65 requested local authorities to prepare and submit plans for reorganisation on comprehensive lines, and listed six acceptable forms of organisation. These were:

1 the 'orthodox' comprehensive with an 11–18 age range – the 'all through' school;

2 a two tier system of a junior comprehensive which transfers all pupils at fourteen or fifteen to a senior comprehensive;

3 a two tier system of junior comprehensives from which some pupils transfer to a senior comprehensive at thirteen or fourteen and the rest remain in the junior – a version of this method was the original 'Leicestershire plan' (see Griffiths, 1971);

4 a two tier system of junior comprehensives from which some pupils transfer at thirteen or fourteen to one of two kinds of senior school only one of which provides courses beyond the school leaving age;

5 11–16 short-course comprehensive schools from which some leave to enter sixth form colleges – the 'Croydon plan', although it was never used there (see Edwards, 1970a);

6 a three tier system for the whole of school education with transfer from primary schools at eight or nine to comprehensive middle schools, and then at twelve or fourteen to comprehensive senior schools.

The circular pointed out that methods 3 and 4 are not fully comprehensive as they retain separation of children after thirteen or fourteen, and must be regarded as interim stages only. In addition to these schemes the Secretary of State in 1969 accepted proposals involving the use of technical colleges as centres for all post-sixteen education in Exeter and Barnstaple.

Of the six schemes approved in the circular the all-through school is most common but more recent plans include more middle school and two tier systems. There were nearly fifty sixth form colleges in 1974 and many more are planned.

The comprehensive schools' contribution to post-sixteen education has increased enormously in the last ten years (see Table 1.1). A substantial minority of comprehensive sixth formers do not take A level courses. Nearly a quarter are taking or retaking O level, CSE and other examinations. However, although there are now more pupils in comprehensive schools than in grammar schools, the latter still made the bigger contribution to the education of older pupils in 1972. The lower rate of staying on in the comprehensive sector is related to the social characteristics of their pupils. There are very few areas where comprehensive schools do not co-exist with grammar schools, and it is not surprising that the National Foundation for Educational Research (Monks, 1968) found that working class children were over-represented in comprehensive schools, and that they seldom had a reasonable proportion of children in the higher ability ranges.

However, the contribution of comprehensive schools is likely to increase. Apart from the bulge and the trend the rate of increase largely depends on two related factors. First, the availability of money; the move away from the 11–18 school is partly due to the high costs of the new buildings thought essential to the arrangement (although some are run on dual sites). Second, the power relationship between local authorities and the central authority, and their relative acceptance of the comprehensive principle. Whilst there is no tendency for the local authorities which are actively going comprehensive to be Labour controlled, the more reluctant are either independent or Conservative controlled. The existing Education Acts empower the local education authorities to organise the form of the education in their areas; hence the Circular 10/65 only requested the authorities to submit plans. Circular 10/70 issued under the Conservative government cancelled 10/65. This removal of central pressure was associated with a slowing in the rate of comprehensive reorganisation. The rate may be expected to increase with the rescinding of Circular 10/70 by the new Labour Secretary of State and the introduction of Circular 4/74 which instructed local authorities which have retained selection to submit information about reorganisation before the end of 1974.

Grammar schools

The increase in the number of comprehensive schools is associated with a decrease in the number of maintained grammar schools (1,284 in 1960, 675 in 1974). Despite their fewer numbers these schools still make an important contribution to post-sixteen education, however, and the effects of the bulge and the trend have kept fairly constant their contribution since 1961 (see Table 1.1). Grammar school sixth formers are predominantly middle class. About 34 per cent have fathers with manual occupations compared with 51 per cent in comprehensive schools, and they mainly follow A level courses; only one in twelve does not (Morton-Williams et al., 1970).

The future contribution of grammar schools depends on some of the same factors relating to the expansion of comprehensive schools. If their numbers continue to be reduced at the rate they have over the last ten years they could all be gone by the end of the century.

Other maintained schools

The number of secondary modern schools has declined (3,887 in 1961, 1,509 in 1974) as the number of comprehensives has increased. Although they make an important contribution to the number of candidates for O level and CSE they also retain a small number of pupils over sixteen some of whom take A level examinations (see Table 1.1).

The technical schools never did form a significant third sector of the so called tripartite system of secondary education. Their number fell from 228 in 1961 to 35 in 1974. Their sixth formers mainly follow A level courses.

Independent schools

There are about 2,500 independent schools in England and Wales and they vary from small day proprietary schools for mixed juniors to large and sometimes ancient boarding schools known as public schools. About 560 are currently classified as catering for pupils of secondary school age.

Although they are small in number compared with maintained schools, they provide nearly as much post-sixteen education as the comprehensive schools (see Table 1.1). Their high rate of staying on is related to the social origins of their pupils, who are mainly middle class. Among sixth formers in boarding schools 96 per cent have fathers with non-manual occupations (Morton-Williams et al., 1970).

It is not possible to define exactly what is meant by a public school, but characteristically they are single sex boarding schools which are members of one or more of the protective associations of the high status sector of private education, including the Head Masters' Conference; in all about 200 schools.

The future of these schools was the subject of the Public Schools Commission set up in 1965. In its 'First Report' the commission recommended the integration of 'suitable and willing' public schools into the maintained sector of education, by their admitting LEA assisted pupils, assessed to be in need of boarding, to at least half their places, by the end of a seven year period. A Boarding Schools Corporation would manage the integration programme.

As with the more modest integration proposed by the Fleming report in 1944, this report has had little effect. In addition to the subsequent change to a Conservative government with no ideological objections to private education, neither the public schools nor the LEAs greatly favour the proposals, and the high cost of the integration is likely to deter any Labour government in the near future.

There are 176 direct grant schools catering for secondary school pupils. These schools occupy an anomalous position in the educational system in that they are financed from both private and public sources. In return for accepting a quota of pupils whose fees are paid by LEAs each school receives a grant directly from the Department of Education and Science. The 'Second Report' of the Public Schools Commission (1970) suggested that these schools should be given the option of becoming parts of comprehensive systems or becoming entirely privately financed. Very few direct grant schools have voluntarily entered into reorganisation schemes. Following the return of a Conservative government in 1970 there were no attempts to implement the recommendations of the report, but in 1975 the Labour Secretary of State announced that to be the last year of the award of the direct grant.

The public and direct grant schools form a small fraction of the total number of independent schools. The numbers of these schools have fallen by about a thousand in the last decade. This is a reflection of the financial precariousness of some of these schools which do not have the trusts, covenants and charity reliefs which protect the public schools, or the DES allowances made to the direct grant schools.

Technical colleges

The term technical college has been used to describe a variety of institutions. Following the White Paper of 1966 30 polytechnics have been created from some of the high status technical institutions. Apart from a small number of national colleges, art and agricultural colleges, the rest are designated either area or local colleges, 480 in all. These are not necessarily called technical colleges but are also known as colleges of further education and commercial colleges. They provide a wide range of courses both full- and part-time, as well as sandwich and day release courses.

It is these colleges that make an important contribution to full-time post-sixteen education, greater than that of grammar schools and rivalling that of comprehensive schools, a contribution that has more than trebled since 1961 (see Table 1.1).

Their full-time students come from working class backgrounds more often than sixth formers in grammar schools (55 per cent compared with 34 per cent). They come to college from a variety of schools; grammar 23 per cent, modern 47 per cent, independent and direct grant 20 per cent (Morton-Williams et al., 1970). They follow a wide range of courses including the usual academic subjects, business studies, commercial and secretarial, engineering and technical, nursing and child care, catering and hairdressing. Apart from O and A level examinations students also take the Ordinary National Diploma and professional qualifying examinations.

Most independent schools are single sex schools, as are two-thirds of grammar schools. A minority of comprehensive schools are single sex but virtually all technical colleges are mixed sex institutions.

The expansion of post-sixteen education

Expansion and diversity

Children up to the age of sixteen are legally obliged to attend school, but beyond that age education is voluntary. The bulge in the birth rate and the trend towards a longer educational life have lead to an unprecedented expansion of post-sixteen education. This has been permitted by policies which assume that educational opportunities should be provided for those who wish to have them. This was made explicit for higher education by the Robbins report in 1963: '... courses should be made available for all those who are qualified by ability and attainment to pursue them and who wish to do so.'

The expansion of the education of 16–19 year olds has fed that of higher education and has given rise to a diversity of institutions within the public domain. The chapters that follow concern the emergence of these different forms of school and college. The cases for and against each of them are presented and examined using research results and other material. Particular attention is paid to those whose arguments are seldom heard and whose opinions are often presumed – the students and pupils.

Chapter 2

The traditional sixth form

The sixth form is the crown of the grammar school, almost its justification. From the sixth form will come the scholars and the administrators. Here the intelligent minority will be trained to take responsibility. Here the thinkers are at home. Such, outside the profession, is the common stereotype.

Frances Stevens, 'The Living Tradition'

Frances Stevens neatly describes the traditional idea of the sixth form. Two aspects of the idea will be explored. First, and briefly, its origins; second, and more extensively, the reality behind it in terms of the experience and opinions of teachers and pupils in sixth forms.

The idea of the sixth form

Many of the established ideas in English secondary education have their origins in the public schools of the nineteenth century. The ancient foundation schools had been strongly criticised during the period of the Napoleonic wars and after. The criticisms included those of narrow curriculum and poor teaching, but much concern was expressed about the delinquent behaviour of their upper middle class pupils, leading on several occasions to rebellions. One, at Winchester in 1808, was only ended by the intervention of the militia with bayonets (Mack, 1938).

The structural reforms particularly associated with Thomas Arnold of Rugby were mainly intended to assert social control and obtain order. The private boarding houses were incorporated into the schools and formed the basis of the House system. Secular and sacred authority were fused in the elevation of chapel attendance as a major element of school life. As Weinberg (1967) puts it, 'God almost became the public school interpretation of the correct social order.' When new schools were later established, to meet the demands by the newly emergent middle classes for a gentleman's education for their sons, they were built in rural areas, not only for economic reasons but also to isolate the pupils from the temptations of town. These and other changes cohered around the idea of the school as a community, one of the most powerful ideas in English education and one that has an important part to play in the later discussion of forms of post-sixteen education.

As with many successful innovations those in the nineteenth century public schools became institutionalised and came to be regarded as being intrinsically worthwhile. Measures taken to establish control were valued not only as a means to this end but also as ends in themselves. The social isolation of the schools as communities of men and boys with similar social origins, the tight organisation of all pupil activities, and the emphasis on conformity, both formal and informal, were justified in terms of their generating the qualities required in the pupils' eventual careers as army officers and senior Civil Servants, often in the outposts of the Empire. This was the fusion of education for leadership and what Royston Lambert (1966) was later to call, 'the stiff upper lip syndrome'.

The idea of the sixth form as what Arnold called 'an aristocracy of talent and worth ... an organised and responsible nobility' (Briggs, 1965) was part of these reforms, and like them was integrated and institutionalised within the concept of the school as a community. He and other headmasters turned their older pupils 'from rebel leaders into junior officers and so curbing the disorder common before his time' (Edwards, 1970a). Arnold reformed the prefectorial system so that prefects became 'instruments for carrying his moral ideas into the school' (Mack, 1938).

These ideas about the nature of the school and of the sixth form were rapidly adopted by the new grammar schools set up by the local authorities after the 1902 Education Act. This followed from the appointment of public school masters to the headships of some of the new schools, but also from the general acceptance of the public schools as an appropriate model. Brian Jackson lays the blame for this on the influence of Robert Morant, the chief Civil Servant of the new Board of Education. An ex-public schoolboy, his purpose was to make sure that '... the education system of the twentieth century should be modelled on schools like his own' (Jackson, 1963). In his analysis of the situation Duncan Mitchell (1964) suggests that the established middle classes were broadly satisfied with the provision of education for their children before the Act and were determined that any new form of education would not constitute an alternative or rival, and thus made every effort to make sure it was a pale imitation of their own, to be used should adverse circumstances demand.

Olive Banks (1955) expands this analysis to show that following the 1902 Education Act most of the educational interest groups, including the teachers' union, began to accept the idea that the new grammar schools should concentrate on the provision of liberal, if not classical, education, so that the prospect held out by the short-lived higher elementary schools which specialised in science, mathematics and technical subjects for older pupils, of a distinctly different kind of secondary education, was not fulfilled. Nor only was the public school precedent followed with respect to the content of education (see Taylor et al., 1974) but also its form. Following its foundation in 1907, one maintained grammar school had by 1914 introduced school uniforms, compulsory games, house and prefectorial systems (King, 1969).

Although the sixth forms of the public schools were often a large proportion of the total school population, those of the new grammar schools are best described for the period up to 1920 in the phrase of Edwards (1970a): '... a thin top soil of advanced work'. After a slow growth in the period up to the Second World War, there was a rapid increase in the rate of staying, a trend that has already been commented upon, and which underlies many important considerations.

The apogee of the official acceptance of the traditional idea of the sixth form is found in the report of the Crowther committee (1959) which urged the continued expansion of post-sixteen education. In chapter 21 they distinguished five marks of the sixth form: close links with the universities, subject-mindedness, independent work, intellectual discipleship between teacher and taught, and social responsibility in the life of the school. Since that time all of these marks have changed or have been questioned. Changes in the idea and nature of the sixth form infuse the changes in forms of education provided for 16–19 year olds.

Teachers' ideas of the sixth form

The Schools Council commissioned the then Government Social Survey to carry out an investigation of sixth form pupils and teachers (Morton-Williams et al., 1970). A representative sample of over 1,000 sixth form teachers were interviewed. These were from 154 schools including maintained grammar, technical and comprehensive schools, independent and direct grant schools. In addition 153 headteachers, from the same schools, were also interviewed.

They were asked to describe the benefits to pupils of staying on into the sixth form. Headteachers and teachers from all types of school considered the development of responsibility and maturity the most important benefit. It was mentioned by 85 per cent of headteachers and 79 per cent of teachers. Thus one of the essential elements in the traditional idea of the sixth form is still strongly supported. The benefits relating to academic processes, including working on their own, thinking for themselves, acquiring qualifications for university entrance or getting a job or studying in depth, were mentioned only about half as frequently (Table 2.1).

Table 2.1 *Pupils', teachers' and headteachers' views on the benefits of staying on into the sixth form* (%)

	Heads	Teachers	Pupils
Sense of responsibility, time to mature	85	79	42
Different attitude to work, independent study	45	41	16
Qualifications for university or job	30	36	25
Thorough knowledge of one subject, working in depth	32	24	24

Source: Morton-Williams et al., 1970, pp. 248–9.

The primacy given to these expressive aspects of responsibility and maturity was also apparent in another study (King, 1973a) (which involved interviews of 34 headteachers of schools with sixth forms) as the following quotation from a pamphlet provided by a comprehensive school headteacher shows: 'It [the sixth form] will be composed of young adults. Adult demands will be made upon you and adult responsibility will be expected from you.'

The Schools Council survey also asked teachers to rate for importance suggested objectives of the sixth form. The results are presented in Table 2.2. To varying degrees they endorse four of the five marks of the sixth form suggested by the Crowther report. The characteristics of close links with the universities (items 2 and 7) and independent work (items 1 and 11) are clearly supported. However, the idea of subject-mindedness received less support (items 20, 29), as did that of social responsibility in the life of the school (items 6 and 22). Of particular interest in relation to the Arnoldian model of the sixth form is the modest ranking of 'help them to develop their powers of leadership' (item 22).

Sixth formers' ideas of the sixth form

The Schools Council survey also interviewed over 4,000 sixth formers drawn from the same 154 schools as the teachers. When they were asked about the benefits of staying into the sixth form they too placed the development of responsibility and maturity as the most important, but it was mentioned only half as frequently (Table 2.1). Indeed, most of the benefits were rated lower by pupils than teachers.

The sixth formers were also asked to rate various aspects of sixth form courses (Table 2.2). Most of these were very similar to those asked of their teachers, and so it should be possible to make comparisons between the two groups. Unfortunately, this can only be done in a limited way since the results are reported as percentages of teachers rating items as important, but as percentages of pupils rating them as extremely important. These reservations having been made it can be suggested that there are significant differences between the pupils and their teachers' opinions in certain respects.

The sixth formers' stronger instrumental orientation in terms

The traditional sixth form

of passing examinations and getting a job is shown in their higher
ranking of items 8, 12, 21 and 28. Their weaker expressive
orientation in terms of changing attitudes and personality is
shown in their lower ratings of items 4, 5, 6 and 10.

Table 2.2 *Pupils' and teachers' rankings of the importance
of aspects of sixth form courses*

	Provide, help with, encourage obtain or develop:	Rankings Teachers	Pupils
1	Independent study	1	3
2	Information about higher education	2	2
3	Clear written expression	3	10
4	Personality and character	4	8
5	Questioning attitude	5	22
6	Experience of responsibility	6	9
7	Chance of university place	7	12
8	A level success	8	4
9	Oral expression	9	11
10	Considerate attitudes	10	21
11	Independence	11	7
12	Careers information	12	1
13	Wide subject choice	13	5
14	Enjoyment and stimulation	14	17
15	Not to conform unthinkingly	15	18
16	Think out desired achievements	16	13
17	Interest in non-examination subjects	17	16
18	Interest and understanding of current affairs	18	20
19	Confidence and ease with people	19	14
20	Study in depth	20	19
21	Careers advice	21	6
22	Powers of leadership	22	26
23	How to behave socially	23	23
24	Community service	24	29
25	Numeracy	25	28
26	New subjects introduced	26	25
27	Sex education	27	24
28	Things of use in career or starting work	28	15
29	Thorough knowledge of two or three subjects	29	31
30	Knowledge of rates, taxes, etc	30	27
31	How to bring up children, home repairs, etc	31	30

Derived from Morton-Williams et al., 1970, pp. 122, 273.

Some of the Crowther report's marks of the sixth form are recognised by sixth formers as further results show (Table 2.3).

Table 2.3 *Sixth formers' views on the sixth form* (%)

	Agree that sixth form:	
	was different to rest of school	should be more different
1 Better and close relations between pupils and teachers, more adult treatment	53	12
2 More independent approach to work required	37	5
3 More privileges	41	
4 More freedom and independence	24	20
5 More responsibility and authority	31	5

Source: Morton-Williams et al., 1970, pp. 77, 80.

Item 1, the most commonly mentioned difference between the sixth form and the rest of the school, could be interpreted as referring to Crowther's pupil-teacher discipleship. Although privilege and freedom are judged to be more extensive in the sixth form, there is also a desire for more of them. This is confirmed in the replies to another set of questions in which the sixth formers were asked to give their complaints about the sixth form. The most common, mentioned by 31 per cent of pupils, were to many restrictions and regulations, and not enough freedom and privileges.

The prefectorial system

The prefectorial system is integral to the traditional idea of the sixth form. The prefect-fagging system existed in the public schools before Arnold's time. It operated almost independently of the masters and headmasters, and prefects were often the leaders of rebellion, particularly when their autonomy was threatened as at Winchester in 1808 when the headmaster tried to make a Saint's day a school working day without consulting them (Mack, 1938).

Arnold's reform of the prefectorial system was central to his whole method, which was to make old forms serve new purposes:

> There were two halves to Arnold's transformation of the prefect system. He gave his sixth form both more and less independence than they had had before. On the one hand, he trusted his prefects implicitly and gave them power and importance they had seldom had before. Prefects became young gods. At the same time he made them realize what few had understood before his day, that a prefect must be loyal to ideals and that power implied willingness to spread these ideals abroad. (Mack, 1938, p. 273)

The prefectorial system has become institutionalised in the maintained secondary schools. In a survey of 72 such schools only 4 claimed not to have prefects (King, 1973a). However, these schools did have pupils who had some formal authority over other pupils. In effect the schools had only removed the title of prefect, not the office.

Interviews with the headteachers of the schools showed that they saw the system serving the same two important purposes that Arnold introduced in his reforms. Prefects were to be role-models and to act as agents of social control. The former was expressed in phrases such as, 'act as an example to younger pupils', 'set the tone of the school'. The latter was explicit in the commonly used phrase, 'help maintain order'.

Some headteachers had clear images of the ideal qualities of prefects. They should act in an adult manner with tact, politeness, tolerance, common sense and humanity. They were chosen because they were thought to have these qualities, at least in potential, and the indicators of their existence were good behaviour, good performance in school work and games.

In most schools only the older pupils were eligible for selection as prefects. In some, particularly those for girls, the role was virtually ascribed in that all a given age group were made prefects. In others the method of selection was much less clear. However, the headteacher was always involved and the teachers nearly always. In about a fifth of the schools the existing or retiring prefects played a part, but in only four schools did younger pupils participate. Apart from the general supervision of other

31

pupils, prefects' other duties included acting as guides to visitors and being stewards at school functions. The control of prefects, what was to be done, when and by whom, was in the hands of the head prefect in about half of the schools, otherwise, control was exercised by the headteacher or more commonly, the deputy head.

Prefects were often given privileges over other pupils of the same age. The most common was exemption from the dinner queue or being allowed to be first in the queue. The most prized was an exclusive prefect's room.

Authority relationships in English secondary schools are often ritualised. The office of prefect was frequently marked by special emblems, ties, badges, sashes and girdles. Prefects were often marked off as a special status group in the ceremonials of school assembly. In nearly half the schools they occupied special positions. It was sometimes a prefectorial duty to read the lesson and, less commonly, the whole prefect group processed both in and out. A large proportion of schools held prefect induction ceremonies, usually during a school assembly, or in a few cases as the focus of a special assembly. In most cases the passing of the headteacher's authority was symbolised by the shaking of hands and the presentation emblems of office. In a small number of schools the new prefects swore an oath of allegiance to the school or signed a special prefects' book.

Only the grammar and comprehensive schools in the sample had sixth forms. In these schools, particularly the grammar schools, the prefects had more responsibilities and more sanctions, and were more often under the control of a head prefect, indicating that the full expression of the prefectorial system is thought to be conditional upon the existence of a sixth form. Perhaps not surprisingly, boys' grammar schools were closest to the public school archetype in having most duties and sanctions, many privileges, and also by being the most ritualised.

The prefects' and other pupils' perspectives on the system were investigated in a case study of a boys' grammar school (King, 1969). The headteachers' views on the social control and role-model functions were confirmed in that 78 per cent of the pupils agreed it was the prefect's job to help run the schools and 83 per cent that they should set a good example, although this was considered less important by older pupils.

The effectiveness of prefects as role-models was partially tested by asking pupils how much they would try to be like them if they wanted to get on better in school. Prefects were found to be as effective as subject teachers in this respect. Furthermore, those second year pupils who identified with prefects in this way were more highly committed to the school than others of the same age.

Pupils were asked to give their opinions on the criteria used in the selection of prefects (Table 2.4). It was possible to check some of their views against the facts. Prefects were more often members of school teams than others of the same age, and they did take part in more school activities, but they were no better at school work. The results show that older pupils in the school had a more accurate idea of the criteria of selection than younger ones.

Table 2.4 *Pupils' opinions on the criteria of prefect selection* (%)

	2nd year	5th year	6th year	7th and 8th year	All pupils
Are good at games	8.6	26.5	32.3	37.5	24.1
Are good at school work	63.4	41.4	32.3	25.0	43.4
Do not get into trouble	37.8	29.9	23.1	15.0	28.5
Get on well with teachers	32.9	40.2	47.7	56.4	42.0
Take part in activities	59.0	52.9	56.9	55.0	51.1

Source: King, 1969, p. 120.

The most important advantage of being a prefect was considered to be having a better chance of a university place or getting a good job. This was held more commonly by older pupils and is based upon such obvious signs as the request for information about the holding of official school positions in the UCCA application forms for university entrance. The two other important advantages were thought to be knowing how to handle people better and getting special privileges.

The main disadvantage was considered to be having to do time-consuming duties, followed by difficulties in friendships and having to set a good example, which indicate the negative side of being agents of social control and role-models. Older pupils, and prefects particularly, regarded having to set a good example more of a disadvantage than younger ones.

B

Edwards (1970a) has referred to Arnold's prefects as junior officers. In the one school studied here they were more like NCOs in their manner. The official sanctions available to them were the giving of lines and detentions. In addition many of them used threats, abuse, contempt and ridicule in their relationships with younger pupils.

Apart from this detail of practice, these surveys clearly show the continued existence in maintained secondary schools of prefectorial systems very much like the Arnoldian prototype, and its special association with the sixth form. However, as later discussions will show, its legitimacy and continued existence are at least being questioned.

The sixth form at St Trad's

St Trad's is the pseudonym of one of twelve institutions of post-sixteen education which were the subject of surveys in 1971. As a preliminary to these a number of tape recorded interviews were carried out with students in full-time education. The surveys drew upon the approaches and methods developed in connection with previous research into the organisation of secondary schools and pupils' experience of school (King, 1973a).

One purpose of these new surveys was to obtain information about the organisation of pupil or student behaviour and learning in the various institutions of post-sixteen education. The sixth form at St Trad's grammar school was chosen because organisationally it corresponded very closely to the median or most common kind of mixed grammar school found in the sample used in the previous investigation (King, 1973a). The organization of each of the twelve institutions was investigated using a number of techniques. The headteacher or principal, or his delegate, completed a questionnaire giving some basic facts about the school or college, and sent copies of prospectuses and other documents. The headteacher or principal was later interviewed, as were senior members of staff and others with posts of special responsibility. These included vice-principals, deputy heads, senior masters and mistresses, heads of department, tutors, counsellors and student liaison officers. Where there was a students' union or guild a senior student officer was also interviewed. During the visits to carry out the interviews, observations were made as part of a tour of the plant, and informal contacts made with students. In some cases direct observations of teaching situations were made.

Another purpose of the surveys was to investigate the pupils' or students' experience of school or college. All sixth formers or full-time students in the same age range were given a questionnaire which was completed during the investigators' visit. The items were based upon the interviews already mentioned and upon those used in previous research (King, 1973a). The questionnaire was completed anonymously, and as an extra guarantee of its confidential nature an envelope was provided in which the respondent sealed the completed questionnaire.

St Trad's was a mixed grammar school of nearly 900 pupils of which just over 200 were in the sixth. (Although only about a third of grammar schools are mixed, a mixed school was chosen for comparison purposes as most other forms of post-sixteen education are co-educational.) Entry into the sixth form proper was confined to those with at least four O level passes. Those without could enter a group called lower sixth general where they prepared for the winter session of O level examinations. The group ceased to exist after this time and, depending on their examination results and wishes, pupils could enter the sixth form proper or leave school.

Most pupils reported that they settled down quite quickly into the sixth form; 47.5 per cent in a few days, 29.1 per cent after a few weeks, 18.4 per cent after a term, 1.1 per cent took longer than a term and only 3.9 per cent still felt unsettled at the time the question was asked. About half (51.4 per cent) estimated they felt happier in the sixth form than they had been in the fifth, a third (34.6 per cent) felt they had been equally happy in either, so that only a small proportion (14 per cent) felt they had been happier in the fifth form.

Most of the sixth form were preparing for A level examinations (93 per cent) but nearly half (49 per cent) were also preparing for some O levels as well. Most of them agreed that there was a strong emphasis on exams in the sixth form but did not feel that their teachers were only interested in those who did well. They all followed a minority time programme, and most felt it took up valuable time. The amount of private study time varied according to a pupil's other commitments, but most of them (59.8 per cent) were satisfied with this provision. Most found work in the sixth no harder than they had expected but a majority felt the need for more individual help (58.7 per cent) and the desire for more discussion (66.5 per cent). School work was formally assessed every term for both effort and achievement, and internal examinations were set twice a year. However, most sixth formers agreed that they decided for themselves how much work they did. (See Table 2.5 for details of pupil's opinions.)

Being a sixth former was associated with a number of privileges which in many cases were relaxations of rules continuing for younger pupils. Unlike the rest of the school, uniform was not compulsory. Sixth form boys could wear dark suits or a 'reasonable' sports jacket but had always to wear a tie. They were not allowed to grow facial hair other than sideboards, but could wear their hair to collar length (not shoulder length). Girls too did not have to wear school uniform but could wear skirts or dresses of a number of prescribed styles and a limited range of colours. They were allowed to wear makeup but not trousers.

Sixth formers took their lunch with other pupils but were exempt from the queue. They had to obtain permission to leave the

Table 2.5   *St Trad's sixth formers' opinions about aspects of the school and sixth form* (%) (n = 179)

	Agree	Disagree
I prefer to keep my social life separate from school	40.2	41.9
The work is harder than I expected	21.8	53.1
Doing non-exam subjects takes up valuable time	30.7	54.2
There is a strong emphasis on exams	86.6	7.3
You decide for yourself how much work you do	82.7	14.5
The staff are interested in your personal welfare	67.0	17.9
I feel I know some of the staff well	57.0	22.3
The staff are only interested in those who do well	14.5	69.8
There are unnecessary restrictions in the sixth	71.5	24.0
It is easy to make friends in the sixth	73.7	12.3
In the sixth form you are treated as an adult	34.6	49.2
You have to look after yourself in the sixth	65.9	19.6
The school expects sixth formers to set a good example	81.6	6.7
The sixth form is too much like the rest of the school	14.5	69.8
The sixth form is isolated from the rest of the school	59.2	29.6
Having to help with younger pupils interferes with work	20.1	46.4
Having responsibilities for younger pupils is an important part of education	58.1	16.8

Note: A third allowed response, not reported, was either 'Can't say' or 'No strong feelings'.

premises at any time including the lunch hour. The daily assembly was compulsory except for those with religious exemption, and they registered in tutor groups at the beginning of the morning and afternoon sessions.

The rooms used exclusively for sixth form teaching also served as social rooms, where, unlike other pupils, sixth formers could stay in during the breaks. They could work or talk in these rooms but eating or drinking was not allowed, nor radio and record playing, except after school hours. Games were not compulsory; the alternative was supervised private study.

The balance of privileges and controls was not to most sixth formers' liking. Most felt that there were unnecessary restrictions and only a third felt they were being treated as adults. However, most of them disagreed with the proposition that the sixth form was too much like the rest of the school but agreed that it was isolated (see Table 2.5).

Prefects were chosen by the staff from the upper sixth; they and other sixth formers played an important part in the house system, used for intra-school competition, and as table monitors at lunch time. They were often the officers of school clubs and societies; 29 per cent held responsibilities which brought them into contact with younger pupils.

Most sixth formers agreed that having responsibility for younger pupils was an important part of education, although there was some feeling that it interfered with their own work. Their acknowledgment of their being role-models is shown in the high level of agreement to the idea that the school expects them to set a good example (Table 2.5). Overall, they felt that both sixth formers and younger pupils gain from these relationships, with greater advantage to the latter.

A sixth form committee of self-elected members was responsible for the organisation of social events including dances. They could spend money gained as profit from a drinks machine in the school, under the supervision of the deputy head. Any major decisions required the headteacher's approval.

School played an important part in the social life of many sixth formers. There was a fairly even spread of opinion on their preference for keeping their social life separate from the school (Table 2.5). However, most felt it was easy to make friends in school (Table 2.5), and a majority (82.6 per cent) reported that most of their friends were at the school, and nearly a third (29.6 per cent) that all their friends were in the sixth form.

Any member of staff was available to deal with problems concerning academic work, future education, careers or personal problems. The incidence of such consultations is shown in Table 2.6 which shows that in general sixth formers consulted their friends and parents more often than particular institutional advisers, especially in the case of personal problems. However, over half (54 per cent) found the advice offered by the school about future education to be useful, and 22 per cent found it useful in choosing a career. Most agreed that they knew some of the staff well and that staff were interested in their personal welfare. But they also felt 'you have to look after yourself in the sixth' (Table 2.5).

The majority of sixth formers (83 per cent) expected to continue their full-time education after leaving school, particularly at universities (45 per cent), polytechnics (24 per cent) or colleges of education (24 per cent).

Table 2.6 St Trad's sixth formers' self-reported incidences of consultations (%) (n = 179)

Consulted	Consultation			
	Academic work	Future education	Career	Personal problem
Headteacher	15.6	14.0	11.7	5.0
Deputy head/senior master or mistress	15.1	35.2	41.9	8.4
Tutor	22.3	26.3	21.8	11.2
Subject teacher	53.6	24.6	24.6	6.7
Careers teacher	9.5	30.6	48.0	2.8
Friends	25.1	26.8	36.9	47.5
Parents	39.7	49.2	57.0	38.5

As far as previous research and experience allows, the sixth form of St Trad's may be considered to be reasonably typical of many grammar schools in recent times: academically and university orientated, with responsibilities accepted with minor reservations, but with the granting of largely token privileges which do not offset what are felt to be unnecessary restrictions. Both the Arnoldian prototype and Frances Stevens's popular image of the sixth form are fairly clearly discernible.

The traditional sixth form

Despite the declining number of maintained grammar schools this kind of sixth form has a double importance. First, it has formed the starting point of the newer forms of post-sixteen education, both literally during the course of reorganisation and as examples to be followed or rejected. Second, the survey of St Trad's, as representative of this genre, can be used in the comparison of the different forms of organisation for 16–19 year olds, and also in the comparison of the students' experience of these different forms.

Chapter 3

The changing sixth form

The sixth forms of the nineteenth century public schools were, socially and educationally, relatively homogeneous. Studies such as Bishop and Wilkinson's (1967) show the pupils came from similar social backgrounds, entered a limited range of high status occupations, and followed the same curriculum of classical studies. Since their creation the sixth forms of maintained schools have become more diverse in each of these respects. This increasing diversity and the recent changes in the social position of young people in society in general, have contributed towards innovations in the organisation of sixth forms. Some commentators see these changes as reforms. They can also be viewed as modifications of the traditional idea of the sixth form.

The social origins of sixth formers

Children from middle class families have always been over-represented in the sixth forms of maintained secondary schools. However, since their foundation this gap between the social classes has been slowly closing. This has been shown in the work of Little and Westergaard (1964) who collated data from a number of surveys to provide a historical perspective. Their most recent figures, taken from the Robbins report (1963), referred to the early 1960s. Unfortunately there have been no large scale surveys since that time and so it is not possible to document the continued closing of the gap.

The increasing proportion of working class children in the sixth form has been suggested to be an important source of change. Frances Stevens's (1960) examination of the social and educational assumptions of the grammar school is pervaded by a nostalgia for the pre-war situation. She does not specifically refer to working class children in her description of the 'new' entrants after the war. 'They came not knowing the ropes, and having few clear expectations or cultural ambitions.' This new generation, '... sometimes lively and curious. sometimes casual and apathetic ... comes with little respect for education or teachers, has no regard for the virtues of perseverance and hard work'. These qualities are contrasted with those of the children lost with the abolition of fees: '... steady cooperative ... [with] unquestioning support of the school'. These too are given no social designation, but several studies, including Banks (1955) and King (1969), have shown them to be almost exclusively middle class. Stevens felt that the 'living tradition' of the grammar school was too valuable to be changed, and suggested that the tensions caused by 'social differences could only be resolved in a common interest in the world of the mind'.

Harry Davies (1965), drawing upon his experience as head-master of the High Pavement school in Nottingham, also preferred not to analyse the changes in recruitment in social class terms. Instead, he referred to the new kind of pupil as 'first generation grammar school'. (In a study of a single school (King, 1969) 63.2 per cent of first generation boys had fathers in manual occupations; 90.0 per cent of second generation boys had fathers in non-manual occupations.) He rejected Jackson and Marsden's conclusion that 'the grammar schools have foundered on a rock – the working class', but did admit that there were tensions in the situation and suggested that 'reforms', especially at sixth form level, were necessary. He described the first generation pupils as sometimes appearing brash and argumentative but saw in this the merit of not being dull conformists, and urged schools to become more tolerant. He advocated the making of games voluntary for sixth formers, and a changed attitude to extra-curricular activities. 'The schools must not however take offence if a senior pupil rejects the opportunities which it has provided, and prefers his own activities apart from the school.' In addition he suggested that the schools should escape the 'middle class pre-occupation with conventional appearance and good manners'.

There are no large scale surveys which have investigated the

41

outcomes of the increasing proportion of working class pupils in sixth forms. However, the Schools Council survey (Morton-Williams et al., 1970) did ask sixth form teachers their opinions about the way home environment may be disadvantageous to some sixth formers. Nearly a third felt that none of their pupils was disadvantaged in this account, but the higher the proportion of working class pupils each type of school had in the sixth form, the higher was the proportion of pupils who were felt to be disadvantaged. At the extremes, 78 per cent of teachers in comprehensive schools, which had 51 per cent of working class pupils in their sixth forms, felt there were disadvantaged pupils, compared with 42 per cent of teachers in independent boarding schools with only 4 per cent of working class pupils. This suggests that teachers tend to judge working class pupils as being disadvantaged in the sixth form. This suggestion is supported when an examination is made of their views on the nature of the disadvantages. The most important was lack of parental interest and support in school work, followed by inadequate facilities for studying at home and restricted cultural and intellectual backgrounds, all stereotypical aspects of the working class rather than the middle class.

The evidence to suggest that working class or 'first generation' pupils have a different evaluation of the sixth form compared with others is not very strong. In a study of a single grammar school it was found that first generation sixth formers were among the most highly involved boys in the school (King, 1969). Few differences were found between working class and middle class sixth formers in a sample of schools, in terms of their disposition towards school (King, 1973a). However, one of Davies's (1965) observations was borne out, in that working class sixth formers showed lower levels of acceptance of the house system.

Two related explanations may be suggested to account for this absence of striking differences between the social classes in their experience of the sixth form: the first concerns selection, the second, socialisation. The many studies of early leavers show that they are predominantly working class. Furthermore, they are more often those working class pupils who are often at odds with the school in terms of their values and attitudes towards authority. As a previous case study showed (King, 1969), this means that those working class pupils who stay on into the sixth form tend to be more conformist and be the more highly involved in all aspects of the school, and show general convergence in these respects to pupils from middle class homes. This may be because, as Jackson and Marsden (1962) and Floud et al. (1957) suggest, they come from socially aspiring working class homes, 'sunken' middle class homes where the grandparents are middle class, or working class homes where the mother has married down. Thus the process of selection for the sixth form tends to produce a more socially homogeneous group of pupils.

This homogeneity may also be produced as a result of the pupils' experience of school before the sixth form. This is the shared experience for pupils of all backgrounds, although its meaning may differ from one social group to another. As a result of this socialisation process some working class pupils may become, as the research of Jackson and Marsden (1962) and King (1969) suggests, more royal than the king in their acceptance of the school.

If our knowledge of working class sixth formers is less than satisfactory then that concerning immigrant sixth formers is even less so. Until 1966 no national statistics were kept of the numbers of immigrant children in British schools, and these records were stopped in 1973. In 1972 just over 4 per cent of children aged sixteen or over in maintained schools were defined as immigrant (DES, 1972). However, the statistics do not report the proportion or number aged seventeen so that the rate of staying on into the sixth form is not available. David Beetham (1968) in a survey in Birmingham found a higher rate of staying on after fifteen among immigrant pupils compared with the indigenous pupils. A study by Durojaiye (1971) suggested that the cultural patterns of Indian and Pakistani families are similar to those of the home-centred, aspiring working class, which studies such as Toomey's (1970) suggest many educationally successful working class children come from. The study by Taylor (1973) in Newcastle upon Tyne showed that both Indian and Pakistani pupils did better at school and stayed on into the sixth form more often than 'English' boys in the same schools.

Whatever the proportion of immigrant sixth formers is nationally, their distribution is not likely to be very even across the country. Sixty-four per cent of schools have no immigrant pupils at all. They are concentrated in a small proportion of schools: 4.5 per cent have over one-fifth immigrant pupils (DES, 1972).

The changed social position of young people

Two contradictory images of young people are commonly described by adult commentators on the educational scene. On the one hand they are seen to be seduced and exploited by the ephemera of a hedonistic, media-created, youth culture. This is Frances Stevens's 'candy floss world', or more literary, 'Vanity Fair'. On the other hand they are seen as becoming more mature and more responsible.

All societies use age as a criterion for the allocation of status, and are therefore age-stratified, usually with higher status for older age groups. In small, non-literate societies without detailed conceptions of chronological age the strata may consist of children, youths, adults and elders, although as Margaret Mead (1958) has pointed out the stage of youth or adolescence is not universal. In Musgrove's (1964) terms, adolescence is a social invention, and he has traced the history of the idea from the enlightenment to its present prominence in modern industrialised societies, where the status of youth is not only defined by common usage but also by the operation of the law governing financial, criminal and parental responsibilities, and the law of education.

In recent times youth or adolescence has not only been viewed as a status group but also a cultural group. Young people, in this analysis, share a way of life, in terms of ideas, beliefs, knowledge and values, which are sufficiently different from that of other age groups as to constitute a distinct sub-culture. As far back as 1932 Willard Waller in his classic 'The Sociology of Teaching' postulated a conflict between the 'play culture' of pupils and the 'adult culture' that their teachers attempt to transmit to them. Talcott Parsons (1943) in his essay on age and sex in American society concluded, 'the orientation of the youth culture is more or less specifically irresponsible'.

The key empirical study in this field is that of James Coleman (1961). As a result of his investigation of ten high schools in the Mid-West of the USA, he concluded (p. 21):

> Our society has within its midst a set of small teenage societies which focus teenage interests and attitudes on things far removed from adult responsibilities, and which may develop standards which lead away from those goals established by the larger society.

There have been many criticisms of Coleman's study. Jahoda and Warren (1965) have pointed out that Coleman did not produce acceptable evidence for the existence of such a youth culture but used the idea of it to explain his results. Previous studies of American youth by Hollingshead (1948), and of Canadians by Elkin and Westley (1955), had reached different conclusions which suggested that social class status in relation to life styles was as important at this age as for adults. Summarising his work in Elmtown, Hollingshead wrote: '... the social behaviour of adolescents is related to the position their families occupy in the social structure of the community'. Epperson (1964) and more recently Kandel and Lesser (1972) have replicated parts of Coleman's original study but have been unable to confirm his conclusions.

In Britain a great deal of research has contradicted Coleman's idea of an anti-adult, anti-academic, unitary, youth culture. Studies of young people by Thelma Veness (1962) and by the Eppels (1966) have shown how strongly conformist many are in terms of their general attitudes and social ambitions. Frank Musgrove (1964) concluded from his own study that, if any conflict exists between the generations, it comes mainly from the adult side. Barry Sugarman's (1967) investigation was of fourteen year old boys in four London Schools. He measured their commitment to an hypothesised youth culture in terms of responses to questions about smoking, going out with girls, pop music, and teenage fashions. Those with a high commitment to the 'teenage culture' tended to have what were judged to be poorer attitudes to school and conduct, and to have lower levels of academic achievement. At first sight these results seem to confirm some of Coleman's ideas, but Sugarman also found that high commitment to the 'teenage culture' was particularly associated with working class boys, and so he preferred to explain their poor conduct and achievement in social class terms. He concluded that, 'Youth culture is the culture of the non-mobile working class youth.'

Murdock and Phelps (1972) have taken Sugarman's analysis further and in a study of a larger number of teenage school children make a distinction between 'street culture' and 'pop media culture'. The former is particularly associated with working class boys in urban areas, and uses the streets, cafés and other public places as its locale. It emphasises physical toughness, looking after yourself, and sticking with your mates. Its activities are commonly summarised in the phrase 'mucking about'. In contrast, the pop media culture is associated with girls, particularly from middle class backgrounds. It is home based and centres upon records, magazines, television and radio programmes concerned with pop music. Murdock and Phelps suggest that adherence to either of these two cultures may be associated with rejection of school.

In an associated piece of research Murdock and McCron (1973) describe a whole range of identities associated with pop music, ranging from the Top 20, followed mainly by younger girls, to progressive rock and underground music listened to by academic, often middle class, older boys. It is this kind of youth culture that may be associated with many sixth formers, and it is not necessarily used as a way of expressing dissent from the school and what it stands for. Given the voluntary nature of staying on in full-time education after sixteen it seems unlikely that adherence to any youth culture would be used to express strong anti-school sentiments.

What may exist in some institutions of post-sixteen education are sub-cultures rather like those described by Martin Trow (1960) in American colleges. First, academic sub-cultures, whose members share an interest in the study of particular subjects. A hint of their existence is shown in the sixth formers' ideas of the benefits of staying on at school reported by Morton-Williams et al. (1970): 24 per cent mentioned gaining a deeper, more thorough knowledge of their main subject. Second, vocational sub-cultures where the main interest is getting on through educational success; 25 per cent of sixth formers mentioned this as a benefit from staying on at school. Third, the collegiate sub-cultures where the main interest is in the non-academic sport and social life of the college; 22 per cent of sixth formers mentioned these as benefits. Finally, the non-conformist or bohemian sub-cultures, which may include some followers of the more esoteric pop music.

The idea that young people are beginning to be more socially mature and responsible was strongly expressed in the Report of the Committee on the Age of Majority (1967), known as the Latey report after its chairman Mr Justice Latey. Drawing upon a wide range of evidence the committee considered, 'That most young people today mature earlier than in the past', and this was the major factor in their recommendation that the age of legal capacity should be lowered from twenty-one to eighteen.

Although this recommendation has been implemented the

arguments made by the committee did not represent a consensus view, as the dissenting report by Howe and Stebbings (see Latey report) made clear at the time. The conflicting views of youth as both serious and hedonistic, as both mature and irresponsible, indicate the dangers of making generalisations about a whole age group. Statements made about young people should be viewed with the same caution as any that might be made about 'middle-aged people'. The young are as socially diverse and varied as any other age group.

Although not dealing in the concepts of youth culture and maturity the Schools Council survey (Morton-Williams et al., 1970) does report the views of teachers on the changes in attitude of sixth formers towards school. Sixty-five per cent of teachers thought that there had been changes in recent years. Of teachers who thought there had been changes, 48 per cent approved of them, 22 per cent disapproved and 28 per cent had mixed feelings. The most important change, in their view, was that sixth formers expected more freedom and are more critical of authority. The survey does not report the extent to which the teachers approved or disapproved of this, or any of the other suggested changes.

The second most important change was that sixth formers were less responsible towards school and more demanding. Some indication of a vocational sub-culture of the kind described by Trow (1960) is made in the next suggested change, 'greater awareness of career prospects, need for qualifications'. The next most important suggestion, 'wider interests outside, not so dependent on school', reflects the observations made by Harry Davies (1965), although this was not associated with the types of school with the higher proportions of working class pupils.

Curricular changes

The increasing proportion of working class pupils and the entry of pupils from immigrant homes may both be regarded as part of the opening up of the sixth form. This opening up process may also be seen in the changing conditions of entry into the sixth form and the changing curricula followed by sixth formers.

In the period before the introduction of the General Certificate of Education examinations in 1951, entry into the sixth form was usually confined to those with at least the General Schools Certificate, and all sixth formers prepared for the Higher Schools

47

Certificate on a two year course. Since that time this kind of entry requirement has become less common so that in some schools the definition of a sixth former is simply a pupil in at least his sixth year at school. Sixth forms now include pupils who are not taking A level subjects (10 per cent), who take O level (40 per cent) or even CSE (18 per cent) (Morton-Williams et al., 1970). The élite quality of the sixth form has been reduced.

Among A level students there has occurred a phenomenon known as the 'swing to the arts' or the 'science shortfall'. The Robbins committee (1963) suggested that by 1967 the ratio of arts to science students in the universities should be slightly adjusted in favour of science (compared with that of 1962) to give 37 per cent arts and 52 per cent science. The actual ratio was even at 44 per cent. Of the 'arts' subjects the social sciences gained most in this swing. The science shortfall has its origin in the schools. In 1953 40 per cent of A level students were preparing for mathematics and science subjects, 48 per cent for arts subjects. In 1974 there were 31 per cent and 49 per cent respectively. Accompanying this swing from science has been an increase in the proportion of sixth formers following mixed arts and science courses (12 per cent in 1963, 20 per cent in 1974). These are what Bernstein (1971) has called impure combinations and regards as part of the opening up of the traditional curriculum.

The assumption that the country's economic growth was related to an adequate supply of scientists and technologists led to concern about this phenomenon, and a number of enquiries were initiated, principally by central bodies. The most important of these were the Dainton and Swann reports. The Dainton report called for an active policy within schools to halt the swing by making science and mathematics more attractive to pupils by stressing their social aspects, and by making mathematics compulsory in the sixth form. Similar recommendations were made by the Swann report for higher education, including the 'humanisation' of science courses. The high levels of graduate unemployment in the early 1970s, including science graduates, contradicts the idea of a direct relationship between economic growth and the supply of scientists, and suggests that the more important concern was about the supply of science undergraduates.

The swing from science is an outcome of freedom of choice of subjects among students. A hint of one factor contributing to the change comes from the Schools Council survey (Morton-Williams et al., 1970), which found that the prevailing image among sixth formers was that those who studied science in the sixth were highest in intelligence and the most hardworking. The corollary might be that the sciences are seen as difficult subjects requiring much hard work.

Another important change in the sixth form curriculum concerns non-examination studies. The Crowther committee (1959), whilst celebrating subject-mindedness in the sixth form, saw dangers in specialisation and proposed the introduction of non-examination programmes to improve the literacy of science students and the numeracy of arts students. At about the same time proposals along similar lines were being made by A. D. C. Peterson and by Boris Ford in his 'A B C' ('Agreement to Broaden the Curriculum' – see Jennings, 1974). In 1960 the 'Third Report' of the Secondary Schools Examination Council also condemned excessive specialisation. The institutionalisation of minority studies in the sixth form has followed the acceptance of the idea by the universities in that applicants must indicate the proportion of time spent on such studies.

The range of courses included under this heading is very wide, from archaeology to the Common Market (see Morton-Williams et al., 1970). Sixth formers' rather mixed evaluation of these courses is indicated in the results of an original survey among over 900 sixth formers from six different kinds of school; 39 per cent agreed and 46 per cent disagreed with the statement, 'Doing non-exam subjects takes up valuable time.'

The sixth form unit

The changes in the general social status of sixth formers, in their social origins and in their studies, have been accompanied by structural changes in the sixth form, often expressed in the creation of sixth form units. These units vary in the degree of their physical and social separation from the rest of the school but usually consist of a number of rooms| for the exclusive use of sixth formers, associated with reduced contact with the lower school and increased privileges. The idea of this type of organisation was preferred by 32 per cent of teachers in the Schools Council survey (Morton-Williams et al., 1970) but more, 55 per cent, preferred the traditional type where the sixth form were 'older members of the school community'.

The teachers' views on the benefits of the traditional and block

Table 3.1 *Teachers' views on the benefits of types of sixth form organisation (% preferences)*

Benefits	Older member of school community	Sixth form block attached to school
Opportunities for leadership, experience of responsibility and authority	87	56
Continuity of teaching and social relationships	34	39
Treated as adults, greater independence, more privileges, less restrictions	1	36
Better facilities and amenities	—	33
Prestige, status, sense of achievement	10	16
Good, better preparation for university/college	—	15
Better opportunity for social relationships within own age group	—	11

Source: Morton-Williams et al., 1970, p. 302.

types of organisation (Table 3.1) suggest that moves towards the latter are a response to the idea that young people are more mature and are less ready to put up with what they feel to be unnecessary restrictions. The idea of the sixth as a source of leadership and responsibility is clearly reduced in importance, whilst other elements of the traditional idea of the sixth form are enhanced in that the sixth form block is considered to confer more prestige and to be a better preparation for university.

It is possible that the changing social composition of the sixth form may also influence these organisational changes. Harry Davies (1965) in his discussion of the first generation grammar school child, '... or if we must express ourselves in class terms, ... the working class child', specifically queries the acceptability of school uniforms, compulsory games and loyalty to school clubs and teams, to such pupils, and questions their continued existence. The sixth form block seems to be associated with a reduction of these three aspects of the traditional sixth form.

The sixth form unit of Newstyle comprehensive school

Newstyle comprehensive school is the pseudonym of the second of the twelve institutions of post-sixteen education which were the subject of original research. Newstyle became a comprehensive school in the mid-1960s by the amalgamation of a mixed grammar and a mixed secondary modern school. The accommodation includes a purpose built block but the sixth form (140 from over 1,000 pupils) is kept as a separate unit in the original grammar school building about a quarter of a mile away.

Unlike St Trad's, entry into the sixth form at Newstyle was completely open so that the sixth form was defined as pupils in their sixth or more year at school. In consequence a smaller proportion of Newstyle sixth formers were preparing for A level (81.1 per cent compared with 92.7 per cent at St Trad's) but a small number were taking and retaking CSE examinations (6.6 per cent). In addition, a slightly smaller proportion expected to continue in full-time education after leaving school (78.7 per cent compared with 83.2 per cent), with a larger proportion setting their sights at further rather than higher education (16.4 per cent compared with 5.6 per cent).

There were no significant differences between the two schools in terms of how quickly the sixth formers reported they settled down, or in their estimate of their relative happiness in the fifth and sixth forms.

As at St Trad's, being a sixth former was associated with a number of privileges. Unlike the rest of the school the uniform was not compulsory and, unlike St Trad's, boys did not have to wear jackets or ties, and girls could wear trousers. At the time of our observations, jeans, T-shirts and sweaters were in favour with both sexes. Games were not compulsory; they could choose from a range of activities including games. They took their lunches quite separately from younger pupils. There was no daily assembly but the pupils had arranged a voluntary attendance service at a local church, once a week. They did have to register with their tutors at the beginning of the morning and afternoon sessions but did not have to seek permission to leave school at lunch time, unlike St Trad's.

The whole sixth form unit was exclusive to sixth formers and their teachers. They had three common rooms in which they could work, play games, records or radios, eat and drink, but not smoke. The control of these rooms was in the hands of a sixth form committee which was elected by a secret ballot and contained no staff ex officio members.

The balance of privileges and controls was more to the liking of Newstyle sixth formers than those of St Trad's were to sixth formers there. Nearly half the Newstyle students agreed they were treated as adults, and only a minority agreed that there were unnecessary restrictions (see Table 3.2). Not surprisingly Newstyle pupils agreed less often that the sixth form was too much like the rest of the school, and agreed more often that it was isolated from the rest of the school (Table 3.2).

There was no prefectorial system; the physical separation of the sixth form unit and the rest of the school was thought to make it impossible. However, the house system was very strong and sixth formers were often officials, and they also played an important part in the School Council which consisted of staff and elected pupil members. There were no significant differences in the extent to which Newsyle and St Trad's sixth formers agreed with the expectation that they should set a good example, or with the importance of having responsibilities for younger pupils. The proportion of sixth formers with such responsibilities, through societies, committees and the house system, was similar in both schools (33.6 per cent in Newstyle, 29.1 per cent in St Trad's). In Newstyle this was brought about by a deliberate policy of basing most activities on the main school and having few exclusively for sixth formers. In consequence, whereas 84.4 per cent of sixth formers at St Trad's belonged to at least one club or society exclusive to them, only 15.6 per cent did so at Newstyle. It is possible that the St Trad's sixth formers' involvement with younger pupils as prefects partly accounts for their higher agreement to the propositions that both sixth formers and younger pupils lose by being part of the same school (Table 3.2).

Two indications of differences in the relationships within the two institutions are shown in the greater preference of Newstyle sixth formers to keep their social life separate from the school, and their lower agreement to the proposition that the staff were interested in their personal welfare (Table 3.2). Perhaps the latter was related to their stronger feelings of being treated as adults?

Although there was less control of sixth formers' behaviour at Newstyle, control of school work was much the same as at St Trad's. Formal assessments of achievement and effort were made three times a year for each subject, together with twice yearly

Table 3.2 *Newstyle and St Trad's sixth formers' opinions on the school and sixth form (% agreement)*

	Newstyle (n = 122)	St Trad's (n = 179)	Significance (%) (chi square)
I prefer to keep my social life separate from school	57.4	40.2	1
The sixth form staff are in-interested in your personal welfare	52.5	67.0	5
There are unnecessary restrictions in the sixth	27.0	71.5	0.1
In the sixth form you are treated as an adult	46.7	34.6	5
There is a strong emphasis on exams	89.3	86.6	ns
You decide for yourself how much work you do	86.1	82.7	ns
Doing non-exam subjects takes up valuable time	35.2	30.7	ns
The sixth form is a good preparation for future education	80.2	84.4	ns
The school expects sixth formers to set a good example	75.4	81.6	ns
The sixth form is too much like the rest of the school	5.7	14.5	5
The sixth form is isolated from the rest of the school	75.4	59.2	2
Having responsibilities for younger pupils is an important part of education	51.6	58.1	ns
Helping with younger pupils interferes with work	12.3	20.1	5
Sixth formers gain by being part of the same school as younger pupils	28.5	30.3	ns
Sixth formers lose by being part of the same school as younger pupils	3.3	14.0	2
Younger pupils gain by having sixth formers in the same school	54.1	54.2	ns
Younger pupils lose by having sixth formers in the same school	3.3	9.5	5

examinations, and every student followed a programme of minority studies. Opinions about the emphasis on exams, deciding how much work to do and non-examination subjects, were similar in the two institutions (Table 3.2). Contrary to the opinions expressed by the teachers in the Schools Council survey (Morton-Williams et al., 1970) there was no significant difference between the two sets of pupils as to the usefulness of the different organisations as a good preparation for future education (Table 3.2).

The Newstyle sixth form unit was regarded by the senior staff as an attempt to bring about compatability between what were seen to be the desire of sixth formers for more freedom and privileges, and the traditional idea of the sixth form as an example on view to the rest of the school. The physical isolation of the sixth form block made the relaxation of the rules of appearance and behaviour easier because these were not constantly visible to younger pupils and would keep low any resentments based upon comparison. Sixth formers were less important as role-models and as agents of social control: 'How can a prefect in jeans tell off a younger pupil for not wearing the correct uniform?' (teacher in interview). However, by integrating extra-curricular activities across the age range a version of the idea of the sixth form as leaders and holders of positions of responsibility was maintained, although mainly in semi-formal, out-of-school situations, and usually in voluntary capacities and relationships. D'Aeth (1973) has posed the paradox of earlier maturity and the prolongation of school. Here, and elsewhere, a solution is sought by changing the nature of the school.

Chapter 4

The sixth form centre

Most British secondary schools do not have sixth forms. Before the moves towards reorganisation on comprehensive lines all grammar schools had sixth forms but virtually no modern schools had them. The earliest comprehensive schools were the all-through 11–18 type, and might have been seen as the forerunners of a national system of schools all of which had sixth forms. However, subsequent schemes and current plans feature this kind of school less often, and among the more common alternatives is the sixth form centre (see Benn, 1972).

In this arrangement, only a limited number of schools have sixth forms, and these centres receive pupils into their sixth forms from associated short-course feeder schools catering for the 11–16 or 12–16 age range. The emergence of this kind of consortium is associated with a factor which has come to be more important in relation to the provision of post-sixteen education: the availability and utilisation of resources.

Reorganisation and resources

Ideas about the relationship between education and the economy have changed radically in a short period of time. The Crowther committee (1959) saw a fairly simple functional relationship in referring to the need 'to provide an adequate supply of brains and skill to sustain economic productivity'. This view of education as a national investment industry was also part of the sociology

of the time as this quotation from Musgrave (1964) shows: '...
as a country grows into an advanced industrial society the educational system ceases to be determined by the state of the
economy and becomes a determinant of the rate of economic
development'. This kind of analysis was used by Crowther and
others to justify the expansion of educational opportunity, which
would therefore benefit both the individual and society. Although
not following so simple a functionalist argument Floud and Halsey
(1956) were in accord with it in their qualified advocacy of the
'common secondary school' as 'best suited to the needs of technological society'. The comprehensive system was seen as the way
to greater equality of opportunity and continued economic expansion.

By 1963 the supposed economic benefits of educational expansion were given less importance in the arguments made by the
Robbins committee, and most stress was placed upon access to
higher education as a right of any 'suitably qualified' individual.
In sociology the critique of functionalist theories, such as that of
Collins (1971), has led to a modification of the idea of a simple
causal relationship between education and the economy. In educational circles the increasing educational expenditure associated
with the recent expansion has lead to a change in the salient
question, which is no longer, Can we afford not to expand education? but, How can we afford to expand?

In 1951 6.8 per cent of public expenditure in the United
Kingdom was on education. This rose to 12.9 per cent by 1973,
when the total expenditure was over £4,000 million; more than
the cost of either defence or health and personal services. More
specifically, the cost of educating each secondary school pupil
over sixteen was £362 for 1972–3 (all figures from Nissel, 1974).
Woodhall and Blaug (1968) made an input-output analysis of
British secondary education for the period 1950–63 and concluded
that the productivity of that sector of education had declined.
Education was judged to have taken more out of the economy
than it put back.

There is scope for argument about the validity of this kind of
analysis and also of the use of economic criteria in judgments of
the value of education, but this conclusion is echoed in the continued tightening of educational expenditure by the central
authority, shown clearly in the White Paper of 1972: 'The total
resources available will always be limited. Everything can not
be done at once. Each [educational] programme is in a very real

sense in competition for its share of resources with other programmes, both within and outside the education service.'

In this economic context several forms of post-sixteen education, including the use of sixth form centres, are claimed to
involve a more efficient use of scarce resources than the all-
through school with integral sixth form. These claims are seldom
backed by sophisticated analyses of relative costs but at a national
level the expansion of post-sixteen education, in many different
forms of institution, has been accomplished with virtually no
increase in expenditure per pupil. The official calculation (Nissel,
1974) is that expenditure per pupil over sixteen in maintained
schools actually fell by 1 per cent between 1964 and 1973, at constant 1964 prices. This compares with increases of 13 per cent
for pupils under sixteen and 23 per cent for university students
(excluding grants).

A particular aspect of the utilisation of scarce resources has
been the cost of building new schools. In 1973 nearly £200 million
was spent on completed building projects for maintained
schools, and more than £400 million worth were still under construction at the end of that period (DES, 1973). The move away
from the all-through 11–18 comprehensive school is strongly
related to the presumption that it requires new custom-built
accommodation, shown in the criticisms of 'botched up' schemes
utilising existing buildings too small to accommodate all the
pupils, and therefore involving split sites. The various tiered
systems of reorganisation and the introduction of sixth form
centres may use existing buildings because they are often the
right size for the numbers of pupils in each unit.

A second aspect of the economic utilisation of resources concerns the supply of specialist, usually graduate, teachers. It had
been thought in the late 1950s that the teacher supply situation
was well in hand, but the increase in the birth rate together with
the wastage rate among married women teachers indicated that
a crisis was imminent. As a result a target of 80,000 college
places by 1970–1 was set. This was endorsed by the Robbins
committee (1963), which set a further target of 111,000 places by
1973–4. The 80,000 places programme was in fact exceeded by
26 per cent in 1967–8. This stemmed from the impetus given to
the teacher education programme by the Report of the National
Advisory Council on the Training and Supply of Teachers in 1965,
which forecast an even graver problem of supply than the Robbins
committee, so that the Robbins target for 1973–4 was nearly

reached by 1967–8. The number of qualified teachers in maintained schools increased from 281,000 in 1963 to 350,000 in 1971, and the pupil teacher ratio fell from 24.6 to 21.4 over the same period.

During this time the proportion of graduates in the teaching force rose only slightly, from 34.4 per cent in 1960 to 38.6 per cent in 1973. Particular concern has been expressed about the decreasing proportion of science and mathematics graduates in teaching. In 1961 they formed 36.1 per cent of graduate teachers in maintained schools, but 32.2 per cent in 1973. In 1971 a group of university vice-chancellors wrote to 'The Times' (see Benn and Simon, 1972) expressing concern about the way in which a national system of 11–18 comprehensive schools would stretch the available graduate teachers too thinly to be effective. In 1968 Egner calculated that each school in such a system would have two-thirds of a graduate mathematics teacher, one third of a physicist and one-quarter of a chemist. Estimates made at a local level by Taylor (1971) seem to bear out this analysis. Although the closing of opportunities for new graduates in industry and an increasing output of BEd holders from colleges of education may improve the recruitment of science and mathematics teachers, another argument for alternatives to the all-through comprehensive has been the more efficient utilisation of available specialist manpower.

Sixth form centres

It is doubtful that any school could claim to be the first sixth form centre. Ever since a few secondary modern schools began to enter some of their pupils for external examinations, first O level and later CSE, some of the successful candidates have entered the sixth forms of local grammar schools. What was claimed by its headmaster to be 'the first sixth form college' (Shield, 1964) was in fact at the time acting as just such a sixth form centre.

A number of local authorities have introduced sixth form centres with short-course comprehensive feeder schools, including Cambridgeshire, Cardiff, Croydon, Lancashire, Northamptonshire, Norwich, Somerset and Warwickshire (Benn, 1972). Peterson (1973) has referred to these schemes as 'mushroom type' bearing the marks of a 'transitional expedient'. This judgment is supported in that some local authorities seem to be planning one of two kinds of future development: either for the sixth form centre to become a sixth form college, or for the feeder schools to develop their own sixth forms. Critical to such changes is the notion of the viable sixth form. Early critics of the comprehensive school, such as Eric James (1951) and Harry Rée (1956) argued that an 11–18 school would have to be unacceptably large to support a viable sixth form. These crititcisms were based upon the traditional idea of a selective sixth form, and were made at a time when the trend to stay on after sixteen was quite modest. In 1968 an ILEA working party in reviewing sixth form opportunities in Inner London proposed the parameters of the viable sixth form, which would be effective and economic. It would offer at least ten A level subjects, have a staffing ratio of 1 : 12 and have no group of students smaller than five. On these criteria its minimum size would be between forty and sixty pupils. The size of intake required to support such a sixth form would depend on the rate at which fifth formers stayed on to take A levels, and would therefore vary with the social composition of the school. If the rate were 15 per cent then a seven form entry intake would suffice, giving a school of over 1,000 pupils. (Similar calculations are made by Gunn, 1972 and Davies, 1971.) This would be higher with a more working class intake, lower with a more middle class one.

The primary justification of the sixth form centre/feeder school consortium is that of the best use of available resources particularly buildings and specialist staff, both points made by the Headmasters' Association (1968) and the ILEA (1968). The traditional value of the sixth form is endorsed even if only some schools in the consortium have one, so that, for example, Shield (1964) considered that the rest of the Mexborough School, at the time, benefited from the presence of the sixth form.

Monks (1968) and Benn and Simon (1972) have shown that sixth form centres are usually former grammar schools, and the feeder schools formerly modern schools. Peterson (1973) and the HMA (1968) see political advantages in this, in that the grammar school interest groups will be satisfied in the retention of the sixth form, whilst the modern school staff are given improved status as teachers in a comprehensive school of a kind.

The supposed disadvantages of the arrangement are corollaries of some of the advantages. The HMA (1968) feared that the 'concentration of first class minds' (sixth form teachers) in one school would be a deprivation for bright children in other schools. Although Shield (1964) saw value in there being continuity between the fifth and sixth forms for some pupils, Peterson (1973) predicted tension between the 'home grown' and 'immigrant' sixth formers, and feared that fifth formers from the feeder schools would be less likely to transfer to the sixth form at another school than to the one in their own.

The strongest critics of the arrangement have been Benn and Simon (1972). They fear the perpetuation of the disparity of esteem associated with the modern school/grammar school distinction: 'The short-course schools may be permanently disadvantaged by smaller size, fewer facilities, narrower ability intake, inadequate staffing, or inability to offer as great a range of courses' (Benn, 1972). The HMA (1968) saw advantages in the small size of feeder schools, and preferred them to middle school arrangements. In a small survey by Caroline Benn (1972) of nine short-course comprehensive schools in a range of schemes, three head-teachers reported that they felt their schools were unfairly treated by the local authority. A more detailed consideration of these and other aspects of short-course schools will be made in chapter 6.

Central School sixth form centre

Central School sixth form centre was another of the twelve institutions of post-sixteen education which were the subject of original investigation. Central School was one of a consortium of six schools, consisting of four feeder schools (11–16) and two sixth form centre schools (11–18). As is common in these schemes both sixth form centres were originally grammar schools and the four feeder schools had been modern schools. The Central sixth form had 140 pupils of whom over 40 per cent had transferred from feeder schools. Unfortunately, whereas in each of the other eleven institutions it was possible to survey virtually all the full-time students, at Central only a sample was available. However, three other 11–18 schools that were surveyed also acted as sixth form centres in that they each took pupils from other schools into their sixth forms. The sixth form of St Trad's contained 25 per cent newcomers, Newstyle 10 per cent, and the Cooperative School (to be discussed fully later) had 30 per cent. Therefore, in considering the educational experiences of what Peterson (1973) called the 'home grown' and 'immigrant' sixth formers, it is possible to draw upon data from four schools.

There were no minimum academic requirements for entry into the sixth form of Central School. Potential pupils from the feeder schools were invited with their parents to talks and tours of the school, and the heads of the feeder schools provided extensive reports on each transferring pupil. Central School senior staff anticipated all of the problems of integration suggested by Shield (1964) and Peterson (1973), and in the period following their arrival the new sixth formers were given particular attention by their tutors, and by the deputy head and senior mistress. They were encouraged to join clubs and take up positions of responsibility, and the gesture was made of appointing one of them the deputy head prefect.

In all four schools the sixth formers' estimates of how long they took to settle into the sixth did not vary significantly between those from the fifth form in the same school and those from elsewhere, except that more of the latter reported that they still felt unsettled at the time of the survey. The percentage for those who transferred was 11.8 compared with 5.1 for the others, which is statistically significant at the 5 per cent level. There were no consistent or significant differences in their estimates of their relative happiness in the fifth and in the sixth form.

Although there were no differences in their opinions about how easy it was to make friends, not surprisingly there were differences in their friendship patterns. Those who transferred were more likely to have friends studying elsewhere, to have made new friends since coming to the school, but to have less friends in the sixth form (Table 4.1). However, there were no significant differences between the two groups in their desire to keep their social lives separate from the school, or in their general attitudes to school and relationships with teachers. Furthermore, there were no significant or consistent differences in the rates at which they joined school clubs or held positions of responsibility.

These results suggest that the transfer from an outside school to the sixth form is an experience that most pupils find fairly easy to cope with, although a small number may find it more permanently unsettling. There is both a persistence of old friendship patterns and a making of new ones, and there is a successful integration into the social life of the school and an acceptance of the responsibilities of the sixth form. In general those who transfer into the sixth form have an evaluation of their school experience similar to those who entered from the fifth form of the same school.

Table 4.1 *Friendship patterns in four sixth forms, by school of origin* (%)

	Transfers from school's fifth year ($n = 331$)	Transfers from other schools' fifth year ($n = 102$)
Most friends in sixth form	81.0	55.9
No friends made at school before coming into the sixth form	1.2	33.3
All friends made before entering sixth form	14.0	1.0
Most friends studying full-time elsewhere	5.4	20.6
All friends made since entering sixth form	1.5	29.4

All differences significant at the 1 per cent level by chi square.

Chapter 5

Sixth form colleges

Of the various forms of post-sixteen education, the sixth form college is probably the most glamorous. Although they are as yet few in number a great deal has been written both for and against them. The complete separation of the sixth form from the rest of the school, in terms of administration, organisation and staffing, represents a further step away from the public school model and a significant change in the idea of the sixth form. Although the private Atlantic College and the War Office's Welbeck College were set up for post-sixteen education before the creation of the first sixth form colleges, they do not seem to have been used as prototypes or as sources of legitimacy.

The Croydon plan

The origin of the idea of the sixth form college is generally associated with the Croydon plan for the introduction of such a college – a plan that was never put into operation. Kenneth Urwin was a Croydon Borough councillor during the period that the plan was introduced and discussed, and his published account (in Donnison et al., 1965) is based upon his active participation in the events, upon diaries and other records.

In the immediate post-war period courses leading to external examinations in maintained schools in Croydon were confined to two grammar schools. Large increases in the population led to the conversion of five central schools to grammar schools, the creation of selective technical schools, and eventually to the introduction of certificate courses in some secondary modern schools. These changes were a response to what was felt to be the pressure for selective education, and it was this that also led to the first attempt at the reorganisation of secondary education.

In 1954 the Croydon Council accepted a motion put forward by two members of the minority Labour group, which requested the Education Committee to inform the council what steps it proposed to take in the near future to increase the proportion of grammar school places, which was below the national average. In response, the Education Committee set up a sub-committee to review the situation, and later the same year a memorandum was prepared by the then newly appointed chief education officer and the chief inspector, which proposed the amalgamation of the grammar school sixth forms to create a two-year 'Junior College' providing courses for pupils from all the sixteen maintained schools which would all offer O level courses. Two main arguments were used to support the plan. First, it would represent the best use of available staffing and equipment. Second, such a college would meet the desire of young people to be treated in a more adult manner. (The report forms an appendix to R. W. King, 1969.)

Urwin reports that the contents of the memorandum were somehow leaked to the local press before it was presented to the sub-committee. In his own account of the affair the chief education officer blamed the leak on a Labour member who suspected that the chairman would 'kill the scheme in embryo' (R. W. King, 1969). It had not been discussed with any representative groups of teachers, and there was an angry response from the grammar school headteachers, who wrote, defensively: 'The sixth form is the backbone of every grammar school. Its standard reflects the standard of the school as a whole.' Their opposition was made more resolute by the memorandum's comparison of the size of the sixth forms in maintained grammar schools with those of public schools. The former's smaller size was part of the argument for their separation and amalgamation in the college. This was a sore point with the headteachers who felt (with some justification) that their sixth forms were depleted by the local authority's policy of taking up places in the numerous direct grant and independent schools in the area. The headteachers of the secondary modern schools were more favourably disposed towards the scheme, and most welcomed it as an opportunity to develop examination work and to reduce the status differences between the schools in the area.

Representative deputations of teachers met the sub-committee and, as a result of this and other pressures, the director of the Oxford Institute of Education was invited in the spring of 1955, at the suggestion of the chief education officer, to act as a consultant in the matter. Although he was asked to report on the educational aspects of the plan and not on the economic ones, the consultant did favour the idea of pooling sixth form resources, but opposed the plan overall. His objections were concerned with the discontinuity between fifth and sixth form studies, the desirability for teachers to teach at all age levels, and the lack of opportunities for responsibility and authority in the college. These aspects of the traditional idea of the sixth form were too valuable to be changed.

The Education Committee presented his report to the council and after a series of discussions the scheme was rejected. The grammar schools were not 'decapitated'. The response to the demand for more selective school places was met by taking over the premises of two polytechnics which closed soon after this time.

The second attempt at reorganisation in Croydon was begun in 1961. Two new factors were part of the situation, the first being the growing doubts about the reliability of the eleven-plus selection procedure and the related concern about the 'wastage' of grammar school places. Since 1956 the Croydon Education Department had made records of the levels of success at O level in the grammar schools, and, using their own rather arbitrary criteria, concluded that there was a measure of under-achievement. The corollary was the necessity for the reorganisation of secondary education on comprehensive lines, the argument being that the abolition of the unfair eleven-plus would reduce the wastage of opportunity. When in 1961 the Education Committee asked for a general report on the 'state of the schools', a plan was produced by the chief education officer proposing the formation of 11–16 'common schools', capped, as before, by a junior college.

Two outside consultants, the director of the National Foundation for Educational Research and the director of the University of London Institute of Education, were asked to comment on the plan, and the latter was broadly in favour of its ideas. The report of the sub-committee in 1962 was also positive in tone and its

65

detailed presentation gave the widespread but false impression that the scheme was being put into effect, despite the report's prefacing words: 'The Sub-Committee have in mind. . . .'

The report was received by the Education Committee which initiated discussions with the Ministry of Education and the head-teachers concerned. Although local reaction was quite favourable, the headteachers took much the same views as in 1954–5. Through the deputations and written memorandum of their various professional associations the modern school headteachers expressed favourability, and the grammar school heads dissent. The latter's opposition was strengthened by the actions of two headteachers who, on the face of it, had no interest in the matter. The head-teachers of a local independent school and a local direct grant school issued a statement arguing that eleven was not too early to select the 'really bright child' and that the education of such children was only possible in a selective establishment. It is possible they feared that the implementation of the plan would lead the local authority to withdraw its sponsorship of pupils to their schools, but their statement convinced the grammar school head-teachers that they could never compete with their old rivals under the proposed reorganisation.

In their meetings with representatives of the Ministry of Education, members of the sub-committee had their attention drawn to the impending reorganisation of local authorities leading to the creation of a new London Borough of Croydon. Any implementation of the scheme would have to wait until this came into existence. In 1963 the chief education officer retired early due to ill-health, and his successor was invited to submit further plans for reorganisation. The original Croydon plan has not been implemented in the new borough. The comprehensive pattern is a mixed one of 11–14, 14–18 and 11–16 schools. Places are still taken up in the direct grant and independent schools and there are two denominational grammar schools (Benn, 1972).

Although Caroline Benn (1969) attributes the first suggestion for a sixth form college to F. I. Jones in 1942, Kenneth Urwin has provided an account of the effective origin of the idea, of the important part played by the chief education officer, who claims to have first thought of the idea in 1939 (R. W. King, 1969), and of its reception by the various interest groups. Patterns similar to those Urwin outlined will be seen again in later accounts of the implementation of another form of separate post-sixteen education in North Devon and Exeter.

The emergence of sixth form colleges

It is doubtful if any claim to be Britain's first maintained sixth form college could be substantiated. The headmaster of the Mexborough Grammar School did make such a claim (Shield, 1964), but it is clear from his description that what had been set up was a sixth form unit, operating in a limited way as a sixth form centre in relation to local non-selective schools. The lower school now has a comprehensive intake but the sixth form, although physically separate, shares headmaster and staff and provides some prefects (Shield, 1970). This retention of links with the lower school is seen by the headmaster as being advantageous, and it is applauded by Robin Davis (1967), a defender of the grammar school tradition. This confusion of the meaning of sixth form college with sixth form unit and sixth form centre is not uncommon and is found in the ILEA (1968) report in which centres are called colleges.

The history of the Mexborough School does, however, illustrate a familiar pattern. Most sixth form colleges were originally grammar schools (Benn and Simon, 1972; Monks, 1968; Phillips, 1972). At an early stage they tend to operate as sixth form centres in relation to modern schools. The selective intake is then either stopped and worked through until only those over sixteen are left, so forming a college, or a comprehensive intake is made to form eventually a sixth form centre. The former has been the sort of pattern of emergence of sixth form colleges in Southampton (see Vale, 1972, 1973; Lennard, 1972), Hampshire (see Gawthorpe, 1972), Luton (see Bailey, 1972) and Scunthorpe (see Edmonds, 1972). Sixth form colleges are seldom born (Stoke-on-Trent seems to be one of the few purpose-built colleges, see Little, 1972); they are produced by metamorphosis. The stages are complete when the college intake comes from associated, fully comprehensive schools. One claimant for the title of being the first sixth form college system, by this definition, would be Southampton. In 1972 the three 'secondary colleges' received students from their associated short-course schools which were the first of the virtually non-selected intake into the schools (see Vale, 1972, 1973; Lennard, 1972; Browning, 1972). One reservation on this claim would be that the former Southampton local authority did continue to take up some places at the boys' voluntary aided grammar school.

Whatever the precise stage of development or form of existing sixth form colleges, most observers agree that the prospects are that more are being planned and that this represents a swing away from the previously favoured all-through school (see, for example, Benn, 1972; Lynch, 1972a, 1972b; Phillips, 1972; McGrath, 1973).

Types of sixth form college

On the basis of accounts made mainly by headteachers and education officers, it is clear that sixth form colleges vary in size, organisation and, most significantly in the view of some commentators, in their conditions of entry (see, for example, Benn and Simon, 1972; Marsden, 1969).

The organisation of student behaviour varies from the traditional sixth form style to what is usually described as more adult treatment. Thus, for example, Ichen College permits smoking (private communication) but Rotherham does not (Prust, 1970). Similar variations are reported in relation to freedom to leave the college during the day and in relation to appearance, the terms 'acceptable' or 'suitable' being subject to many interpretations. Most colleges are co-educational, two exceptions being the Southampton College for girls and the Richard Taunton College for boys, also in Southampton (see Lennard, 1972).

The variations in size are quite marked. The Stoke-on-Trent College will eventually provide over 1,000 places (Little, 1972), whereas the Southampton College has a little under 600 (Vale, 1973). Most sixth form colleges will be considerably bigger than any sixth form integral to a school.

The conditions of entry vary from open access in Southampton (Vale, 1972, 1973; Lennard, 1972; Browning, 1972) to a fairly tightly defined minimum entrance requirement as at Stoke-on-Trent (Little, 1972). Dennis Marsden (1969) regards these two forms of college as representing different philosophies or ideologies of comprehensive education. The selective college is an expression of a meritocratic ideology in which emphasis is placed upon assisting children to succeed, through the examination system, in the prevailing social system. John Bright's (1972) account of 'Stoke-on-Trent's A level Academy' supports Marsden's view. He describes the 'semi-university environment': 'The atmosphere is certainly going to develop into one of unrelieved competitiveness.' Benn and Simon (1972) describe the Stoke College as, 'specifically designed to act as a high powered grammar school sixth form'. Although it is not made explicit in the official description of the college (Little, 1972) it may be inferred that the introduction of a selective sixth form college, in which at least four O levels are usually required for entry and virtually everyone follows an A level course, was seen as a means to maximise the motivation and so the academic success of as many as possible of the bright children in a largely working class area. This is a version of Harry Davies's (1965) defence of the grammar school in relation to the working class: it represents their best chance of getting on.

Marsden (1969) regards open access sixth form colleges as expressions of an egalitarian comprehensive philosophy, in which emphasis is placed upon attempts to transform the nature of society. As previous research has shown (King, 1973a), headteachers of some (but not all) comprehensive schools feel this social engineering may be achieved as a result of the experience of school. Children from many different social backgrounds share a common educational experience, and this may lead to changed relationships in the outside world they eventually enter. Marsden's view is not, however, clearly confirmed in the accounts of Southampton's open access system (Vale, 1972, 1973; Lennard, 1972; Browning, 1972). Any sixteen year old may enter one of the three colleges, which provide CSE as well as O and A level courses and a small number of vocational courses. This is also seen as a way of maximising educational success but at a number of different levels: 'It has been said that open access will mean levelling down. In our experience it has meant the opposite, since many girls have been encouraged to attempt more than they previously dared to, and have succeeded' (Vale, 1972).

Brian Simon (1969) considers that the egalitarian or social engineering element in the comprehensive movement has become associated with left wing political views; this may account for the ascendancy of the meritocratic element – comprehensive schools as the best providers of educational opportunities. There is perhaps a hint of an egalitarian sentiment in relation to the open access colleges of Southampton: 'They [the most able] have not become arrogant, because they have also learned to value the strong practical common sense and powers of organisation, of the others in their community' (Vale, 1972).

The case for the sixth form college

The literature of the sixth form college is in part descriptive but mainly consists of discussions of the cases for and against the arrangement. The general sentiments of teachers towards the idea of the college are indicated in the results of the Schools Council survey (Morton-Williams et al., 1970). Only 10 per cent of sixth form teachers and 5 per cent of headteachers considered sixth form colleges to be the most beneficial for pupils of sixth form age; both much lower levels of approval than for either the integral sixth form or the sixth form block (see chapter 3). The reservations made about sixth form colleges have sometimes 'met the abuse commonly reserved for blasphemy' ('Times Educational Supplement', 1965). As the heresy is the proposal to 'decapitate' the traditional all-through school, the arguments for and against the 'radical break with tradition' (Edwards, 1970b) are inseparable from those for and against the integral sixth form.

The principal argument used in the unsuccessful attempt to introduce the sixth form college in Croydon was one concerned with the efficient utilisation of educational resources (Urwin, 1965; R. W. King, 1969). Many of the more recent, detailed arguments along this line are very similar to those used in relation to sixth form centres. The colleges' better use of scarce, skilled teachers and their power to attract high quality staff are frequently mentioned (for example, NUT, 1966; Taylor, 1965; Little, 1972). However, the National Union of Teachers (1966) and the Headmasters' Association (1968) see in this the possibility of a 'split profession' and point out, as does O'Connor (1967), that this may isolate younger pupils from what are thought to be the benefits of contact with the better qualified, graduate teachers. Whilst Peterson (1973) considered that sixth form college teaching is an attractive idea to existing sixth form teachers (a proposition not strongly supported by the Schools Council survey already quoted), Beynon (1966) felt that the introduction of the arrangement may be unsettling to staff, who may move to other areas. Both the Headmasters' Association (1968) and the Assistant Masters' Association (1974), and also Taylor (1965), considered that most staff prefer to teach a wide age range.

The NUT (1966) and Benn (1972) point out that the introduction of sixth form colleges may be made using existing buildings; this is in fact nearly always the case. The HMA (1968), Gawthorpe (1972) and Little (1972) use the viable sixth form argument in suggesting that colleges are suitable where integral sixth forms would be too small. The ILEA enquiry (1968) calculated that a college would need at least 400 students to provide what was considered to be a viable range of A level courses. This number was based upon the assumption that mainly A level courses would be provided, but the more 'open' colleges also provide full O level or even CSE courses, thus meeting a reservation made by the HMA (1968) concerning the education of those who take six years to O level. The efficient use of resources is seen by some to lead to a greater choice of subjects for the pupils (NUT, 1966; HMA, 1968).

The original Croydon plan was also justified in terms of the desire for young people to be treated in a more adult way (Urwin, 1965). (This is also used to justify sixth form units and further education colleges.) This view is often endorsed (for example, Vale, 1973; Gawthorpe, 1972; Taylor, 1965) and the teachers in the Schools Council survey saw this as the greatest benefit of the sixth form college (Morton-Williams et al., 1970). Nearly half (47 per cent) saw advantages in terms of adult treatment, greater independence, more privileges and less restrictions; much higher ratings than those for the integral sixth form or sixth form block (see Table 3.1, p. 50).

Following from this, the college is argued to be a better preparation for higher education (see, for example, Bailey, 1972; Little, 1972; Peterson, 1973). The teachers in the Schools Council survey agreed with this view; 37 per cent of them felt this was a benefit of sixth form colleges compared with 15 per cent in relation to sixth form units. As an additional benefit 31 per cent felt that the colleges would provide better opportunities for social relationships within the students' own age group. This is again higher than for sixth form units (11 per cent). The AMA (1965), however, feared the colleges may involve too much freedom, 'offering immature minds a pseudo-adult atmosphere'.

The transition from the fifth form to the sixth form college is seen as a disadvantage by some commentators. The NUT (1966) and HMA (1968) suggest that some may fail 'to jump the gap' and so be lost to post-sixteen education, the proposition being that children are more likely to stay on in a school they know. Dalton (1969) feels this may be particularly true for potential, first generation sixth formers. Others see disadvantages for those who do jump the gap. Taylor (1965) Corbett (1969), Miller (1964) and Murphy (1972), all argue that sixteen is a bad time for a break, that adolescents need continuity and need to relate the people they have known for a long time. The relatively short period spent in a college (one to three years) is thought to create the danger of a 'transit camp atmosphere', which would pose problems of pastoral care (see, for example, HMA, 1968; Taylor, 1965; Thomas, 1972; Ruffle, 1973).

A defence of the traditional idea of the sixth form is strongly implied in the criticisms of sixth form colleges which centre upon the loss of opportunities for leadership and responsibility (e.g. NUT, 1966; HMA, 1968). Some see this not only as a loss to younger pupils but as a loss to the sixth formers themselves (HMA, 1968; Corbett, 1969). Woodward (1970), in a survey of sixth form colleges in Hampshire, found some dismay among PE teachers concerning what they saw to be the students' indifference to team games, and their difficulties in getting teams together on a voluntary basis. The advent of sixth form colleges has been claimed to be 'killing rugby at its roots', as students, given a choice, do not want to play team games (Frost, 1973).

The idea of the sixth form college represents a further departure from the traditional idea of the sixth form. The social control and role-model purposes in relation to younger pupils have gone. The traditional academic elements, including the special relationship with the universities, are quite clearly preserved in the selective college, which is seen by some to be 'a sort of academic Noah's ark to carry traditional academic values over the flood tide of declining academic standards' (Carter, 1970). But in the idea of the open access sixth form college this aspect is less important so that this type of college is the more heretical. It is interesting to note that although the cachet of 'sixth form' is widely used, with very little logic, in the names of colleges, 'junior college' (as originally proposed for Croydon) and 'secondary college' (as in Southampton) are becoming more common.

Two sixth form colleges

Two contrasted sixth form colleges and their students were the subjects of original research. Both 'Open' College and 'Selective' College were originally grammar schools. Open College is a clear example of the open access type of college, in that there were no entry requirements; indeed, this was officially seen as being a second chance institution for those who did not do well at school. Selective College's pseudonym is not entirely accurate. Officially there was no bar to entry, and the stated criterion was the ability and sense of purpose to benefit from the courses provided. These courses were 'concerned with preparation for the Advanced level examinations in order to allow candidates to qualify for higher education . . . or for the professions' (official handbook). The entry procedure would be fairly described as guided choice, the alternative for a fifth form leaver being the local technical college.

These differences in entry procedure are reflected in the proportions of students taking different courses in the two colleges. In Open College 75 per cent were taking O levels, 57 per cent A levels. Figures for Selective College were 49 per cent and 86 per cent respectively. Open College also provided CSE courses and a secretarial course. The orientation of Selective College students was more strongly towards full-time higher education, which 82 per cent expected to take up, compared with 55 per cent in Open College.

There were also broad differences in the general organisation of student behaviour between the two colleges. Although senior staff in interview and official documents referred to the adult atmosphere in both colleges, the control of students was generally less tight in Open College, more traditional in Selective College. Selective boys were required to wear jackets and ties, but at Open College the criterion for appearance was 'not too scruffy', and jeans were permitted. After what seems to have been a struggle, girls at Selective College were allowed to wear trousers, but not jeans, which girls at Open College were allowed to wear. Both colleges provided common rooms run for and by the students. The rules for Open College permitted smoking at certain times and were more permissive in relation to the playing of records and radios. Both colleges allowed students to go out without permission during the lunch hour, and at Open College they could do so at other times as well.

The experience of the students reflects these differences in organisation. Open students were more likely to feel they were treated as adults, but less likely to feel there were unnecessary restrictions. They also agreed more often that the college was good preparation for work, that the staff were interested in their

Table 5.1 *Students' opinions in two sixth form colleges*
(% agreement)

	Open College (n = 171)	Selective College (n = 313)	Significance (%) (chi square)
Staff are interested in your personal welfare	59.6	47.0	5
In the college you are treated as an adult	69.6	51.4	1
There is a real sense of belonging	45.6	30.0	1
The work is harder than I expected	18.1	28.8	5
There is a strong emphasis on exams	71.3	82.7	5
The college is a good preparation for going to work	48.5	29.7	1
There are unnecessary restrictions in college	13.5	55.5	0.1
Doing non-exam subjects takes up valuable time	49.7	38.0	5
Happier in the fifth year of previous school than in college	9.9	22.0	1

personal welfare, and that they felt a sense of belonging (Table 5.1).

The control of school work was very similar in both colleges, ensuring the regular collection of marks, sessional examinations and reports. However, students of Selective College agreed more often that there was a strong emphasis on exams and that the work was harder than they expected, but they were less inclined to feel that doing non-exam subjects took up valuable time (Table 5.1).

More students at Selective College felt they had been happier in the fifth form than in the college (Table 5.1), although the rates at which they estimated they settled in were similar in both colleges. Although the Selective College was a slightly more important centre for student friendships, Open students were more likely to make new friends in college (Table 5.2).

In both colleges games were compulsory, although a wide choice was available. Both provided a wide range of extra-curricular activities; 57 per cent of Open students joined at least one of these, as did 63 per cent of Selective students. These

Table 5.2 *Friendship patterns in two sixth form colleges* (%)

	Open College (n = 171)	Selective College (n = 313)	Significance (%) (chi square)
Most friends at the college	72.5	81.5	5
No friends made at school before coming to college	18.7	5.8	1
All friends made since coming to college	18.7	4.8	1

activities and the committees associated with the running of the student common rooms provided opportunities for positions of responsibility; 21 per cent of students in both colleges held at least one such position.

Neither college had a house or prefectorial system. One of the headteachers commented on this: 'Little account need be taken of the loss of the prefect or house systems. These arose at a time when day grammar schools (and others) thought it advantageous to ape the nineteenth century public schools.' However, both colleges had compulsory attendance at school assembly and a prize giving ceremony, so that some of the traditional rituals were retained.

Several interesting differences were found in the sexes' experience of the colleges (Table 5.3). In both colleges girls estimated they took longer to settle in than did boys. Boys in both colleges agreed more often than girls that there were unnecessary restrictions. The difference is reflected in the girls more often agreeing that they decided how much work they did. However, girls were more likely to disagree that they knew some of the staff well. This may be related to their slower settling in. These results show how the experience of the same organisation can vary with the sex of the participant.

The two colleges represent different degrees of modification of the traditional idea of the sixth form. Selective College was nearer to this but Open College was associated with higher levels of student satisfaction, although in both colleges boys settled in more quickly than girls, but girls seemed to feel a greater sense of freedom.

Table 5.3 *Sex differences and students' opinions in two sixth form colleges* (%)

	Boys (n = 274)	Girls (n = 210)	Significance (%) (chi square)
Settled in a few days	62.8	35.2	1
Settled in a few weeks	26.6	40.5	1
Settled after about a term	5.8	12.9	5
Still feel unsettled	2.2	3.8	ns
Agree there are unnecessary restrictions	53.3	23.3	1
Agree they decide how much work they do	80.3	90.5	5
Disagree they know some of the staff well	20.1	30.0	5

The integral sixth forms and the sixth form colleges compared

A comparison of the organisation of student learning and behaviour in the four schools with integral sixth forms (St Trad's, Newstyle, Central and Cooperative), with the two sixth form colleges, shows that neither type of institution is associated with particular forms of control. In many ways the sixth form unit at Newstyle could be regarded as having the least restrictions on behaviour, although the control of school work was very similar in all six institutions. Any overall differences in the students' experience of the two forms of provision may therefore be cautiously associated with the presence or absence of younger pupils. When comparisons of the experiences of students in sixth form colleges were made with those in schools considerable variations in the percentage levels of response to particular questions were found across the six institutions. Only if the percentages in both sixth form colleges were either higher or lower than those in each of the four schools was the average for both colleges compared with that for the four schools. (A more detailed discussion of this procedure is made in chapter 11.)

Although the control of school work was similar in all six institutions, students in the four schools felt there was a greater

Table 5.4 *Students' opinions and experiences in sixth form colleges and integral sixth forms* (%)

	Sixth formers in colleges (*n* = 484)	Sixth formers in schools (*n* = 436)	Significance (%) (chi square)
Agree there is a strong emphasis on exams	78.7	87.8	5
Agree they prefer to keep social life separate from school or college	32.0	44.5	2
Disagree that school/college a good preparation for work	35.1	47.7	5
No friends of the opposite sex in sixth or college	11.0	2.3	5
All friends made before entering sixth or college	3.5	11.0	2
Still feel unsettled in sixth form/college	2.9	6.7	5
When sixth forms are part of the same school as younger pupils:			
The sixth formers gain	14.3	30.2	1
The sixth formers lose	27.9	11.9	1
The younger pupils gain	37.2	57.8	1
The younger pupils lose	18.4	5.3	1

emphasis on exams than did those in the two colleges (Table 5.4). Boys in the schools felt more often than boys in the colleges that the staff were only interested in those who did well (Table 5.5). Girls in the schools disagreed more often than girls in colleges that they could decide how much work they did (Table 5.5). Sixth form colleges are not A level factories to their students.

At the time of asking, more students in school than in colleges still felt unsettled, this being particularly true for boys (Tables 5.4 and 5.5). More boys felt they had settled in quickly in the colleges than in the schools (Table 5.5). Clearly, the fears expressed about the transition involved in the use of sixth form colleges are not substantiated.

There were a number of interesting differences in friendship patterns between the two types of institution, some expected and some not so easily explained. Students in schools, especially girls,

Table 5.5 *Sex differences and students' opinions and experiences in sixth form colleges and integral sixth forms* (%)

	Boys			Girls		
	College (n = 274)	School (n = 205)	Significance (%) (chi square)	College (n = 210)	School (n = 231)	Significance (%) (chi square)
Agree prefer to keep social life separate from school or college	34.7	44.9	5	28.6	44.1	1
Agree staff only interested in those who do well	12.4	21.0	1	—	—	—
Disagree you decide how much work you do	—	—	—	4.3	12.1	1
Agree it is easy to make friends in school or college	88.3	66.3	0.1	—	—	—
Agree they are treated as adults	—	—	—	67.6	40.3	0.1
All friends made before entering sixth or college	3.7	8.8	ns	3.3	13.0	0.1
No friends of opposite sex in sixth or college	12.0	2.4	0.1	9.5	2.2	0.1
Settled in a few days	62.8	45.9	0.1	35.2	38.1	ns
Still feel unsettled	2.2	6.8	2	3.8	6.5	ns

Note: Blank sections of the Table indicate that there were not consistent differences between the colleges and the schools.

preferred to keep their social lives separate from the institution more often than those in colleges, thus supporting the contention of the teachers in the Schools Council survey (Morton-Williams et al., 1970) that the sixth form college would provide better opportunities for students to form relationships with their age-mates (Tables 5.4 and 5.5). This is supported by the finding that college boys found it easier to make friends than those in school (Table 5.5). A little surprisingly, more students in college, both boys and girls, reported they had no friends of the opposite sex (Tables 5.4 and 5.5). Obviously the long term contacts between the sexes in the schools had not produced anything like an incest taboo, nor had the newness of relationships in the colleges (Tables 5.4 and 5.5) strongly enhanced the attractiveness of the opposite sex.

There were no consistent or significant differences in the rates at which college or school students voluntarily joined clubs or other activities, nor, contrary to opinions mentioned before, do they vary in the number of positions of responsibility held. As may be expected, college students were less likely to see benefits in the integral sixth form organisation, for either sixth formers or younger pupils (Table 5.4).

Interesting as some of these results may be, it is important to stress that there are many similarities in students' experience of the two forms of post-sixteen education. There were no consistent or significant differences in their reported relationships with teachers (other than that already mentioned for boys), in their dispositions towards school work (other than that reported for girls), or in their feelings of belonging. The sixth form college is no more a transit camp than the sixth form. The protagonists of the college stress its more relaxed control and its adult atmosphere, but there were no consistent or significant differences in students' assessments of the extent of unnecessary restrictions. Only the girls in the colleges agreed more often than those in schools that they were treated as adults (Table 5.5).

These results, based upon a small sample of institutions but a larger one of students, show that neither the integral sixth form nor the sixth form college has the monopoly of student satisfaction. However, they do suggest that contrary to expectation, students, especially boys, may find it easier to settle in to the college organisation. In addition, the colleges may form more important centres for the social lives of their students, even if they are associated with less friendships between the sexes.

The results also draw attention to a phenomenon not mentioned in the school versus sixth form college debate; the sex differences in the experience of educational organisations. This refers to the experiences of the same sex in different organisations, and the two sexes in the same organisation. This is strikingly shown in the way in which girls in the colleges feel they have more control over the amount of school work they do than boys in colleges, and also more than do girls in schools.

Chapter 6

Short-course comprehensives

A corollary of the establishment of any kind of separate post-sixteen education is the creation of short-course comprehensive schools for 11 or 12–16 year olds. These schools may exist in two basic organisational settings: either in association with sixth form centres, or in association with sixth form colleges, and, as in Exeter and North Devon, in association with colleges of further education used as centres for all post-sixteen education. Some of the concerns about short-course comprehensives apply to only the former arrangement; others apply to both.

The case for the short-course school

Many of the suggested advantages of short-course schools are really those of sixth form centres or colleges, especially the effective utilisation of scarce educational resources. The schools are also seen as permitting the generation of an adult atmosphere in the colleges.

The absence of a sixth form as a source of leaders and as a reference group for younger pupils is seen as a disadvantage by the NUT (1966), HMA (1968), Corbett (1969) and Taylor (1965), but some of the headteachers of short-course schools in Benn's (1971) small survey of nine such schools saw advantages in their absence in that it gave fifteen and sixteen year olds opportunities for leadership otherwise denied them. One headteacher felt that an academic sixth form was more a discouragement to the less able than a stimulus. Others pointed out that since all pupils of the same age left school at the same time, those taking up jobs did not feel inferior to those going on to continued full-time education. Edmonds (1972), referring to short-course schools in the Scunthorpe scheme, reports that the removal of the sixth form had not affected discipline.

Another criticism concerns staffing. It is argued that sixth form colleges or centres will attract graduate teachers, and that younger pupils will be deprived of contact with them (see, for example, HMA, 1968; NUT, 1966). Some of the headteachers in Benn's (1971) survey shared these views, one suggesting that O level teaching suffered where there was no A level work. However, others saw advantages, pointing to the possibilities of greater job satisfaction for non-graduate teachers, and the easier adjustment to reorganisation for secondary modern teachers. One headteacher suggested that the sort of heads of department appointed for sixth form work were not always the best for younger pupils.

One of their few advantages seen by the HMA (1968) was that short-course schools could be small schools, a point endorsed by some of the headteachers (Benn, 1971). However, small size and the absence of older pupils leads to a small points allocation for scale posts in such schools, and this too is thought to lead to a shortage of good applicants for posts (HMA, 1968). Edmonds (1972) claims it has been possible to attract able staff to the short-course schools in Scunthorpe, but some of the headteachers in Benn's (1971) survey shared the HMA's fears.

Benn and Simon (1972) also express concern about the academic viability of such schools, not only in terms of the quality of the teachers, but also in their provision of curriculum and examination opportunities. In their survey they found that a sample of short-course schools offered an average of seven O level subjects – only half that offered by long-course schools. Related to this is a concern about the transition rates to continued full-time education from such schools (for example, NUT, 1966; HMA, 1968). Benn and Simon found that the short-course comprehensives in their sample had the lowest rate of staying on of any type of comprehensive. This is to some extent explained by their head-teachers' estimate of the percentage of their intake in the top 20 per cent of the ability range. That, for short-course schools, was lowest at 13 per cent.

Short-course schools in association with sixth form centres

The strongest critics of the arrangement of sixth form centres (long-course schools) with short-course feeder schools have been Benn and Simon (1972). They fear the perpetuation of the disparity of esteem associated with the origins of the schools: most short-course schools were secondary moderns, most long-course were grammar schools. 'The short-course schools may be permanently disadvantaged by smaller size, few facilities, narrower ability intake, inadequate staffing or inability to offer as great a range of courses' (Benn, 1972). In the small survey by Caroline Benn (1971) of nine short-course schools in a range of schemes, three headteachers did report that they felt their schools were unfairly treated by the local authority. One of the headteachers of a feeder school confirmed Benn and Simon's fear that parents may also tend to regard the short-course school as second best.

Short-course comprehensives in a single local authority

Some of the propositions about short-course schools were put to the test in a survey in one local authority area, a county borough in the South of England, now reorganised to become part of a larger unit. (Some aspects of this research have been published in King, 1974a, 1974b.)

The basic structure of the school system is as follows: first schools (ages 5–8), middle schools (8–12), short-course comprehensive schools (12–16) and open access sixth form colleges (16–19). As is common in such systems, the 12–16 schools were originally modern schools, and the sixth form colleges originally grammar schools. The secondary comprehensives are neighbourhood schools, each receiving pupils from associated first and middle schools. Parents may choose to send their children to a comprehensive in another area but this is not officially encouraged. Two specific constraints are that parents must take the initiative in applying for a transfer, which must be made on a special form obtained from the middle school headteacher and which must be returned by a specified date early in the school year before the time of transfer. In addition, pupils attending schools outside their area are not eligible for free travel.

Over 95 per cent of thirteen year olds attend these comprehensive schools. The local authority continued to send about 120 boys (3.9 per cent of all twelve year olds) to one aided grammar school. Ignoring the small numbers going to this selective school, the comprehensive schools have had a 'non-selected' intake since 1967. The examination candidates of 1972 were drawn from the intake of 1967.

Over a number of years the authority ranked among the highest for expenditure on secondary pupils, and was among the lowest for pupil/teacher ratios (Institute of Municipal Treasurers and Accountants, 1972). These relatively high indices of levels of expenditure, together with the relatively early entry into secondary reorganisation and the creation of open access sixth form colleges, indicate that this local education authority was probably characterised by what Byrne and Williamson (1972b) suggest is an anti-élitist or egalitarian ideology. The retention of places in the grammar schools should be seen as a reflection of the general problem of co-operation of aided schools in schemes of secondary reorganisation, rather than an élitist ideology.

The sample consisted of all the sixteen short-course neighbourhood comprehensive schools in the local education authority. Three are for boys, three for girls, and ten are mixed. The headteacher or his designate completed a detailed questionnaire concerned with provision and organisation. The public examination results of summer 1972 for each pupil were also provided by the schools, together with their incidence of continued full-time education in one of the sixth form colleges, the local technical college or in the sixth forms of other schools outside the area. The chief education officer provided copies of annual reports and statistics, brochures for parents describing educational provision in the area, confidential memoranda and informal comment on the system.

The overall pupil/teacher ratio was 16.3, which is lower than the national average of 17.7 for comprehensive schools. Graduates formed 26.7 per cent of the teaching staff (range 6.3–53.8 per cent). This is less than the national average of 40 per cent for all comprehensive schools (DES, 1971), but comparable to the mean of 23 per cent for those in junior high school comprehensives, reported by Monks (1968). The proportion of full-time teachers was 89.1 per cent (range 85.3–93.9 per cent), which is comparable to the national average of 87.6 per cent for secondary schools. Without necessarily accepting the implicit value-judgment that contact with graduate teachers is a good thing, it is clear that in most of the short-course schools in this system the majority of teachers were non-graduates, whereas virtually all the staff of the sixth form colleges were graduates, with the exception of PE and technical subjects specialists.

The mean size of the schools was 631 pupils (range 449–1.014 pupils), and compares fairly closely with the mean of 587 for 11 or 12–16 schools in the Benn and Simon (1972) survey. Four schools in the present survey had posts at the scale five level (six posts in all), and every school had posts at the scale four level. Altogether, 26.9 per cent of the teachers were on scale four or five (range 13.5–39.3 per cent). There are no national or other statistics available for comparison purposes but it is clear that some opportunities did exist for access to higher levels of remuneration. It is of interest to note that non-graduates were just as likely to hold high level posts as graduates were, but, as was noted by Mays et al. (1968), in a study of a single comprehensive, there was a tendency for graduates to be heads of department and for non-graduates to hold head of house and head of year group types of appointment.

Every school was able to offer at least two foreign languages, six offered three, and one, four. All were able to offer three separate sciences. All prepared pupils for both O level and CSE examinations. The mean number of O level subjects entered for was 16.3 (range 13–22). This is more than double that for the short-course comprehensives in Benn and Simon's (1972) sample, and higher than that for all-through comprehensives with an average of 15. The mean number of CSE subjects entered for was 17.6 (range 13–24). This compares favourably with an average of 19 for the sample of mainly all-through schools studied by King (1973a).

Apart from the proportion of graduates in the schools, their academic provision was, therefore, good by any available standards, in terms of curriculum and examination opportunities. A better test of their academic viability is to analyse the examination performances of the pupils. This was done for the results for all pupils in the examinations of 1972. Six levels of attainment were used, each derived from those used by examining boards in making their statistical reports and from the regulations governing entry requirements to employment and post-school education. Each, therefore, has a fairly distinct social meaning; for example, the highest level is thought to indicate potential for higher education.

Level A: Five passes at O level, or CSE grade 1, or combinations of both, to include English, mathematics and a language.

Level B: Five passes at O level, or CSE grade 1, or combinations of both, for any subjects.

Level C: Three passes at O level, or CSE grade 1, or combinations of both, for any subjects.

Level D: Five CSE passes at grades between 1 and 4, to include O level passes as equivalent to grade 1 CSE.

Level E: Three CSE passes at grades between 1 and 4, to include O level passes as before.

Level F: One CSE pass grade 1–4, or one O level pass.

The results (Table 6.1) compare favourably with the national levels as far as equivalence between the statistics allows. Of leavers from comprehensive schools in 1970, 14.5 per cent had five or more O level passes – roughly equivalent to level B with an average of 13.0 per cent. Nationally, 21.4 per cent of comprehensive school leavers had three or more O levels (DES, 1971). This is roughly equivalent to level C with a mean of 22.2 per cent.

Table 6.1 *Percentage of fourth year pupils of 1971 with examination passes in 1972*

Attainment level	Boys $(n = 772)$	Girls $(n = 731)$	All $(n = 1,503)$	Range (all)
A	1.6	8.9	5.3	0.0–16.7
B	9.8	16.0	13.0	3.6–29.6
C	19.0	25.2	22.2	8.8–36.9
D	44.9	44.2	44.5	17.5–62.0
E	53.9	50.3	52.1	26.3–67.5
F	58.0	52.7	55.3	37.2–69.5

Note: The Table follows the schools' use of fourth year to refer to the third year in the school.

The discrepancies between boys and girls at the higher levels of attainment are probably due to the recruitment of boys to the aided grammar school, and also, at Level A, to the generally lower levels of attainment for boys in languages.

Five indices of continued education were derived from the pupil data (Table 6.2).

Table 6.2 *Continued education* (%)

		Boys	Girls	All	Range (all)
1	4th year staying for 5th year	63.3	54.2	58.8	46.0–78.4
2	4th year in f/t education after 16	24.8	35.6	30.3	19.7–44.7
3	4th year with exam results at levels A and B in f/t education after 16	76.1	87.2	83.0	65.4–96.0
4	4th year with exam results at levels D and F or no pass continuing in f/t education after 16	27.2	50.0	36.8	18.2–63.6
5	5th year in f/t education after 16	38.5	62.4	49.9	33.3–72.1

Note: The Table follows the schools' use of fifth year to refer to the final year in the school. See also note to Table 6.1.

Index 3 shows that the majority of the successful pupils did continue their education after sixteen, and Index 4 shows that a substantial proportion of the less successful did so as well.

It is possible in this case to make direct comparisons with national statistics. In 1972 sixteen year old pupils formed 35.5 per cent of thirteen year olds three years previously (boys 35.7 per cent, girls 35.2 per cent). In the local authority studied the figure was 38.2 per cent (boys 37.1 per cent, girls 39.4 per cent). In the same year seventeen year old pupils formed 19.6 per cent of thirteen year olds four years previously (boys 19.8 per cent, girls 19.4 per cent). The local authority figures were 24.5 per cent (boys 25.1 per cent, girls 24.0 per cent) (DES, 1973). It is clear that this system of short-course comprehensive schools was associated with levels of academic success that compare well nationally, and with high levels of continued education.

The absence of sixth forms as a source of leaders and exemplars was not considered a problem by the headteachers, possibly because they had never had sixth forms, their schools having been originally secondary moderns. Thirteen of the sixteen had prefects and, despite the absence of sixth formers, ten produced an annual play, twelve a regular school magazine, and thirteen an annual school concert. Comparisons with other comprehensive schools and with schools in general show the incidence of most of these activities to be above average or quite high (see King, 1973a; King and Fry, 1972).

It is clear from the results presented that the fears about the educational provision and the academic and expressive viability of short-course schools were not realised in this system of schools. This may have been due to the local authority's generous financial policies and its commitment to the comprehensive ideology. As Caroline Benn (1971) has expressed it: 'With short-course comprehensive schools – as with all other comprehensive schemes – it is the policy that counts, not the age-range.'

Educational provision and educational attainment

The data from this survey may also be used to comment further upon Benn and Simon's (1972) conclusion that short-course schools are associated with a low retention of pupils in full-time education. This may be correct for a national sample of such schools but the results of those presented show that there are big variations between individual schools even within the same local authority area (Tables 6.1 and 6.2). One possible source of variation is indicated by Benn and Simon: the imputed ability of the pupils. The lower the average ability, the lower the average uptake of continued education. A more important and related source of variation are the social class origins of the pupils.

The schools in the survey were neighbourhood schools so the social composition of each school was roughly the same as that of its catchment area. (It might be suggested that the element of parental choice available in allocation to the schools may have led to some middle class pupils attending school outside their own area serving a more middle class population. The correlations between social composition and headteachers' estimates of the proportion of 'poached' pupils were not statistically significant.) The chief education officer provided details of the catchment areas of the schools, and the social composition of the areas was obtained from the 1966 sample census ward reports. Two indices were obtained: the percentage of economically active males in occupations corresponding to the Registrar General's Social Classes I and II, and Classes IV and V. They are not altogether satisfactory in that they do not use all the data available; social class III is not represented. Any classification of social class that uses a single index (in this case occupation) has an arbitrary element, but a more important problem was to create measurements which were susceptible to correlational analyses. Social class is not a continuous variable, but a categoric one, where the categories are rather arbitrary. There are, however, many precedents for the treatment of social class as a continuous variable in correlational analysis, including that of Byrne and Williamson (1972a, 1972b) and Wiseman (1964). What these reservations suggest is that caution must be used in interpreting the precise magnitude of correlations involving social class, and in the use of more sophisticated analyses which attempt to quantify the 'effects' of social class in relation to other supposed factors.

Table 6.3 shows that all the correlations between attainment and percentage of social classes I and II are positive, and all the correlations between attainment and the percentage of social classes IV and V are negative. The correlations for boys and girls separately were all of the same order as those for both sexes, despite the loss of boys to the aided grammar school. These results indicate that the more working class the social composition of the school the less well the pupils performed in examinations, and the less often they continued their full-time education. This is very much in line with expectations based upon the enormous literature of social class differences in educational attainment (see, for example, King, 1971). In largely ignoring the social characteristics of pupils entering their schools Benn and Simon (1972) explain the variation in the rates of staying on in terms of the type of school. This is the view that the nature of the school determines its educational output. A similar view is held by Elizabeth Halsall (1973).

However, the evidence to suggest a connection between educational provision and attainment is not conclusive. Davies (1968), in an analysis of local education authorities, found that variations in expenditure per pupil, both in secondary and in primary schools, were small in relation to variations in attainment. More specifically, expenditures per secondary pupil were hardly correlated with the rate of staying on in school until the age of seventeen. The variations in the rates of staying on and of going

Table 6.3 *Product moment correlations between social class composition and pupil educational attainment (n = 16)*

	Attainment variables	Social class composition % SC I & II	% SC IV & V
1	% 4th year staying on	0.24	−0.54
2	% 4th year with exam results at level A	0.24	−0.28
3	% 4th year with exam results at level B	0.35	−0.38
4	% 4th year with exam results at level C	0.46	−0.51
5	% 4th year with exam results at level D	0.31	−0.67
6	% 4th year with exam results at level E	0.24	−0.66
7	% 4th year with exam results at level F	0.28	−0.59
8	% 4th year continuing in f/t education after 16	0.48	−0.25
9	% 5th year continuing in f/t education after 16	0.44	−0.05
10	% 4th year with exam results at level A and B continuing in f/t education after 16	0.26	−0.12
11	% 4th year with exam results at level D and F or no passes continuing f/t education after 16	0.48	−0.06

on to higher education were, however, strongly related to high social class and the proportions of pupils in selective schools. Several studies, including that of Little et al. (1971), have contradicted teachers' conventional wisdom in demonstrating positive correlations between attainment and size of class in school. Coleman (1966) concluded, 'differences between schools account for only a small fraction of differences in pupil achievement'.

This conclusion has been queried by Byrne and Williamson (1972a, 1972b). Following the work of Eggleston (1967), they made a statistical exploration of the relationships between the educational expenditure, the rate of staying on at school, and the social composition of selected local authority areas. In line with expectation they found that middle class areas were characterised by higher levels of expenditure and higher levels of staying on than working class areas. In a partial correlation analysis they claim that part of the variation in the rates of staying on may be explained by differences in educational expenditure. This claim is not strongly supported by Davies's (1968) similar kind of analysis.

In the survey of short-course comprehensives ten indices of educational provision were obtained (see Table 6.5). Ancillary staff (number 6) excludes caretakers but includes secretaries, bursars, laboratory technicians and librarians (range 1–6). The score for material provision (number 10) was only distantly related to the scale for material provision used by Eggleston (1967) following that of the Newsom report (1963). It was based upon a simple analysis of the collated provision for schools. The attempt was to produce a simple additive scale which would discriminate with the sample. One point was awarded for each of the following, giving an eight point scale: gymnasium, careers room, language laboratory, swimming pool, second gymnasium, second library, music room (range 2–5).

Some of these variables are provision indices in the sense used by Byrne and Williamson (1972a, 1972b) to refer to the use of resources. These include the pupil-teacher ratio and the percentage of graduate teachers (graduates are paid more than non-graduates). Others are what Eggleston (1967) calls administrative variables, referring to organisational arrangements at the school level e.g. the number of out-of-school activities (range 9–26). The term 'provision' as used in this analysis was defined in terms of what the schools provided for the pupils irrespective of whether expenditure of money was involved. It is recognised that the inclusion of every one of these indices is associated with an institutionalised value-judgment, for example, graduate teachers are 'better' than non-graduates.

The correlations between the educational provision and attainment variables are given in Table 6.4, and seven important observations may be made about them. First, all the correlations between pupil attainment and the percentage of full-time staff are negative. The highest value, $r = -0.48$, gives a coefficient of determination of 23.0 per cent where $d = r^2 \times 100$, indicating that just over 20 per cent of the variance in attainment is associated with the proportion of full-time staff. Second, all the correlations for staff stability are negative; the highest value -0.50 giving a coefficient of determination of 25.0 per cent. Third, all the correlations for number of subjects available at O level are negative, the highest of -0.50 giving a value of 25.0 per cent for d. Fourth, all the correlations for the number of subjects available for CSE are negative. The highest correlation is -0.43 where $d = 18.5$ per cent. Fifth, all the correlations for attainment and pupil/teacher ratio are positive; the highest correlation is 0.81, which gives a coefficient of determination of 65.6 per cent. Sixth, the correlations for attainment and the number of languages

Table 6.4 *Product moment correlations between educational attainment and educational provision (n = 16)*

Attainment variables*	Provision variables†									
	1	2	3	4	5	6	7	8	9	10
1	−0.06	0.44	−0.47	−0.59	0.06	−0.21	−0.20	−0.41	0.75	−0.09
2	−0.43	0.42	−0.32	−0.20	0.42	0.21	−0.50	−0.35	0.36	0.35
3	−0.48	0.22	−0.49	0.16	0.15	0.17	−0.34	−0.28	0.57	0.25
4	−0.47	0.30	−0.55	0.16	0.02	0.16	−0.24	−0.27	0.67	0.18
5	−0.32	0.36	−0.50	0.60	0.17	0.13	−0.26	−0.42	0.79	−0.03
6	−0.30	0.36	−0.52	0.56	0.13	0.10	−0.27	−0.43	0.81	−0.08
7	−0.33	0.30	−0.40	0.46	0.20	0.11	−0.26	−0.38	0.75	−0.16
8	−0.41	0.27	−0.39	0.05	0.06	0.01	−0.28	−0.25	0.55	0.13
9	−0.34	0.27	−0.27	−0.19	−0.02	−0.05	−0.26	−0.18	0.32	0.14
10	−0.13	−0.05	−0.02	−0.38	0.03	−0.10	−0.02	−0.08	0.33	−0.21
11	−0.13	0.12	−0.13	0.13	−0.05	−0.18	−0.19	−0.07	0.23	−0.14

*See Table 6.3.   † See Table 6.5.

taught are both negative and positive. There is probably some social significance in the value of 0.42 (d = 17.6 per cent) for the highest level of attainment. High imputed ability is assumed to be a pre-requisite for the study of languages. Seventh, all except one of the correlations for attainment and the percentage of graduates are positive. The highest value, 0.44 gives a coefficient of determination of 19.4 per cent.

These results indicate that the differences in the mean levels of pupil attainment in the schools are not in general associated with differences in their educational provision, but that low levels of attainment are associated with low proportions of full-time staff, high staff stability and low pupil/teacher ratios, all contradictions of teacherly conventional wisdom.

Pupil attainment at the higher levels is associated with high proportions of graduate teachers, but this 'explains' less variance than the proportion of full-time staff, staff stability, provision of O level or CSE subjects, and pupil/teacher ratio. The separate correlations for boys and girls were of a similar order to those for both sexes.

It would be unfortunate if these results were to be used to justify the continued existence of inequalities of provision between schools, or, worse still, a lowering of the general provision for education. Three important points should be made in this connection. First, extensive educational provision, in the form of the availability of subjects and range of examination courses, may be valued in terms of the greater degree of choice offered to the pupil. Second, schools are concerned with more than just helping pupils to pass examinations, important though this function is. The generous provision of staff may therefore be valued in terms of its contribution to the quality of relationships within the school. At a prosaic but sometimes urgent level, smaller classes may mean less problems of control for the teacher. Third, such things as pleasant buildings and good facilities for games and other non-academic activities may be intrinsically valued. This is the sentiment expressed by Christopher Jencks (et al., 1973, p. 256):

> Instead of evaluating schools in terms of long-term effects on their alumni, which appear to be relatively uniform, we think it wiser to evaluate schools in terms of their immediate effects on teachers and students, which appear to be more variable. Some schools are dull, depressing even terrifying places, while others are lively, comfortable and reassuring.

If we think of school life as an end in itself rather than a means to some other end, such differences are enormously important.

These apparent contradictions of teachers' conventional wisdom concerning educational provision and attainment may be partly explained by examining the distribution of provision by the social class composition of the schools. The correlations between the two variables are given in Table 6.5.

Three sets of correlations are at a level that suggests social significance. The more working class the social composition of the school the more the teachers tended to stay five or more years.

Table 6.5 *Product moment correlations of social composition and educational provision (n = 16)*

	Provision variables	Social class composition	
		% SC I & II	% SC IV & V
1	Percentage staff full-time	−0.18	0.25
2	Percentage staff with degrees	0.16	−0.34
3	Percentage staff still in school after five years	−0.22	0.64
4	Number of out-of-school activities	−0.17	−0.26
5	Number of languages taught	−0.13	0.17
6	Number of ancillary staff	−0.09	−0.03
7	Number of subjects available at O level	0.08	0.15
8	Number of subjects available at CSE	−0.20	0.56
9	Pupil/teacher ratio	0.37	−0.69
10	Material provision score	0.00	−0.17

The coefficient of determination d for the correlation value of 0.64 is 41.0 per cent indicating that more than 40 per cent of variance in teacher retentivity is associated with the proportion of lower class pupils. It is a common part of educational thinking to assume that a degree of staff stability is a good thing in a school. The evidence of the Newsom report (1963) and the work of Herriot and St John (1966) suggests that staff turnover is higher in schools in working class areas. This was clearly not true within this local authority area. Whether the teachers were content to stay on, or were unable to obtain other posts, is not known.

The pupil/teacher ratio was negatively correlated with the percentage of working class pupils. The value of d for the correlation value of -0.69 is 47.6 per cent. This larger proportion of teachers in the more working class schools was the result of the local authority policy of making generous staffing provision for schools with 'special problems'. There is little evidence to show that small pupil/teacher ratios have advantages in terms of attainment (see, for example, Little et al., 1971), but it can be inferred in this particular case that the concomitant reduction of class size was independently valued as a contribution to the maintenance of order within the schools serving what the headteachers themselves referred to as the 'downtown area'.

The number of subjects available for CSE was positively correlated with working class composition ($r = 0.56$, $d = 31.4$ per cent). This may be seen as part of the policy of such schools to extend opportunities for examination success at the level that they perceive to be suitable for many of their pupils.

It is important to note that the other correlations reported in Table 6.5 indicate that schools in working class areas of the authority were not significantly associated with more part-time teachers, less out-of-school activities, less ancillary staff, less subjects available for O level, less foreign languages in the curriculum or poorer material provision (as defined in the scale), than schools in middle class areas.

The correlations for the percentage of teachers with degrees are perhaps marginal in this consideration. The value of d for the correlation with the percentage of middle class pupils is very low at 2.6 per cent, but that for percentage of working class is higher at 11.6 per cent.

It is clear that in this system of neighbourhood comprehensives the schools in working class areas were better provided for in some respects than those in middle class areas. This is an unusual conclusion, most previous research having reached the opposite conclusion. Floud, Halsey and Martin (1957) found poorer material provision in the primary schools serving working class areas, and similar results were obtained for secondary modern schools in the surveys carried out for the Newsom committee (1963) and by the National Union of Teachers (1962). In America both the Coleman report (1966) and the survey by Herriot and St John (1966) confirm the general correlation between low social class and poor provision.

These further correlations suggest that some of the negative correlations between provision and attainment may be in part attributed to the better provision, in some aspects, made for the working class schools, whose pupils on average did less well in examinations. The relationships between the social composition of the schools, educational provision and attainment are summaried in Figure 6.1. Further statistical analysis on the relationships between the three sets of variables taken together was not carried out, mainly because of the crudity of some of the data and the poor fit between some of them and the methods of analysis, especially those for social class.

Social Composition of School

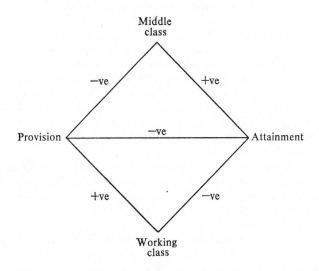

Figure 6.1 *Social composition, provision and attainment*

Once again, it would be unfortunate if these results were used to argue against policies such as those used by the local authority in question, which make more generous material provision for schools in working class areas; the policy of positive discrimination. They have all the limitations of the use of correlational analysis in sociology, which may include doubtful assumptions about the distribution of the variables, and the interpretation of causality and social significance. Even if these results do not show an attainment pay-off from increased provision, this does mean that such benefits may not be attained by continued or greater positive discrimination. Correlations only relate to two variables within the extent of those variables. To take an absurd example: because there is a negative correlation between the number of O level courses provided by a school and the average number of O levels passed by the pupils, it does not follow that a school providing no O level facilities will have the highest number of passes. Using the same line it could be spuriously argued, on the basis of these correlations, that working class schools would produce better results if they were less well provided for; all of which illustrates how cautiously correlations must be interpreted, and how complex and little understood is the relationship between educational provision and educational attainment. However, the correlations do illustrate that the common assumption that 'better' provision is associated with 'better' attainment is not true in all circumstances.

Chapter 7

Technical colleges

Since the White Paper of 1966 the name of technical college or college of further education has been mainly applied to the local and area colleges which provide courses below degree level. They form part of what Gerald Fowler (1973) has called 'the forgotten sector of public education'. In terms of the lack of public debate and the scarcity of educational studies his sobriquet is quite justified, but the colleges have been discovered by an increasing number of young people seeking full-time education outside the school system; what Armytage (1970) describes as 'the steady tramp to the "Tech"'.

The further education tradition

The further education tradition in England is based upon two principles: voluntarism and consumerism. The earliest agencies in the nineteenth century for the education of adults outside the universities were the voluntary foundations of such protagonists as Thomas Hodgkinson and George Birkbeck. Later, local authorities and industrial firms set up their own colleges and institutions. The statutory basis for the present provision of further education by local authorities in England and Wales is section 41 of the 1944 Education Act which laid upon them the duty of securing 'the provision for their area of adequate facilities for further education', defined as full- and part-time education for persons over compulsory school age and 'leisure-time occupations'. This obli-

gation does curtail the voluntary nature of the provision of further
education, but the extent of that provision varies greatly from
one local authority to another. This is partly explained by the
pooling system of finance to which authorities contribute according to a set formula based upon the school population and
the rateable value of the property in the area. An authority can
therefore put on courses, subject to the approval of the Regional
Advisory Council, without having to bear the full cost of the
enterprise.

Voluntarism of provision is matched by voluntarism of attendance. The early Mechanics Institutes attracted audiences of
artisans for lectures on scientific, and later, political subjects
(although by 1850 they were attracting the middle classes for
more reactional and popular courses). This provision and attendance was the institutionalisation of the Samuel Smiles spirit
of self help. The ambitious working classes used the emerging
system of further education as a way to improve their career
chances. In this century promotion in many industries has become
related to the successful completion of courses leading to awards,
which have proliferated into the 'maze through which only the
old and experienced are likely to find their way without error'
(Fowler, 1973). A consequence, illustrated by Stephen Cotgrove
(1958), was that the successful completion of craft courses was
being used as a criterion of suitability for supervisory jobs.

A strong link exists between voluntarism and consumerism in
further education. When students may choose to attend, and,
where in recent times, local firms may choose to release workers
to attend, then the attractiveness of the courses becomes important. The orientation towards their consumers, potential students
and potential sponsoring employers, is expressed in the entrepreneurial character of much of the work of college principals
and heads of departments, sounding out local demands and
matching them with proposed courses. As one principal has expressed it, 'A technical college exists primarily to serve the heads
of industry, commerce and the professions' (Bristow, 1970). This
expression of what Beryl Tipton (1972) calls 'environmental determinism' is common as a justification of the colleges. As she points
out, this ignores the way in which senior staff may stimulate and
shape demands by their activities on committees, and by the extensive use of advertising through prospectuses and the local press.

The evolution of further education, particularly in its truly
technical aspects, is strongly linked to the parallel emergence of

the maintained system of secondary education. The use of public schools as models for the new grammar schools was associated with a lack of interest or even disapproval of anything specifically vocational in their curriculum. The same ideas were associated with the lack of development of technical schools as the third part of the never-existent tripartite system, and the way in which they acted as second tier grammar schools.

Since the Samuelson report of 1884 the central government authority has been making the same basic analysis about the connection between technical education and industrial advance. 'Our industrial empire is vigorously attacked all over the world. We find that our most formidable assailants are the best educated peoples.' Musgrave's (1967) analysis of the development of the iron and steel industries of Britain and Germany, our principal 'assailant' at the time, suggests that the latter's greater progress was associated with a centrally established, national system of technical education. This connection between technical education and industrialisation was, however, in conflict with the belief in self-help. Smiles' doctrine was insidious and helped to feed the myth that England's greatness was due to the discipline and character of individuals improving themselves by individual efforts' (Roderick and Stephens, 1972). Industrial power sprang from the special qualities of being British and not from anything taught at school.

This apathy towards technical education was shared by industrialists. Cotgrove (1958) concluded, 'there is no evidence of any pressure by industry before the 1930's for any extension of technical education.' Despite a succession of government reports and papers reiterating the thesis of technical education as the basis for industrial expansion, including the White Paper of 1966 and the Crowther report, the continued apathy of industry is shown in the solution attempted in the Industrial Training Act of 1964. The Act empowered the Ministry of Labour to set up Industrial Training Boards for each major industry, under a Central Training Council. The Boards contain representatives of employers, trade unions, nationalised industries and educationalists, and are obliged to impose a levy on employers. Grants are paid to employers who arrange for their employees to receive training approved by the Board. Thus a firm sponsoring many employees stands to gain financially, perhaps appropriately, since only non-vocational education is considered intrinsically valuable. Vocational education is to be propagated by putting it into a cash nexus.

The implementation of the ITA clearly reduces the traditional voluntarism and consumerism of further education. The importance of these changes, and their relation to the colleges' provision of full-time academic education is discussed in chapter 10.

The 'flight to the college'

The recent rapid expansion of students following full-time courses in colleges of further education illustrates the consumerism capacity of the colleges to adapt to new demands, and the voluntary nature of the students' attendance has stimulated a certain amount of interest. The most popular explanation has been in terms of the search for 'adult freedom' ('Times Educational Supplement', 1972) on the part of young people who 'shun the restrictions and alleged privileges of the traditional sixth form for the more relaxed but still work-orientated atmosphere of further education' (Moore, 1972). Small-scale surveys of full-time students in colleges by Trustam (1967) and Cook (1970) tend to support the explanation, which has become particularly associated with former grammar school pupils. In a case study of a single college Swinhoe (1967) concluded that students on full-time academic courses were mainly 'grammar school recusants'.

The Crowther report (1959) also suggested the existence in colleges not only of 'those who had got inevitably tired of school' but also of 'those whose schools have no sixth forms', that is, secondary modern school leavers. This was confirmed by a survey conducted by Peter Lawrence (1973) who found that the most important reason given by ex-secondary modern pupils for going to college was that advanced level courses were not available at school. Lawrence also showed the existence of a third group of students, the ex-independent school pupils, who seemed to stand between the former modern and grammar school students in terms of their reasons for going to college. Lack of advanced courses at school was the most important reason, closely followed by dislike of school.

The existence of these three groups of students was confirmed in a survey of over 4,000 full-time students from 131 colleges, commissioned by the Schools Council (Sharp, 1970). Dislike of school was the most important reason given by ex-grammar school pupils for leaving. For ex-modern school pupils it was, 'had got to the end of what the school had to offer educationally'. Dislike of school and limited opportunities were also important in relation to ex-independent school pupils leaving, but in addition they also mentioned the expense of school fees.

The survey also showed strong relationships between school of origin and course of study at the college. Former modern school pupils were most likely to be taking O level courses, but boys often followed courses in technical subjects leading to Ordinary National Diplomas or City and Guilds, and girls secretarial and commercial courses, especially Royal Society of Arts qualifications. Former independent school pupils were most likely to be taking A level courses; boys were also commonly on business studies OND courses, and girls on secretarial courses. Ex-grammar school boys were fairly evenly spread over A level, business studies and to a lesser extent engineering courses. Girls from these schools were most commonly on A level or secretarial courses. Most students following pre-nursing, catering and hair-dressing courses were from modern schools.

The students' experience of college

Surveys were made of the full-time students in six colleges of further education, given the pseudonyms of North, East, South and West Colleges, Cooperative College, so called because it was involved in a cooperative arrangement with a local school (to be discussed in chapter 8), and Pro-Tertiary College, so called because it was to become what has been called a tertiary college, providing all the post-sixteen education in the area (see chapter 9).

Table 7.1 provides some indications of the students' experience of college, and also shows that there can be considerable variation from one college to another. In every college there were high levels of agreement to the proposition that you had to look after yourself in college, and this is reflected in that in only one college did more than half the students agree that the staff were interested in their personal welfare, and in only one college did more than half feel they knew some of the staff well. In every college the rate of disagreement to the feeling of belonging in the college was higher than that of agreement.

All of the colleges provided, what would be called in schools,

Table 7.1 *Students' opinions of college* (%) (*n = 1,771*)

	Agree (Range)	Disagree (Range)
I prefer to keep my social life separate from college	51.6 (46.3–63.3)	26.9 (19.8–32.1)
The staff are interested in your personal welfare	45.9 (31.7–50.1)	20.7 (18.1–32.5)
There are unnecessary restrictions in college	31.6 (24.4–57.1)	51.5 (26.2–58.7)
I feel I know some of the staff well	43.6 (35.7–64.2)	29.5 (18.3–37.3)
It is easy to make friends in college	70.9 (63.6–81.7)	17.3 (7.9–23.9)
In college you are treated as an adult	55.0 (39.7–63.3)	28.8 (21.8–45.2)
The staff are only interested in those who do well	14.5 (11.3–20.6)	63.5 (52.4–73.3)
Doing non-exam subjects takes up valuable time	48.3 (42.1–58.3)	29.2 (23.2–33.3)
You have to look after yourself in college	77.5 (71.7–79.8)	10.2 (7.1–11.0)
There is a real sense of belonging in college	21.9 (18.3–28.3)	44.3 (32.9–49.2)
You decide for yourself how much work you do	69.4 (48.4–78.0)	22.8 (15.4–40.5)
College is a good preparation for going to work	49.9 (43.7–51.5)	24.6 (20.7–34.9)
College is a good preparation for future education	73.5 (64.2–77.0)	6.9 (3.9–10.0)

Note: The third response, 'Can't say', is omitted from the Table.

pastoral care. This was based upon the tutorial system in which every student belonged to a tutorial group, usually with students on the same course. The course tutor usually also taught the group members, and the group met once or twice a day for registration and other administrative purposes, and at least once a week for a more extended meeting. Every college had a careers adviser and a welfare officer, and the Pro-Tertiary College also had a counsellor. The tutors were the most frequently consulted members of staff over matters of careers, college work or personal problems, but there was in every college a higher incidence of parents and friends being consulted about such matters. Among the institutional advisers, heads of department were consulted next most frequently, although seldom about personal problems.

Although in every college it was possible for any student to consult the principal, only a handful of students in any college reported having done so.

Although overall most students agreed they were treated as adults, in two colleges less than half did so, and in West College more disagreed with the proposition than agreed with it. The claim to an adult atmosphere is clearly not justified in all colleges. Although in five colleges half or nearly half the students disagreed that there were unnecessary restrictions, in West College this was a minority opinion, nearly half the students being in agreement with the proposition (Table 7.1).

No college forbade students leaving the premises during the lunch break, and in only one was permission required at other times. In every college smoking was limited to certain times and places; never in classes. Only one college had a general rule about student appearance. East College expected boys to wear a tie; most did. Other rules about appearance were generated at the departmental level. Engineering departments controlled the length of hair for safety reasons, and catering departments for reasons of hygiene. Business studies departments usually had the highest level of control, the criterion being 'office dress'. Every department had a woman member of staff, often known as the 'dragon', whose self-appointed duty was to ensure standards of dress and appearance were maintained among girls. At the time of our interviews the mini skirt was defined as appropriate office dress, and girls in several colleges were forbidden to wear maxi skirts. Trousers on girls were also forbidden in these departments and, as in schools, other departments in some colleges forbade the wearing of jeans by both sexes. This was so in the general studies department of East College where boys were expected to wear jackets and ties. Failure to do so involved an interview with the head of department, who reported that his usual approach was to ask them not to 'let me and the department down'. Our interviews with college students show these regulations to be a source of irritation among students, who saw them as a contradiction of what they report to be the college staff's claim that they were being treated as adults. One exception to this was the students' ready acceptance of the wearing of specialist or protective clothing particularly in catering departments.

There were mixed levels of satisfaction with the work aspects of college life. In all but one college more than half the students agreed they decided how much work they did, and in every college most students disagreed that the staff were only interested in those who did well. In every college there were high levels of agreement to the proposition that college was a good preparation for future education, but less to its being a good preparation for work (Table 7.1). However, in every college a substantial proportion felt they had too little individual help (the range was 44–54 per cent) and too little private study time (range 44–69 per cent).

The control of student learning was fairly tight in all the colleges. This stemmed from the process of setting up courses requiring the approval of the Regional Advisory Council. Submissions included a detailed breakdown of the proposed course, including the number of contact hours between teachers and students and the amount of homework to be completed. This approach was generally extended to O and A level courses as well. In every case there was the notion of the college day, usually nine to five (the resemblance to the working day was often stressed in interview by college senior staff), and every student was supposed to have a timetable making provision for the whole of that time.

As Pugh and his associates (1968) have pointed out, there is often a difference between what is intended to happen in an organisation, what is allowed to happen, and what actually happens. This kind of disparity is clearest in the colleges with respect to non-examination studies, which in every college most students felt took up too much valuable time (Table 7.1). The principle operating was that of the full timetable. If a student's course programme had gaps in it they were filled with non-course studies, variously called complementary studies, options or activities, and usually run by the general studies department. However, within departments and courses staff sometimes let off students if they pleaded a heavy timetable. In interviews with both staff and students it was sometimes clear that a blind eye had been turned towards fairly regular absences from these activities.

In every college more students agreed than disagreed that they preferred to keep their social life separate from the college. However, in all colleges a majority of students felt it was easy to make friends (Table 7.1). Across the six colleges between 56 and 72 per cent of students reported that most of their friends also attended the college. As may be expected these were mainly other full-time students, particularly those in the same department and on the same course. In our group interviews with students we invited them on a departmental basis. On one occasion we had to introduce two first year OND engineering students to two second year students; they had never met in college.

Differences in the students' experience of college – sex and school of origin

Not only were there differences in the students' experience between colleges but also within colleges. In every college there were a number of differences in the opinions expressed by boys and girls, which indicate, with one exception, the greater acceptability of college life to boys. They felt more often than did girls that they knew the staff well, that there was a sense of belonging, and that it was easy to make friends. Girls disagreed more often than did boys that they were treated like adults, but agreed more often that they had to look after themselves in college. Only in the girls' higher agreement that college was a good preparation for work was the pattern of greater male satisfaction not confirmed (Table 7.2).

Table 7.2   *Sex differences and students' opinions of college (%) (Boys n = 790, Girls n = 981)*

	Agree		Significance (%) (chi square)	Disagree		Significance (%) (chi square)
	Boys	Girls		Boys	Girls	
Know some staff well	47.8	40.1	1	23.9	34.0	0.1
Easy to make friends	74.8	67.7	1	—	—	—
Treated as adults	—	—	—	24.2	32.5	0.1
Have to look after yourself	73.7	80.4	0.1	10.7	7.2	0.1
Sense of belonging	25.2	19.4	1	39.7	47.8	0.1
Good preparation for work	39.1	58.5	0.1	28.9	21.2	0.1

Note: Blank sections of the Table indicate that there were not consistent differences between the sexes in all colleges.

Although boys found it easier to make friends in college, girls had more friends in college among other full-time students.

However, they were less likely to have friends among the part-time students, or among the small number of overseas students (between 0 and 7.1 per cent of full-time students), both predominately male groups (Table 7.3).

It might be expected that the students' opinions about college would vary by department or course. This was so in only a limited way and mainly in relation to their studies. Characteristically, students on practical courses such as OND engineering, wanted more practical work. In particular colleges, students in certain departments showed high levels of satisfaction in their relationships with staff. This was often, but not always, true of catering departments.

Table 7.3 *Sex differences and students' friendship patterns* (%)

	Boys (n = 790)	Girls (n = 981)	Significance (%) (chi square)
Most friends studying full-time in college	54.4	63.5	1
Most friends studying part-time in college	9.9	2.8	2
No friends studying part-time in college	40.6	50.9	1
No friends from overseas in college	58.7	66.4	2

A more important source of variation in the students' opinions of college was their school of origin. Each college recruited students from grammar, independent and modern schools. In general, those from grammar schools had the most satisfactory experience of college, those from modern schools, the least. But, as the previous results may suggest, sex differences in opinion existed within groups of pupils from the same kind of school. Thus it is possible to document, to varying degrees, six types of student experience: those of grammar school boys, grammar school girls, independent school boys, independent school girls, modern school boys and modern school girls. Of the six, the clearest in each college were the grammar school boys, showing the highest levels of satisfaction, and the modern school girls, with the lowest.

Compared with girls from grammar schools, boys from the same kind of school felt a greater sense of belonging to the college, found it easier to make friends and more often considered it to be a good preparation for future education (Table 7.4, c, i and k). Compared with all other full-time students in the college, grammar school boys found it easier to make friends, did not feel they had to look after themselves as much, did not feel that staff were only interested in those who did well or that non-examination subjects took up valuable time (Table 7.4, c, d, f, g and h).

Girls from modern schools were more likely than boys from the same type of school to feel that non-examination subjects took up valuable time and that college was a good preparation for work (Table 7.4, f and j). The girls also felt less often that they knew some of the staff well (Table 7.4, a and b). Compared with all other students in the college, girls from modern schools felt more strongly about non-examination subjects as a waste of time, felt they knew the staff less well, but agreed more often that college was a good preparation for work (Table 7.4 a, b, e and j).

These differences in levels of satisfaction with college were related to the students' retrospective experience of school. In general, the higher the level of satisfaction with college, the lower was that of school. This observation refers to groups of students, defined by sex and school of origin, not necessarily to individuals.

Thus ex-grammar school boys, the group with the highest levels of satisfaction in each college, agreed less often than girls from the same type of school, that their teachers had been interested in their personal welfare, that they had known some of the teachers well and that they had felt a sense of belonging (Table 7.5, c, g and j). They felt more often than the girls that there had been unnecessary restrictions and that they had found the work harder than others (Table 7.5, b and e). Although both boys and girls from grammar schools felt happier in college than in school, more boys claimed to be happier in college (Table 7.5, k and l). Compared with all other students in the college the ex-grammar school boys reported the least satisfactory relationships with staff at school and the least feeling of belonging, and had the highest proportion of those who felt happier in college compared with school (Table 7.5 c, d, g, h, i, j, k and l).

Girls from secondary modern schools, the group with the least satisfactory experience of college, had in retrospect the most satisfactory of school experiences. Compared with boys from the

Table 7.4 Sex differences and students' opinions of college, by school of origin (%)

	Grammar		Independent		Modern	
	Boys (n = 127)	Girls (n = 251)	Boys (n = 129)	Girls (n = 190)	Boys (n = 435)	Girls (n = 497)
(a) Agree know staff well	54.3	47.4	47.3	43.7	44.6	35.8
(b) Disagree know some staff well	25.2	30.3	24.8	32.1	25.3	37.2
(c) Agree it is easy to make friends	81.9	61.0	65.1	67.4	76.3	72.8
(d) Disagree staff only interested in those who do well	73.2	68.9	58.9	67.4	59.3	61.8
(e) Agree non-exam subjects take up valuable time	43.3	45.8	45.7	42.1	50.8	54.3
(f) Disagree non-exam subjects take up valuable time	37.8	39.8	26.4	32.6	21.6	27.4
(g) Agree you have to look after yourselves	66.9	78.1	79.8	83.7	75.6	80.5
(h) Disagree you have to look after yourselves	18.9	9.6	3.1	4.7	10.3	6.8
(i) Agree there is a real sense of belonging	28.3	14.3	—	—	—	—
(j) Agree good preparation for work	37.8	51.4	34.9	50.5	41.2	64.0
(k) Agree good preparation for future education	74.0	63.7	71.3	72.1	79.3	75.5

Significances (chi square):
(a) Modern boys/modern girls 1%, modern girls/other students 1%.
(b) Modern boys/modern girls 0.1%, modern girls/other students 1%.
(c) Grammar boys/grammar girls 0.1%, grammar boys/other students 0.1%.
(d) Grammar boys/other boys 0.1%, grammar boys/other students 5%.
(e) Modern girls/other girls 1%, modern girls/other students 2%.
(f) Grammar boys and girls/other students 0.1%, grammar girls/other girls 1%, modern boys/modern girls 5%, grammar boys/other students 5%.
(g) Grammar boys/other students 1%.
(h) Grammar boys/other students 0.1%.
(i) Grammar boys/grammar girls 1%.
(j) Grammar girls/grammar boys 1%, independent girls/independent boys 1%, modern girls/modern boys 0.1%, modern girls/other students 0.1%.
(k) Grammar boys/grammar girls 5%.

Note: Blank sections of the Table indicate that there were not consistent differences between the sexes in all colleges.

Table 7.5 *Students' retrospective experience of school* (%)
(*n as Table 7.4*)

	Grammar		Independent		Modern	
	Boys	Girls	Boys	Girls	Boys	Girls
(a) Found the work easier than most	13.4	10.0	16.3	10.5	28.3	14.7
(b) Found the work harder than most	11.8	3.2	7.8	8.9	3.4	3.0
(c) Agree staff were interested in personal welfare	29.1	45.4	55.8	61.1	46.9	53.5
(d) Disagree staff were interested in personal welfare	39.4	23.5	21.7	18.4	24.1	21.2
(e) Agree there were unnecessary restrictions	82.7	58.6	65.9	68.4	61.8	56.4
(f) Disagree there were unnecessary restrictions	12.6	35.5	25.6	25.3	26.7	34.5
(g) Agree they knew some staff well	39.4	50.6	55.8	58.4	62.2	54.1
(h) Disagree they knew some staff well	41.7	33.5	27.1	23.7	17.5	27.2
(i) Agree there was a real sense of belonging	17.3	34.3	39.5	45.3	32.4	37.4
(j) Disagree there was a real sense of belonging	57.5	46.2	32.6	28.9	37.7	31.6
(k) Happier in college	63.7	42.6	54.3	40.5	48.0	33.7
(l) Happier in school	5.5	21.5	10.1	15.3	15.4	20.3

Significances (chi square):
(a) Boys/girls 0.1%, modern boys/modern girls 0.1%, modern boys/other boys 0.1%.
(b) Grammar boys/grammar girls 0.1%, grammar boys/other students 1%.
(c) Girls/boys 0.1%, grammar girls/grammar boys 1%, modern girls/modern boys 5%, independent/modern/grammar 0.1%, grammar boys/other boys 0.1%, independent girls/other girls 2%, grammar boys/other students 0.1%.
(d) Boys/girls 1%, grammar boys/other students 0.1%.
(e) Grammar boys/grammar girls 0.1%, grammar boys/other boys 0.1%, grammar boys/other students 0.1%, modern girls/other students 2%.
(f) Modern girls/modern boys 2%, grammar boys/other students 0.1%.
(g) Grammar girls/grammar boys 5%, modern boys/modern girls 1%, grammar/other students 0.1%, grammar boys/other boys 0.1%, grammar boys/other students 1%.
(h) Modern girls/modern boys 5%, grammar/other students 0.1%, grammar boys/other students 0.1%.
(i) Girls/boys 1%, independent/modern/grammar 0.1%, grammar boys/other students 0.1%.
(j) Grammar boys/grammar girls 5%, grammar/other students 0.1%, grammar boys/other students 0.1%, grammar girls/other girls 0.1%, grammar boys/other boys 0.1%.
(k) Boys/girls 0.1%, independent girls/independent girls 2%, grammar boys/grammar girls 0.1%, modern boys/modern girls 0.1%, grammar/other students 1%, grammar boys/other boys 1%, grammar boys/other students 0.1%, modern girls/other students 0.1%.
(l) Girls/boys 0.1%, grammar girls/grammar boys 0.1%, grammar boys/other students 0.1%.

same sort of school they felt less restricted, although the boys reported more often that they found the work easier than most, and knew the staff well (Table 7.5, a, c, g and h). Both boys and girls felt they were happier in college than in school but the proportion of girls doing so was lower (Table 7.5, k). Compared with all other students ex-modern school girls were the least likely to feel there were unnecessary restrictions at school, and had a lower proportion reporting themselves to be happier in college (Table 7.5, e and k).

In general girls had more favourable retrospective opinions about school than boys from the same type of school, although they less often felt that they had found the work easier than most others (Table 7.5, a, c, g and i). In addition, a lower proportion of girls felt happier in college compared with school (Table 7.5, k).

Students of both sexes from independent schools reported higher levels of satisfaction with some aspects of school compared with those from modern and grammar schools, especially the girls (Table 7.5, c, i and k).

The significance of these results is that they show that the experience of college is not determined by its formal organisation but is related to the sexual identities of the students, and to the nature of their previous experience of school. These sources of variation, together with the differences found between individual colleges, mean that any generalisations about students' experience of college must be suitably qualified. Some of these comments are amplified in the comparisons of schools and college in chapter 11.

Students' unions and voluntary participation

Each college had a students' union or guild, membership of which was compulsory for all full-time students in two of the colleges. Virtually all the positions of responsibility were associated with the unions. The proportion of full-time students with such responsibilities varied from 4.6 per cent in Pro-Tertiary College to 17.5 per cent in Cooperative College, with an average of 10.2 per cent in all colleges. In every college more boys than girls held these positions, although girls had more often held such positions when at school (Table 7.6). There was no tendency for students from particular school backgrounds to hold union positions, although those from modern schools, of both sexes, were more likely to have held positions of responsibility at school than those from independent or grammar schools (72.5 per cent, 63.4 per cent and 48.7 per cent respectively). Boys from independent schools were, however, more likely to do so than girls (19.5 per cent compared with 3.2 per cent).

There was no general tendency for particular departments to be over-represented in these positions although it did happen in particular colleges. In Pro-Tertiary College the union committee had been dominated by business studies students for some years, but soon after our initial enquiries there was a successful putsch by the engineering department, the plans of which had been revealed in our interviews with students.

At the individual level there was no tendency for those who had had responsibilities in school to hold such posts in college more often than those who had not had responsibilities in school. This is a situation in which the previous experience of school did not have direct consequences for that in college.

The officers of the student unions were elected. We were unable to obtain reliable estimates of the turnouts at these elections, but they seem to be rather low. The successful coup by engineering students at Pro-Tertiary college was brought about by canvassing and whipping in the vote in their own department.

Table 7.6 *Sex differences and students' participation* (%)

	Boys ($n = 790$)	Girls ($n = 981$)	Significance (%) (chi square)
Had positions of responsibility at school	61.6	66.8	5
Have positions of responsibility in college	12.8	8.2	1
Joined voluntary activities at school	55.8	46.8	2
Joined voluntary activities in college	28.7	21.1	0.1
Want more activities provided by college	23.2	16.8	0.1
Want more union activities	11.9	7.4	1

In four of the six colleges there was a student president or chairman; in the other two it was the principal, ex officio. Only one college had a student treasurer, and one of the staff representatives on the committee, found in all but one college, kept effective control of expenditure, since all of the unions' activities were extensively subsidised, membership fees being nominal to encourage joining. The main function of the union committees was to arrange social activities, particularly discos. In four colleges they had representatives on the canteen committee, in three they ran the student common rooms, and in one a coffee bar.

In addition, what in schools would be called extra-curricular activities were usually associated with the union, although they were almost always under the effective control of college staff when they were at all extensive or permanent, as at South College which provided thirty-six activities, including team and individual sports.

Most students did not take part in any of these voluntary activities. The average rate for taking part in at least one was 24.4 per cent, the range across the colleges being 18.4-36.3 per cent. In each college, boys from all types of school joined more often than did girls (Table 7.6). There was a tendency for those who had joined clubs at school to join college activities more often than those who had not joined at school. (64.1 per cent who joined school clubs joined college clubs (n = 898). 17.8 per cent of those who did not join school clubs joined college clubs (n = 873). The difference is significant at the 0.1 per cent level by chi square.) In view of the sex differences in participation in both union responsibilities and college provided activities, it is not surprising to find more boys than girls wanted more union and college activities provided, although the demand by each was low (Table 7.6), indicating either contentment or, more likely, in view of the evidence of low levels of participation, apathy.

The general level of interest in the unions' activities is indicated by more than one-third agreeing that students don't care what the union does, and about the same proportion agreeing that the union has done a lot to help students (Table 7.7). In slight contradiction, more than half agreed that there is not enough student participation in the union, and a communication problem is indicated in the proportion agreeing that the union doesn't let them know what's happening. The value of union participation in terms of the usefulness of the experience was balanced by the feeling that it is difficult to do your work and be on committees (Table 7.7). In line with their higher participation in union affairs boys felt more often than girls that students don't care what the union does (45.8 per cent and 31.1 per cent respectively).

Table 7.7   *Students' opinions about the union or guild (%*
agreement, n = 1,771)

	Range
Students don't care what the union does	37.7 (29.2–50.7)
The union doesn't tell the students what is happening	41.2 (29.3–52.9)
The union has done a lot to help the students	35.8 (22.9–42.1)
There isn't enough student participation in the union	57.1 (46.8–68.8)
Being on union committees is a useful experience	23.9 (19.5–28.3)
It is difficult to do your work and be on union committees	27.1 (10.8–35.3)

As may be expected, those students who were active in Union affairs took a more favourable view of its activities than others and felt more strongly the apathy of other students (Table 7.8). Most found membership of committees a useful experience, but more often than non-activists considered it was difficult to work and be on committees.

Students' unions and guilds provide opportunities for a minority of interested students to exercise limited responsibility under tolerant staff supervision. Like many other areas of college life, they tend to be male domains.

Table 7.8   *Students' opinions about the union or guild, by*
participation (%)

	Activists (n = 179)	Others (n = 1,592)	Significance (%) (chi square)
Students don't care what the union does	53.1	35.9	0.1
The union doesn't tell students what is happening	32.4	42.2	5
The union has done a lot to help the students	49.2	34.4	0.1
There isn't enough student participation in the union	63.7	56.3	ns
Being on union committees is a useful experience	56.9	20.3	0.1
It is difficult to do your work and be on union committees	36.3	23.7	1

Chapter 8

School-college cooperation

The maintained school and further education sections of the dual system of post-sixteen education have different origins, ideologies, traditions and regulations. Links between the parts are slight, tentative but growing, although as Whitehouse (1962) has pointed out, some mutual ignorance and prejudice exists between the staffs concerned. The links vary from a fairly general incidence of ad hoc, small scale helping, mainly from college to school, to the rarer, permanent and more extensive cooperation involving joint policies, but preserving a great deal of institutional identity and autonomy.

School-college links

Links between schools and colleges have some of the characteristics of many college activities in varying a great deal from one area to another, and provide an example of the adaptability of further education to local demands, and to a new class of consumer, its neighbouring schools.

The most comprehensive account of these links is given in an appendix to the survey commissioned by the Schools Council, based upon interviews with a sample of college principals (Sharp, 1970). The most common contact by college staff with schools was to provide information about courses and stimulate recruitment, carried out by 92 per cent of colleges, the main targets being modern schools. Nearly a quarter of the colleges had arrangements for their staff to teach in local schools, usually to teach specific subjects, often where the school was short-staffed. There seems to be little evidence of school staff teaching in colleges.

Nearly three-quarters of the colleges had pupils coming to them, most commonly for vocationally orientated courses of various lengths, for example, 'industrial studies', or for subjects not available in their schools, often commercial studies or the less common A level subjects. Pupils also attended the colleges to use special equipment only available there, or because of staff shortages. There is little evidence of full-time college students taking part in courses or using the facilities in local schools.

The main arguments in favour of these kinds of arrangement are economic ones, particularly the avoidance of the unnecessary duplication of courses in schools and colleges and the greater use of resources, especially expensive technical equipment (see, for example, Whitehouse, 1962; O'Connor, 1967; Thomas, 1972; London and Home Counties Regional Advisory Council, 1972). The DES (1969) and the HMA (1968) also see such links as broadening the pupils' choice of study.

The difficulties of these arrangements are seen by the HMA (1968) as those of lack of proximity between some colleges and schools, and the problems of joint timetabling. They also express concern that some college staff are not trained teachers, and have fears of the possibility of their pupils being 'poached' by the colleges, 'tempted by quite frivolous considerations—the wish to toss his school cap over the windmill and adopt the less formal garb of the student' (Whitehouse, 1962).

School-college cooperation: the Witney Model

In most contacts between school and college, the college is the more active partner, but in a few cases there is cooperation on a more equal basis involving the full-time education of the 16–19 age group. This has happened at Henley-on-Thames and at Witney.

The 'Witney Model' of school-college cooperation started from links of the sort previously described between the West Oxford-shire Technical College at Witney and the Witney Grammar School, which in 1969 became the Henry Box School with a comprehensive intake, and was fostered by the productive relationship between the principal and headmaster concerned (Wilcock, 1969). Later, three other schools entered the scheme, two modern schools becoming comprehensive and a longer established comprehensive school. The four schools and the college constitute a consortium called the West Oxfordshire Centre of Advanced Education. The Centre's five joint directors are the headteachers and principal, its two joint secretaries come from the college and the Henry Box School. The directors and secretaries constitute the Consortium Management Panel which has a rotating chairman from among the directors, and reports to both the secondary and further education sub-committees of the education committee.

The impetus for the setting up of the centre was the avoidance of unnecessary duplication of courses by school and college, particularly at A level, and also to provide better educational guidance for intending full-time students over sixteen, by presenting them with information about all of the courses available in the two, and later five, institutions. As the booklet produced by the centre puts it, 'the idea of the Centre is to help people – especially young people – find the course of further full-time education best suited to their abilities, interests and careers ambitions'.

The booklet gives prominence to the courses available rather than to which institution is providing the course. The principal of the college is clearly aware of the differences in the traditions and of those of schools and colleges (Wilcock, 1969), but at the formal level there seems to be no attempt to present the college and the school sixth forms as alternative forms of experience. Fears, such as those of the HMA (1968), of 'body snatching' from schools by colleges, appear to have been recognised in this form of presentation.

Fifth formers in local schools apply through their headteachers for entry to a course provided by the centre. Applications are then considered by the joint secretaries. Every candidate is then interviewed (sometimes accompanied by their parents) by heads of departments from a school or college, by one of the joint secretaries, or members of college or school staff, assisted by careers advisory officers.

All of the five institutions provide, or will provide, A level courses, the largest number at the college, and some specialisation occurs with respect to the less commonly chosen subjects, including music and religious education. This arrangement involves each institution surrendering a certain amount of autonomy in relation to its curriculum and timetable, since it is planned for students to be able to study in more than one institution. Only the college provides vocational courses, including OND in business studies and RSA secretarial studies (Wilcock, 1973).

The Witney plan represents one of the few operationalisations of the belief expressed by the Schools Council Sixth Form Working Party that the 16–19 stage of education is the joint concern of the schools and colleges of further education, and that cooperation between them will be reached on an increasing scale (Schools Council, 1972).

Cooperative School and Cooperative College

Cooperative School and Cooperative College are the pseudonyms of institutions that have been in active formal cooperation over a number of years as the 'Nossex Consortium of Continued Education'. The cooperation mainly concerns a joint application procedure for entry into the college or the school sixth form by intending full-time students at sixteen, and a certain amount of planning in relation to the economic provision of A level courses and joint timetabling. About a quarter of all students decided upon the course of their choice on the basis of advice given at the formal interview part of the entry procedure.

At the time of the survey Cooperative School was becoming comprehensive and still received into its sixth form pupils from neighbouring modern schools, also in the process of becoming comprehensive. Virtually all (98.9 per cent) sixth formers at Cooperative School were following A level courses, and 21.3 per cent followed O level courses. The percentages at the college were 38.3 and 68.3 respectively, with 12.5 per cent on an OND business studies course and 44.2 per cent on RSA courses, mainly for secretarial qualifications. The distribution of O and A level students was partly due to the policy of allowing into the sixth form only those modern school pupils intending to take A level; O level candidates had to go to the college. Of ex-fifth formers from the school still in full-time education, two-thirds stayed on into the sixth form and one third transferred to the college.

Table 8.1 compares the students' opinions about the institutions they attended. The experience of the sixth form compared with that of the college was one where students felt themselves to have more control over their work, and where they felt a stronger emphasis on exams and a stronger meritocratic interest on the part of their teachers (Table 8.1, e, g and i). Not surprisingly, the college was felt to be the better preparation for work, but there was no significant difference between the two groups' opinions about their institutions as a preparation for future education. College students felt more often that they had too little private study, 68.3 per cent compared with 12.8 per cent among the sixth formers, and they felt less often than those at school that they had too little individual help (48.3 per cent compared with 60.6 per cent).

Table 8.1 *Students' opinions about school or college (% agreement)*

	Cooperative		Significance (%) (chi square)
	School ($n = 94$)	College ($n = 120$)	
(a) Prefer to keep social life separate from school/college	39.4	63.3	0.1
(b) Unnecessary restrictions in school/college	54.3	36.7	1
(c) Easy to make friends in school/college	46.8	68.3	1
(d) Treated as an adult in school/college	27.7	63.3	0.1
(e) Staff only interested in those who do well	25.5	14.2	5
(f) You have to look after yourself in school/college	50.0	65.0	5
(g) There is a strong emphasis on exams	85.1	75.0	5
(h) There is a real sense of belonging	4.3	28.3	0.1
(i) Decide for yourself how much work you do	83.0	65.0	1
(j) School/college is a good preparation for work	9.6	48.3	0.1
(k) School/college is a good preparation for future education	70.2	64.2	ns

College students felt it easier to make friends in college than did sixth formers in school but preferred more often to keep their social life separate from their institution (Table 8.1). However, the proportion of students from both groups reporting that most of their friends were from the college or sixth form was much the same (72 per cent and 73 per cent respectively).

Although school students felt less often than those in college that they had to look after themselves, the experience of school was less satisfactory in that it was felt to be more restrictive, less adult in its treatment of students, and evoking less sense of belonging (b, d, f, h). This less pleasant experience of the sixth formers is confirmed in that only a minority (36 per cent) of them felt themselves to be happier in the sixth form than they had been in the fifth form. This may be compared with the 58 per cent of college students who felt themselves happier in college than in their previous school.

The control of student behaviour was tighter in the school than in the college. College students could wear what they liked, but boys in the sixth form, although not compelled to wear the school uniform, had to wear jackets and ties; girls were not allowed to wear trousers, and their skirts or dresses had to be the regulation colour. The length of boys' hair was subject to control in the school, as was the wearing of jewellery or any other than 'discreet' makeup. Both groups could leave the premises in the lunch break but those in school had to sign a book or inform their tutor.

Although the school provided more extra-curricular activities than the college, the proportion of students joining at least one was similar in both (33 per cent and 31 per cent respectively). Rather surprisingly, Cooperative School students took longer to settle down in the sixth form than students did in college, despite all the college students being new to the institution compared with only 20 per cent of school students (Table 8.2). The pattern of the differences between school and college students was very similar when the sexes were compared separately.

It has already been shown in chapter 7 that the experience of college is different for students from different educational backgrounds, and in chapter 4 that the experience of the sixth form is slightly different for those who come from the schools' own fifth form rather than from other schools'. The differences between Cooperative School and Cooperative College could therefore be attributed to the nature of their students' previous educational experience, rather than the differences in their control of student behaviour and relationships with staff. This proposition can be tested by comparing the experiences of those ex-fifth formers from Cooperative School staying on in the schools' sixth form and those transferring to Cooperative College.

Table 8.2   *Time taken to settle in Cooperative College and Cooperative School* (%)

	School (n = 94)	College (n = 120)	Significance (%) (chi square)
A few days	23.4	40.8	2
A few weeks	31.9	41.7	5
About a term	21.3	10.8	5
More than a term	13.8	0.0	1
Still feel unsettled	8.5	5.8	5

Table 8.3   *Cooperative School ex-fifth formers' opinions about sixth form or college* (% agreement)

	Stayed on at school (n = 65)	Went to college (n = 31)	Significance (%) (chi square)
Treated as an adult in sixth form or college	33.8	64.5	1
Staff only interested in those who do well	20.0	6.5	5
There is a real sense of belonging	4.6	38.7	1

Table 8.3 shows that those who transferred to the college more often felt they were treated as adults, more often felt a sense of belonging (after a much shorter exposure to the institution) and felt less often that the staff were only interested in those who did well. Thus the experience of sixth form and college was different for those from the same school background. Those who went to the college actually settled down more quickly, in their own estimate, than their fifth form mates who stayed on in the more familiar sixth form (Table 8.4).

In line with these differences, 65 per cent of those who transferred to the college felt themselves to be happier there than in the fifth form at school, compared with 39 per cent of those who stayed on in the sixth form. Most of the differences between the two groups of students hold for the separate sexes.

Table 8.4 *Cooperative School fifth formers' time taken to settle in at school or college* (%)

	Stayed on at school (n = 65)	Went to college (n = 31)	Significance (%) (chi square)
A few days	26.1	51.6	2
A few weeks	30.8	38.7	ns
About a term	24.6	6.5	2
More than a term	12.3	0.0	5
Still feel unsettled	6.2	0.0	5

Table 8.5 *Sixth formers' opinions – Cooperative School and three other all-through schools* (%)

	Cooperative sixth formers (n = 94)	Other sixth formers (n = 342)	Significance (%) (chi square)
Agree helping younger pupil interferes with work	25.5	16.1	ns
Agree sixth formers lose when in same school as younger pupils	21.3	9.4	1
Disagree responsibilities an important part of education	26.6	15.8	5
Agree sixth form too much like the rest of the school	23.4	12.0	2
Disagree sixth form too much like the rest of the school	57.4	74.0	1
Agree it is easy to make friends	46.8	71.9	0.1
Agree they are treated as adults	27.7	51.2	0.1
Agree staff only interested in those who do well	25.5	13.7	2
Agree non-exam subjects take up valuable time	47.9	32.2	2
Agree you have to look after yourself	50.0	69.0	1
Agree there is a real sense of belonging	4.3	30.7	0.1
Agree school a good preparation for work	9.6	29.5	1

The suggestion that something in the nature of the organisations of Cooperative School and College contributed to these differences in the experiences of their students is partly confirmed when comparisons are made with other schools and colleges. Table 8.5 compares the opinions of students in Cooperative School with those of students from the three other all-through schools in the survey. In every case Cooperative School had either the lowest or highest percentage response of the four schools. It is clear that Cooperative School students had, with one exception, the least satisfactory of experiences of the sixth form, and had the poorest opinions about the place of the sixth form in the school.

The one exception is that they had the lowest agreement to the proposition that you have to look after yourself in the sixth form. Being looked after does not necessarily go with feelings of satisfaction.

In line with the general trend of differences, sixth formers at Cooperative School took longer to settle in than those in any other school (Table 8.6). Most of these differences between Cooperative School and others hold for the separate sexes.

Table 8.6 *Time to settle in – Cooperative School and three other all-through schools* (%)

	Cooperative sixth formers ($n = 94$)	Other sixth formers ($n = 342$)	Significance (%) (chi square)
A few days	23.4	46.8	1
About a term	21.3	13.7	5
More than a term	13.8	2.1	2

In contrast, Cooperative College students were more likely than students in five other colleges to feel they knew some staff well and feel a sense of belonging, and less likely to feel they had to look after themselves. Rather confusingly, they felt most often that they would prefer to keep their social life separate from the college (Table 8.7). In line with the general trend, proportionally more students at Cooperative College felt themselves to be happier in college than at school (57.5 per cent compared with an average of 42.6 per cent).

It is not easy to locate which aspects of their organisations were associated with Cooperative College having the most contented students, not only among the six colleges but also among all twelve institutions studied, and with Cooperative School having the least satisfied. The college was among the least restrictive of colleges, and was also the smallest, although there was no general relation between student satisfaction and size of institution. The school, however, was not the most restrictive of student behaviour, the most demanding of responsibility, or the meanest with privileges.

There is, however, some rather indirect evidence to suggest that the particular relationship between Cooperative School and Cooperative College may have contributed to their students' strongly contrasted evaluations, in a kind of polarisation effect. The analyses of the students' opinions of college suggest that these are an outcome of their comparing their present experience with those of the past in school (chapter 7). The suggestion is that Cooperative School and College students were able to compare their current experience with that of similar students in the other institution.

Students from college and school could meet or just see each other during the dinner hour in the small town where they were both situated, and at other times. A small number of students from the college attended some classes in the school, and vice versa. More than a quarter of college students who had been fifth formers in the school claimed to have most of their friends still at the school and 8 per cent of those who stayed on claimed to have most of their friends in the college. The opportunities for the mutual comparison of their situations did exist, and may have lead to an enhancement of the college students' delight with college and an exacerbation of the sixth formers dislike of school. In response to the open question, 'What do you dislike about the sixth form?', one sixth former wrote: 'A bit too much like the rest of the school considering we are meant to be part of Nossex Consortium of Continued Education, and not being treated as an adult, as they are at the tech.' In reply to the question 'Why did you come to college?', one ex-fifth year pupil of the school now at the college wrote: 'I was pissed off with school, particularly the small-minded dictators who pose as senior masters and mistresses. From what I hear its not much better in the sixth form.'

There is a very speculative analysis of the situation. Whatever its validity the phenomenon it seeks to explain illustrates the way in which social actions often have unintended consequences. The

Cooperative Consortium was set up to economise on resources and maximise student choice. The unforeseen outcome seems to have been the emergence of two highly contrasted institutions in terms of the satisfaction of their students.

Table 8.7   *Students' opinions – Cooperative College and five other colleges (% agreement)*

	Cooperative College ($n = 120$)	Other colleges ($n = 1,651$)	Significance (%) (chi square)
There is a real sense of belonging in college	28.3	21.5	5
Prefer to keep social life separate from college	63.3	50.8	1
Know some staff well	64.2	42.1	0.1
You have to look after yourself in college	65.0	78.4	2

125

Chapter 9

The tertiary college

A logical extension of the cooperation between school and colleges of further education is the proposal that the two streams of post-sixteen education should become one. This merging would produce what Sir William Alexander (1969) has called a tertiary college system, a new stratum between secondary and higher education. Exeter College and North Devon College were the first of the few institutions which could be seen as prototypes of this proposed system, although they operate under further education regulations and from this point of view may be seen by some as a takeover of part of the school system rather than a merger.

The idea of the tertiary college

The use of the term tertiary college is particularly associated with Alexander (1969) but other advocates of the idea, including Mumford (1965, 1970, 1972), prefer the term junior college, although this has been used for sixth form colleges. Sir William made his proposals at a time when a new education Act was widely expected, and his plan for a new tertiary stratum of education for all 16–19 year olds is based upon some of the same sort of arguments used in relation to sixth form centres, sixth form colleges and some school-college cooperative schemes. These are also used in the justification of the realised examples of tertiary colleges in which all post-sixteen education is based upon a college of further education; Alexander saw both colleges and schools becoming tertiary colleges under new regulations.

The economic advantages in terms of better use of scarce staff and equipment and the avoidance of unnecessary duplication of courses in different types of post-sixteen institution are stressed by Alexander (1969) and Mumford (1970). At a more concrete level they are also used by the principal of Exeter College (Merfield, 1973) and by the former deputy (now chief) education officer of Devon in relation to the North Devon College (Owen, 1970, 1972). They also point to the wider choice of subjects and courses such arrangements make possible, and Mumford also suggests that transfer between courses would be easily accomplished.

Alexander argues that the increasing maturity of young people demands an institution separate from younger pupils. Mumford and Merfield claim that post-sixteen education based on the technical college could and does provide the desired adult atmosphere. A number of advocates including Owen (1972) consider that such a college would attract more students to stay on in full-time education, and at a time when there was thought to be a shortage of scientists and technologists, the Association of Technical Institutions (1969) felt this might be alleviated as more students entered an institution with a 'positive view' of technology. A further advantage of this atmosphere would be to provide a better preparation for higher education (Rolfe, 1969).

A claim special to the tertiary or junior college is that it would be more comprehensive, in both the social and educational sense, than existing forms of post-sixteen education. The principal of Exeter College (Merfield, 1973) suggests: 'There are social advantages in gathering all students together in a comprehensive college: academic and technical, full-time and part-time, adolescent and mature, local and "foreign" (whether out of town or overseas.' This version of what Marsden (1969) calls the egalitarian philosophy of comprehensive education is also supported by Mumford (1970), Owen (1970, 1972), Benn and Simon (1972), the ATI (1969) and the APTI (1972). Alexander (1969) also felt that in this sense tertiary colleges would be more comprehensive than a divided system of academic and technical education, but his opinion must be set against his view that the 2 per cent of children who are 'unusually gifted academically' should be educated in a separate institution.

The comprehensive qualities of the tertiary or junior college have also been endorsed by a long-standing advocate of comprehensive education, Robin Pedley (1973), who was one of the earliest to make reservations about the place of the sixth form in a system of all-through schools (1956). However, he qualifies his advocacy by pointing out some deficiencies of technical colleges as centres for the education of all young people (1973, p. 246):

> Pastoral care, clubs and societies strengthened and supported by members of staff, and a strong community life and spirit, are invaluable in these years. There are exceptions in this or that technical college, and in this or that department of particular colleges, but much remains to be done over the whole field.

Some defenders of the colleges, such as Moore (1972) and the ATI (1969) refute this, but the criticisms are at least partly acknowledged in the changes made at the Exeter College by its principal. In a letter to the 'Times Educational Supplement' (Merfield, 1969), when the plan to set up the college had just been announced, he wrote of his own future role as, 'embodying the best traditions of headmasterly pastoral care and college liberalism', and stressed that the college would change 'in nature and in name'. In a later report of the college in action he describes the arrangement of tutors, counsellors and other institutional advisers as ways in which, 'a large and rather amorphous college can be reduced to human proportions' (Merfield, 1973). He also reports the development of more clubs, societies, and sports activities, and the college prospectus (1974–5) refers to a well-established choir and developing orchestra.

Pedley (1973) also refers to the technical colleges', 'low standing in the public eye' as needing correction. In the implementation of the Exeter scheme this was centred on the discussion of the name to be given to the new establishment to be based on the then Exeter Technical College. The name Exeter College was chosen by the Education Committee as correcting any disadvantage its students may have had in applying for university places. As the chairman was quoted as saying, '... the university people may look down their noses. We like to think ours is a bit more than a college of further education' (Exeter 'Express and Echo', 4 February 1972).

Both the Exeter and North Devon college operate under the

Further Education Regulations (1969). Fears that young people would benefit less under these than under school regulations were quickly dismissed by the then director of education for Exeter and the principal of Exeter College (Merfield, 1969). Full-time students aged 16–19 at the Exeter and North Devon colleges, receive similar dispensations to those in schools with regard to meals, medical services and travel.

The pastoral aspects of the treatment of students are, in the school system, part of the concept of the school as a community. In both Exeter and North Devon the existing links between college and industry have formed the basis of a more extended notion of the college serving the local community. The principal of the Exeter College refers to 'community advantages in focusing attention upon an educational centrepiece' (Merfield, 1973). The principal of the North Devon College is quoted as saying, 'we want the college to become a centre of things in the district' (Mo, 1972).

Two lines of criticism of the use of technical colleges as centres of post-sixteen education have been expressed. The first, made by the NUT (1969), the HMA (1968) and the ILEA (1968), is that the dual system of colleges provides a choice of type of institution for the student, a view endorsed by at least one college principal (Trustam, 1967). The second criticism looks to the corollary of any scheme to segregate post-sixteen education: the end of the all-through school. The criticism becomes a defence of the traditional idea of the sixth form and a criticism of short-course schools, and has been made by the HMA (1968), AMA (1974) and by a number of headteachers of schools with sixth forms, including Murphy (1972) and Ruffle (1973).

The idea of the tertiary college was put to a sample of students and teachers in the survey by Smith (1974). Among sixth formers, 30 per cent felt there would be advantages, 11 per cent disadvantages, whilst most (42 per cent) felt there would be both. The most commonly perceived advantages were more choice of courses and better facilities. Sixth form teachers were much less favourably disposed, only 3 per cent seeing only advantages, and 33 per cent seeing only disadvantages, including the separation from younger pupils, impersonality and lack of individual attention. As may be expected, all but 7 per cent of college of further education students saw advantages in the tertiary college idea; 44 per cent saw only advantages, 36 per cent both advantages

129

and disadvantages. The main disadvantage they saw would be that a technical college may become too much like school when reorganised in this way.

Reorganisation in Exeter

This account of the establishment of the Exeter College is partly based upon a study carried out by Hugh Jones (1972), and upon original research, particularly in the more recent period.

Byrne, Williamson and Fletcher (1973) created a typology of English local education authorities using the technique of cluster analysis. Exeter, during the period under discussion, fell into what could be called their 'mean, middle class, Conservative' category. For many years the Exeter local education authority ranked among the lowest for expenditure. In 1970–1 it was 144th among 148 local authorities, for expenditure per secondary school pupil (IMTA, 1972). Midwinter (1973) has calculated it to be 21st for middle-classness among local authorities. It had a Conservative controlled city council during the period under discussion. All of these characteristics are relevant to an understanding of the processes of reorganisation leading to the establishment of the Exeter College.

In June 1963, at the request of the city council, the then director of education submitted a report on secondary education in Exeter with reference to the possibility of reorganisation along comprehensive lines. At the time the city was served by three girls', three boys' and one mixed modern school, two single sex grammar schools, and places were offered at two direct grant grammar schools. As in Conservative Croydon (Urwin, 1965), the case for comprehensive schools was made more on the grounds of meeting the increased demand for grammar school type education than an acceptance of the comprehensive principle. A second report presented by the director in February 1964 specified the different forms of comprehensive systems then in use, and the city council showed approval towards some kind of two tier system on the basis of the economic utilisation of existing buildings.

In October 1964 the council set up a working party on reorganisation with a majority of education members. Following the guidance given in Circular 10/65 the working party presented its initial proposals in October 1965, which suggested the idea of 11–16 comprehensives with a sixth form college based on the boys' grammar school. Their final scheme was approved by the education committee in June 1966 and discussions with interested parties began. The DES made reservations about the small form entry (4 or 5) of the comprehensive schools and the somewhat academic concept of the sixth form college.

Following the publication of the Plowden Report the idea of turning the city's infant schools into first schools (5–8) and the junior schools into middle schools (8–12) was seen as a way of increasing the form entry into comprehensive schools by re-cruiting at twelve instead of eleven. A new and enlarged working party for both primary and secondary reorganisation was set up in April 1967 and presented its first proposals in November. These recommended the setting up of a system of first, middle, and 12–16 comprehensive schools, and a sixth form college based on the boys' grammar school. This was rejected by the education committee in January 1968, the Conservative majority for the first time voicing the realisation that becoming comprehensive meant the going of the grammar schools.

At the next meeting of the working party, in February, the director of education introduced the idea of using the Exeter Technical College – recently rehoused in new buildings – as a centre for sixth form work. The origin of this idea is not very clear. It had been discussed by the original working party, but the then principal of the college, the only college representative, whose retirement was imminent, was not in favour. It is possible that it arose from informal discussions between the educational administration and the DES. If this is so, it indicates a development of DES policy beyond that of Circular 10/65, which referred only to school/college cooperation.

Despite opposition from the staff of the boys' grammar school and the local branch of the AMA, the director's plan was accepted by the working party, the city council, and on 13 August 1969 by the Secretary of State. The Conservative majority's acceptance of the plan was based mainly upon its presumed costs which were thought to be advantageous, although they were never actually calculated. As the first area to include a technical college in its reorganisation scheme, a great deal of approbation was received for its boldness, but as Edwards (1970b) has commented, 'This boldness is administrative rather than ideological.'

What was called 'the last 11+ in Exeter' occurred in 1971. However, due to problems of accommodation the first transfer to the comprehensive schools happened the next year for eleven year olds and not in 1973 for twelve year olds, as planned. In 1970 girls who would have transferred to the sixth form of their grammar school went to the technical college for A level and other studies, and a similar change occurred in 1971 for the boys' grammar school. In 1972 all post-sixteen students from local schools enrolled at the college.

In the period since the inception of the scheme two incidents have occurred which illuminate the concerns of the Conservative majority on the city council. In October 1970 the council announced that it would continue to take up places at the two direct grant schools, which had offered only token cooperation in the reorganisation discussions, claiming that no 'damage' would be done to the nascent comprehensive schools which were designed for the 'average' child. The Labour and Liberal members protested as did the coopted members of the education committee and the local teachers' associations. The permanence of the decision was made clear with the announcement that after 1974 entry to the direct grant schools would be at twelve and not eleven. As if to add their doubts about the new college to those about the comprehensive schools, in 1973 the council arranged for free places to be taken up in the sixth forms of the direct grant schools, for those, as the Public Notice put it, 'fit to follow A level courses in 3 subjects'. No information is available about the social composition of the direct grant schools in Exeter, but they are not likely to be any less middle class strongholds than those described in the Public Schools' Commission 'Second Report' (1970).

To their own satisfaction the council majority had their cake and ate it; they had reorganised and retained their grammar schools. In their fifty-six square inch notice about the decision in the local paper, the Exeter Conservative Association followed the party line in justifying the retention of direct grant places in terms of parental choice (the schools take 3.5 per cent of thirteen year olds in the area), and did not mention their social or academic selectivity. In October 1971 the boys' direct grant school launched a successful appeal for a £75,000 building fund.

The second incident concerned the expense of the scheme. During late 1970 and throughout 1971 reports of shortages of books and overcrowding at the college led to increases in the financial allocation to the college in December 1971. In January 1972 the education committee's estimates were nearly one million pounds up on the previous year, and most of the increase was for the college. By April increased educational costs were being blamed by the Conservative majority for what was called a 'rates' crisis. In the period before local elections in May they were unwilling to announce rates increases. The Liberal and Labour councillors predicted a breakdown in the educational system of the city if cuts were imposed, and uncorrected forecasts of teacher redundancy were rife. In May, the policy committee announced an enquiry would be made into the finances and administration of the college. Reorganisation was proving to be more expensive than expected and, as the present college principal has written, 'the [Exeter] burghers traditionally seek value for money' (Merfield, 1973).

Whilst the enquiry proceeded, an attempt was made to replace the chairman of the education committee by a more cost-conscious Conservative. The committee then elected one of its coopted members to the chair but this was overruled by the council, and their new chairman, from outside the committee, was installed. The report of the Committee of Enquiry, presented in September 1972, found no major faults in the administration and finances of the college. However, subsequently there were cutbacks in the admission of overseas students and in the provision of courses for evening studies.

A new principal was appointed to the college in 1969. Whereas the Conservative majority on the city council had endorsed the use of the college as a centre for post-sixteen studies mainly on economic grounds, the new principal quickly showed himself to be the ideologue of the scheme (Merfield, 1973). The ideology of comprehensive education was to find its purest expression yet in the college which would not only cater for students of all abilities but also bring together the young and mature, the part-time and full-time, the academic and the vocational. The 'open door' policy that this implied was criticised when the increased college expenditure was seen as the prime element in the financial crisis. Strictly speaking, the 'open door' policy has operated in that anyone can seek enrolment at the college, but entry to courses is governed by detailed requirements in almost every case. The corollary was a wide provision of courses, a policy vigorously pursued by the new principal in the further education entrepreneurial tradition. Although the number of O level subjects and OND courses provided remained fairly constant between 1971–2 and 1974–5, the number of A levels increased from twenty-eight to thirty-nine. The number of full-time staff increased by 28 per cent. There are no plans to introduce CSE, as in some sixth form colleges.

Every student is recruited to a particular course. Here the college has extended two related elements of arrangement of further education courses to those for O and A level. Each course either has a fairly specific vocational title or explicitly points to particular opportunities in higher education, and the curriculum is organised around a related rationale. For example, the pre-professional course in engineering involves five relevant O level studies together with workshop practice, and is designed as a preparation for the OND engineering course. More novel, if not unique, are the courses created around a key A level subject or subjects. For example, the English with history course has a unifying theme of America, which is not only the specialist element in the A level syllabuses followed, but also that of a wide range of ancillary studies including painting, films and religions. The prospectus refers to the number of universities which offer American studies as part of degree courses (fifteen).

In 1970–1 the internal organisation of the college was very similar to other colleges with a similar departmental and course structure (see chapter 7). By 1973 a number of changes had been made, all related to the changing nature of the student intake: the guaranteed supply of sixteen year olds from local schools to take mainly academic courses, particularly A level. The overview of these changes became the responsibility of the new appointment in 1971, from a sixth form college, of an Academic Vice-Principal.

The principal propagated the idea that the college was changing its nature (Merfield, 1967, 1972), and this was meant to be symbolised in the change of name to simply Exeter College in 1972. The college prospectus refers to 'its dual responsibility as Technical College and Sixth Form College'. A curious double identity is in common usage. The college is still commonly referred to as the 'tech', whilst some parents, teachers and local politicians refer to it as 'the sixth form college'. The idea that the former sixth formers are a separate unit within the college is erroneously but quite widely held. These students belong to different departments, are taught by lecturers who also teach students from other backgrounds, and do not occupy a discrete part of the college. The situation is that the college acts as both a technical college and a sixth form college, but these are not structurally differentiated.

Although part of the ideology of the comprehensive college has been to claim that its more 'adult' atmosphere is more acceptable to the faster maturing adolescents than is that of school, the changes in organisation have been to introduce more school-like features. There has been a considerable strengthening of the provision of pastoral care, as suggested by the Secretary of State in approving the scheme. There are two full-time counsellors, a nurse and other advisers. Each student belongs to a tutorial group which meets every day and for a longer period each week – an interesting convergence with comprehensive school practice. The rationale for this has been that students may feel 'lost' in a big, complex institution – again a parallel with the large comprehensive (see King, 1973a). Parents' meetings have also been introduced.

The technical bias implied in its former name has been corrected by the introduction of more Arts elements into the curriculum, and as study options or voluntary activities. A choir and orchestra have been started. The range of what in schools would be called extra-curricular activities has been increased and attempts are being made to run team games. There has also been a considerable strengthening, both financial and administrative, of the students' union (Merfield, 1973).

Reorganisation in North Devon

This account of the establishment of the North Devon College is partly based upon a research report prepared by Professor Richard O. Carlson of the University of Oregon whilst acting as a consultant for the Organisation for Economic Cooperation and Development in 1971. A version of that report, prepared by the secretariat of the Centre for Educational Research and Innovation (a part of OECD), and which acknowledges the help of Dr Brian Holmes of the University of London, was published in 1973. This account also draws upon original research.

In contrast to Exeter the Devon local education authority (before reorganisation in 1974) was among the more generous in its spending, ranking above average for expenditure on secondary pupils in 1970–1 (IMTA, 1972), and although under independent control, it had pursued a policy of going comprehensive since the late 1950s. Until the scheme for North Devon was produced the pattern had been to create all-through 11–18 schools by combining small town grammar schools with one or two associated modern schools, as at Totnes, Tavistock and Exmouth. The situation in North Devon did not seem to lend itself to such a scheme. The mixed grammar school in Barnstaple did have a complementary modern school in the town, but modern schools also existed at South Molton (12 miles away) and Braunton (6 miles away).

In the mid-1960s the headteachers of the three modern schools started to have informal meetings to discuss common problems, particularly relating to the advent of CSE. When the prospect of reorganisation was introduced in 1967 they called themselves the Academic Board, invited the head of the grammar school to join them (and later the Principal of the North Devon Technical College) and set about devising plans. Their first effort, produced in the summer of 1967, was for a sixth form centre at the grammar school (with an 11–18 range), with the three modern schools as feeder 11–16 schools. This was presented to the education officers with reservations made by the modern school headteachers, who felt it perpetuated the existing status differences between the schools in a new form.

Informal contact with the DES produced an unfavourable response to the plan, mainly on the grounds of the cost of improving the facilities at the grammar school site. By February 1968 the Academic Board was split, the grammar school head still favouring the idea of a sixth form centre at his school, and the modern school heads favouring the idea of a sixth form unit based at the North Devon Technical College in Barnstaple.

In March the chief education officer, in consultation with his own senior staff, produced the scheme that was eventually accepted: all post-sixteen education to be centred on the college with the grammar and modern schools forming 11–16 feeder comprehensives. The scheme started its easy passage through the county committees. Carlson suggests that the committee members were well disposed towards the scheme as it would be financed out of the further education budget, and were not fully aware of the implications of the difference between having a sixth form unit at the college, as proposed by some of the Academic Board, and the officer's plan to create, in effect, a comprehensive college. This distinction may not have been fully appreciated by the members of the Academic Board to whom the plan was revealed in the strictest confidence.

In September 1968 the teachers in the four schools involved were informed of the plan by letter. This provoked a shocked and angry reaction from the teachers, parents of pupils and governors of the grammar school, who mounted a campaign of opposition. The grammar school head wrote to each member of the education committee, but was rebuked by the chief education officer. In November the MP for North Devon raised the matter with the Secretary of State. Formal statements of opposition were made by the grammar school staff, and the Parent-Teacher Association arranged a public meeting in Barnstaple for 9 January 1969. On 2 January the county education committee gave its final approval to the scheme as did the county council on 9 January. So when the chief education officer took part in the meeting on the evening of the same day, the situation appeared to be one of fait accompli and he was accused of secretly pushing through his own 'pet scheme', which he denied. The heated meeting involved little dialogue, the audience concentrating on what they thought was being destroyed, the idea of the sixth form and its place in the school, and the officers attempting to justify what they thought was being created, a new idea in education, a comprehensive college.

After negotiations with the DES central approval in principle was given in October 1969, and final approval in May 1970. Carlson attributes the speed of this process to the existence of long-standing productive relationships between the local education authority officers and the DES officials. It may also be due to the Department's experience with the Exeter plan, which had been approved shortly before.

Opposition to the scheme continued during and after this time. Many senior staff resigned from the grammar school, as did the headmaster at the time of final approval, when he publicly expressed his support for comprehensive reorganisation, but not in a form which meant the loss of the sixth form. With the change of government in 1970 and the advent of Circular 10/70, the grammar school parents made representations to the new Conservative Secretary of State, but in September the DES announced they were not prepared to reconsider the plan.

Most of the justification of the scheme was made after its official approval. Whilst, as in Exeter, important arguments were made about the economic use of resources, the ideological element was much more important. This was encapsulated in the phrase invented by the chief education officer, 'the seamless cloak'. This was meant to symbolise the continuities created by the scheme, not only between vocational and academic education, but also between the feeder schools and the college, in terms of cooperation and curriculum planning.

The details of the setting up of the new system were dealt with by the Barnstaple Planning Committee set up in December 1969. Its members included the heads of the schools concerned, the principal and later vice-principal of the college, and various council officers. The chairman was the assistant education officer for further education. The first students under the new scheme entered the renamed North Devon College in September 1972. As at the Exeter College there has been an expansion, mainly of academic courses. In 1970-1 courses were offered in twenty A level subjects and twenty-one O level subjects. By 1974-5 these figures were twenty-nine and thirty-five respectively. The number of OND courses remained constant and there is no provision for CSE.

Since 1972 the Academic Board, consisting of the four head-teachers of the associated schools, the college principal and director of studies, and two local education authority advisers, has acted as 'an initiating and innovating body' in relation to what is called the Barnstaple Reorganisation Complex of the college and secondary schools (Lineham, 1974). The director of studies to the complex describes the college as, 'not a school, not a 6th form college, not a traditional "tech." – it is just North Devon College and caters for all post-16 education in a part of the North Devon Area'. The ideology of the seamless cloak is expressed in the attempts to provide continuity of guidance and pastoral care across the 11–19 age range, and thus across the school-college boundary. The egalitarian aspects of the scheme are expressed in the view that students on the different kinds of courses, 'are aware of each other as students and what is provided for one educationally is neither better nor worse than but different from what is provided for another' (Lineham, 1974).

The Exeter and North Devon schemes are structurally very similar, and the events leading up to their introduction do have some elements in common. The most important of these were the informal, poorly documented, but decisive discussions between the local education authority officers and the DES. The differences are more interesting. The North Devon scheme was mainly locally devised and later propagated by the education department at county hall, and was justified more on ideological than economic grounds. In Exeter the scheme although locally devised (if not originated) by the working party with a majority of non-political coopted members, was accepted by the city council mainly for its presumed economic qualities. The Barnstaple scheme was associated with a great deal of acrimony, but there was much less in Exeter, where most of the outcry was made about the continuing use of the direct grant schools.

Some of these differences centre on the role of the chief education officer. Miriam David (1971, 1973), in a study of the workings of local authority education departments, identified two types of chief education officer. The conciliator types were mainly concerned with dealing with the conflicting demands and pressures made on the education service, and felt themselves to be primarily administrators and servants of their education committees in implementing the committees' policies. In his public comments on the Exeter scheme the then director of education made it fairly clear that this was the way he saw his role. As such he could not be used as a focus of attack on the reorganisation scheme.

The second type of chief education officer in David's analysis is the educator. These are 'very evangelical and have a strong desire to develop and disseminate new ideas, methods and techniques in education' (David, 1971). The chief education officer of Devon during the introduction of the Barnstaple plan was regarded in this way. As the presumed originator of the idea, the Barnstaple scheme could be blamed on him. His own view of his role was partly revealed in his published interview with Maurice Kogan (Kogan and Van Der Eyken, 1973) in which he commented, 'not many committees or councillors think or want to think that the ideas are theirs'.

Another possible factor was spatial proximity. Exeter was a small administrative area and the educational administrators had a great deal of informal contact with the headteachers. It was possible for the deputy director to see each secondary school headteacher about a particular matter, almost before they had the chance to 'phone each other to advise of his coming. In these circumstances a tight, inward-looking loyalty to the administration was developed over the long lengths of service of the headteachers. Barnstaple is 40 miles away from the county education offices in Exeter and although a divisional office with one officer existed for North Devon in Barnstaple, teachers and headteachers generally felt the Exeter administration to be remote and not too sensitive to their local situation.

The lower level of dissent in Exeter may have been partly due to the imminence of retirement for many of the secondary headteachers. By 1974, only one of the original seven was still in office. In addition, it is likely that some of the potential pro-grammar school activists could see that the traditional pattern of the integral academic sixth form would be preserved in the direct grant schools. Middle school headteachers serving the middle class areas of the city have reported that increased pro-portions of their pupils were seeking places in the direct grant schools and in other local private schools. The headteachers of the direct grant schools have publicly commented on the in-creased demand and several other private schools have expanded their numbers. In Croydon the rejection of the scheme to provide a separate post-sixteen institution was associated with the inter-vention of schools not involved in the scheme (Urwin, 1965); in Exeter the guaranteed continued existence of such schools was associated with the acceptance of a similar scheme.

In North Devon the animosity of the pro-grammar school groups towards the 'decapitation' of their school was similar to that in Croydon earlier, but was matched by the modern school headteachers' determination to get the sentence carried out. The emotional charge of the events derived in part from the response to the threat of death to the traditional concept of the sixth form, but was also, as Sara Payne (1969) has suggested, due to '. . . feelings of superiority and inferiority – feelings one is tempted to conclude which lie at the root of all the bitterness'.

The education offices of the former Devon and Exeter local authorities were both in Exeter, with little over a mile between them. At no time during the drawing up of the two very similar plans did consultations occur between the two sets of education officers. After the DES acceptance of the schemes the then director of education for Exeter did attend two meetings of the Barnstaple Planning Committee, although making no contribu-tion. It was left to one of Her Majesties Inspectors to institute a conference of officers and teaching staff from the two areas to discuss common concerns. In April 1974 the two authorities became part of the new county authority of Devon.

Tertiary College

In 1971 Pro-Tertiary Technical College was one of six surveyed colleges. The survey included interviews with the principal, vice-principals, heads of department, members of staff with special responsibilities, officials of the students' union and groups of students; periods of observation in the college; the analysis of documents provided by the college authorities; and the completion of a questionnaire by full-time students. This survey was partly replicated in 1973 when the college had become a centre for all post-sixteen education in the area under further education regulations, and so changed its pseudonym to Tertiary College. Thus the two surveys can be regarded as a before and after design, although changes in relation to the new organisation were occurring and being planned at the before stage, and the high status staff of the college still had plans for future changes at the after stage. The results of both surveys of students were sent to senior staff, and some of the organisational changes made in the period following the first survey drew upon its results.

The heads of the vocational departments, engineering, construction, business studies, and food and fashion, viewed reorganisation with some apprehension, fearing that they would come off worse in the competition for resources, both money and students. As the head of the construction department put it, 'The only ones to benefit will be the grammar school types up in General Studies.' The general studies department did increase in size the most, and was split into two departments, social studies and liberal arts. But the engineering and construction departments also increased in size, although retaining much the same proportion of students, whilst business studies increased its share. (The science and mathematics departments, however, had a reduced share of students; perhaps part of the swing to the Arts.) As part of a deliberate policy to involve vocational departments in the idea of the new Tertiary College, O and A level courses were spread across all departments. Thus the construction department provided an A level pure and applied mathematics course, and the food education department provided one for A level home economics. The heads of the vocational departments began to see advantages in having a reliable supply of students from the local schools.

Overall, the proportion of A level students increased from 30

141

per cent to 46 per cent, whilst that for O level fell from 55 per cent to 38 per cent. OND, RSA, City and Guilds and other vocational courses fell slightly from 56 per cent to 52 per cent. The percentages for both periods add up to more than 100 per cent because both Pro-Tertiary and Tertiary College, and other colleges of further education, allowed some students to enter for related vocational and academic examinations.

There were important changes in what in schools would be called the pastoral care of students. In a long internal memorandum, the vice-principal outlined what was seen to be the problem: 'a change from a small secondary school to a large college can be disconcerting, and it would be irresponsible to leave students to sink or swim'. The importance of the matter was placed very highly: 'the success or failure of the [Tertiary College] scheme, must depend to a high degree upon the success of our tutorial policy'. The policy was to make every student a member of a tutorial group (average size, twelve), with others on the same course, taken by a tutor who also taught the group's course. The groups have a 'home base' used for the twice daily registration and a weekly tutorial meeting. The course tutors were the most commonly consulted of college staff about matters concerned with college work, future education, careers or personal problems. Pro-Tertiary College had a counsellor and a second was added, together with an appointment based on the students' union, called the Students' Welfare Officer, and a college nurse. Only a small number of Tertiary college students reported ever consulting these institutional advisers.

It is extremely difficult to make estimates of the effectiveness of pastoral care or tutorial systems. Were these advisers so little used because the students preferred to take their problems elsewhere, or because few of them had problems? Comparing the views of Pro-Tertiary and Tertiary college students, there were no significance differences in the extent to which they felt they knew the staff well, had to look after themselves, or had a sense of belonging (Table 9.1). To this extent the tutorial provision may be judged to be effective in that the levels of satisfaction had been maintained despite an increase in student numbers.

The college day was officially defined as 9.00–5.15. Most students had a class at 9.00. The average staff/student contact time was twenty-five hours a week, and students were expected to work a forty hour week, that is, to do fifteen hours of homework or private study. It was officially admitted that few students reached this figure. The expansion in numbers put a heavy strain on space for private study, so after a brief struggle against student protests about overcrowding and widespread absences, the ruling was made that private study could be done at home during the college day, and most of it seemed to be done there. This change may be reflected in the greater satisfaction of Tertiary College students, compared with Pro-Tertiary, with respect to the provision of private study (Table 9.1, o). They also felt less often that there was an emphasis on exams, and were less likely to feel they were getting too little individual help (Table 9.1, j and p). Their feelings about college as a preparation for work and future education, and the amount of control they had over their work, remained much the same (Table 9.1, l, m and n).

There was a considerable strengthening of the provision of non-examination activities. Every full-time student had one afternoon timetabled for activities chosen from a wide range, either aesthetic, athletic or social service. Senior staff estimated that about 90 per cent of students did in fact attend regularly, compared with about 70 per cent in the less tightly controlled and less lavishly provided Pro-Tertiary College. Table 9.1 (item h) shows that Tertiary College students were the more appreciative of their arrangements.

The control of student behaviour remained much the same. No restrictions on appearance were made, except on some catering courses, and the business studies department was less insistent upon 'office wear'. As the head of the department commented, 'they all want to be students now'. Table 9.1 (c and f) shows that Tertiary College students did feel less restricted than their predecessors, although their feelings about being treated as adult were much the same.

The union was given a larger budget and more responsibility for student facilities. Table 9.1 (items g, r, s and t) shows some increase in students' concern about the union and a greater appreciation of its activities.

The range of voluntary activities increased, emphasis being put upon cultural activities, including a choir and orchestra, and team games. There was an increase in the proportion of students taking part, from 18.3 per cent to 25.4 per cent. Team games were fostered by the creation of a physical education course. This consisted of all students following O or A level programmes with a special interest in games and PE. In addition to their academic studies they received instruction and coaching in a wide range

Table 9.1 *Students' opinions – Pro-Tertiary College and Tertiary College* (%)

	Pro-tertiary College (*n* = 617)	Tertiary college (*n* = 918)	Significance (%) (chi square)
(a) Prefer to keep social life separate from college	51.8	36.9	0.1
(b) Staff are interested in personal welfare	46.6	48.0	ns
(c) There are unnecessary restrictions	24.4	16.4	1
(d) I feel I know some staff well	43.5	44.4	ns
(e) It is easy to make friends	63.6	66.5	ns
(f) Treated as adults	62.8	65.1	ns
(g) Staff only interested in those who do well	11.3	10.3	ns
(h) Non-exam subjects take up valuable time	42.1	36.2	5
(i) You have to look after yourself	80.9	77.0	ns
(j) There is a strong emphasis on exams	76.7	61.5	0.1
(k) There is a real sense of belonging	20.4	23.5	ns
(l) You decide for yourself how much work you do	78.0	73.0	ns
(m) College is a good preparation for going to work	51.5	49.0	ns
(n) College is a good preparation for future education	73.1	73.8	ns
(o) There is too little private study	44.5	33.3	1
(p) There is too little individual help	44.0	38.7	5
(q) Students don't care about the union	36.4	42.9	5
(r) The union doesn't tell students what is happening	29.6	29.4	ns
(s) The union has done a lot to help students	41.3	51.0	1
(t) There isn't enough student participation in the union	47.2	60.9	1

of sports, and they formed the core of the college teams. The rugby team was unbeaten in the 1972–3 season.

Tertiary College students were less likely to settle very quickly into college: 33.7 per cent reported having done so in a few days, compared with 41.1 per cent of Pro-Tertiary College students. The difference was probably due to the longer induction period in which more students were being allocated to courses and tutorial groups. There were no significant long-term differences in settling in.

Once in, the Tertiary College students were less keen to keep their social lives separate from the college (Table 9.1, a). This confirms what the vice-principal in his memorandum expressed as one of the elements in the atmosphere of the college, 'the pleasure of meeting a lot of people and making friends among them'. This is supported in the changing pattern of student friendships. More Tertiary College students had friends among part-time and overseas students than did those in Pro-Tertiary College, despite the fact that the proportion of these students had fallen slightly (Table 9.2). If these reported friendships are an acceptable indication of social integration then it could be said that the college was fulfilling some of the egalitarian claims made for such colleges. There were also more friendships between the sexes in Tertiary College (Table 9.2). This may be an indication of something other than egalitarianism.

Table 9.2   *Friendships in Pro-Tertiary and Tertiary College*

	Pro-Tertiary college ($n = 617$)	Tertiary college ($n = 918$)	Significance (%) (chi square)
Some friends studying part-time	52.6	68.9	0.1
Some friends from overseas	56.8	70.3	0.1
Some friends of the opposite sex	82.2	91.4	1

Overall, the comparisons of the college before and after reorganisation show that in general there was a slight, and in some areas significant, improvement in student satisfaction. This is confirmed in the students' estimates of their relative happiness in school and college. In Pro-Tertiary College, 17.8 per cent felt happier in school compared with 15.7 per cent in Tertiary College; the figures for those happier in college were 36.2 per cent and 43.5 per cent respectively.

The previous discussion of colleges of further education showed them to be associated with higher levels of satisfaction among boys than girls. Table 9.3 shows that this situation existed in Pro-Tertiary College in that boys reported knowing staff well, ease of making friends and a sense of belonging more often than did girls. In Tertiary College, however, the sex difference was narrowed for relations with staff and had disappeared from significance for ease of making friends and sense of belonging. This is also shown in the rates at which the sexes occupied positions in the union. In Pro-Tertiary College 5.4 per cent of boys held positions compared with 3.8 per cent of girls; in Tertiary College these were 3.7 per cent and 3.2 per cent respectively. However, the higher proportion of boys joining voluntary activities remained; in Pro-Tertiary College these were 24.1 per cent for boys and 14.3 per cent for girls, in Tertiary College 30.5 per cent and 20.6 per cent respectively.

One interesting result concerns the students' feelings about unnecessary restrictions in college. In Pro-Tertiary College, boys actually felt more often than did girls that they were restricted. Although both sexes agreed less often to this feeling in Tertiary College, the difference between the sexes was wider, so that boys were almost twice as likely as girls to feel there were unnecessary restrictions. (Table 9.3). This is a further indication of a swing away from a preponderance of male satisfaction.

The experience of colleges of further education was shown not only to be different for the sexes, but also to vary with the students' school of origin, the two most conspicuous groups being grammar school boys and modern school girls. The feeder schools of Tertiary College were in the process of becoming comprehensive and so the intake did include pupils from what were in effect still grammar and modern schools. When the responses of grammar school boys were compared with those of other boys or with students of both sexes, they did not show any significant differences. The college staff confirmed their impression that the 'recusant' grammar school boy had become a rarity. It was earlier suggested that the 'recusant' grammar school boy's favourable experience of the further education college was associated with his less favourable experience of school, and with his having chosen the college as an alternative to the sixth form. Although the grammar school boys at Tertiary College had chosen to go there the choice had not been between college and sixth form. Furthermore, their retrospective experience of school was no better and no worse than any other group of students.

146

Table 9.3 *Sex differences and students' opinions in Pro-Tertiary and Tertiary College (% agreement)*

	Pro-Tertiary College Boys (n = 261)	Girls (n = 356)	Significance (%) (chi square)	Tertiary College Boys (n = 452)	Girls (n = 466)	Significance (%) (chi square)
There are unnecessary restrictions	29.1	21.1	5	20.1	12.9	1
Feel they know some staff well	49.4	39.3	1	48.0	40.8	5
It is easy to make friends	70.5	58.7	0.1	68.4	64.8	ns
There is a real sense of belonging	25.7	16.6	5	26.1	21.0	ns

In the colleges of further education, ex-secondary modern girls were the least satisfied of students. This was also true of such girls in Tertiary College. Table 9.4 shows that they felt less happy in college than did other students, and felt more often they had been happier in school. The trouble seemed to centre on their relations with the college staff, and although they were no more likely to find unnecessary restrictions in the college than did other students, their retrospective view of school was of it being less restrictive. This persistence of the different experience of the secondary modern girls might be expected. Although the internal organisation of the college had changed the basic choice about entering it was the same: between college or a job.

Table 9.4 *Former secondary modern girls in Tertiary College (% agreement)*

	Ex-modern girls (*n* = 86)	Other students (*n* = 832)	Significance (%) (chi square)
Felt happier at school	24.4	14.8	5
Felt happier in college	27.9	45.2	1
Feel know some college staff well	30.2	45.9	1
Felt knew some school staff well	59.3	42.7	2
Felt unnecessary restrictions in school	39.5	60.9	0.1

In the transition from Pro-Tertiary to Tertiary College the senior staff were concerned to try to preserve what they saw as the best elements of the further education college, and to introduce the best elements of the traditional sixth form. In so doing they were conscious of having to change the public image of the college and of having to meet and even anticipate criticisms made about it. Their attempts did not, at first, receive the support of staff in the vocational studies departments, who were often fiercely proud of the further education tradition, often having been students within the system. One head of department complained, 'We don't want to end up like a bloody school.' Nevertheless, the efforts were made to introduce from the school sixth form tradition a supportive system of pastoral care and the virtue of voluntary participation in cultural and sporting activities. From the college tradition, they tried to retain the adult atmosphere, the vocational relevance and the emphasis on structured learning. If their efforts may be judged by comparing the evaluations and experiences of different students in the periods before and after the reorganisation to achieve these changes, then the conclusion is that they were appreciably successful.

Chapter 10

Ideologies, identity and interest groups

There exist a number of ideas about the organisational forms of post-sixteen education, all of which relate to two dominant, somewhat antithetical, patterns of ideas or ideologies. These are the ideology of the school as a community, and of the technical college as an association. These ideologies are held by groups connected with these different forms of organisation, and are used to explain and justify their social actions which are in accordance with their patterns of ideas. Ideologies are both empirical and evaluative; they not only express what is thought to be, but also, what ought to be. They provide an over-arching conception of social experience which helps to integrate the group members' conceptions of themselves and their place in the social order, that is, their social identities.

The very nature of ideologies makes them difficult to study, but this may be attempted by posing a set of questions based upon the interrogative adverbs. When did these ideas come into existence, which groups hold them, how are they propagated, and the most important and most difficult to answer, why do they hold these ideas?

Ideologies of school and college

The key assumption made by George Baron (1955) in his seminal treatment of 'The English Notion of the School', is that it is or should be a community. A study of maintained secondary schools has shown the acceptance of the ideology of the school as a community among most headteachers. In interviews and in the analysis of documents written by them or produced with their approval, frequent references occurred to the school as a community, commonly in the form of, 'we aim to be a happy, well-ordered community' (King, 1973a).

The concept of community is an important and long-established one in sociology, and like many such key concepts is difficult to define precisely: 'The more he [the sociologist] attempts to define it in his own terms, the more elusively does the essence of it seem to escape him' (Bell and Newby, 1971). This elusive quality of the idea is reduced when it is linked with what in some senses may be considered to be its social antithesis, the idea of association. This apposition of community and association, or Gemeinschaft and Gesellschaft, was first made by Ferdinand Tönnies (1955), to represent two basic forms of social order. The social order of the community is based upon relationships which are intimate, affective, enduring and involuntary, as between parent and child, and thought to be ends in themselves. The culture of the community is relatively homogeneous; 'a community of fate'. Its moral custodians are strong and their injunctions well-internalised. Community sentiments involve close and enduring loyalties, and make for the preservation of traditional ways. In contrast, the social order of the association, as, for example, expressed in modern work situations, is based upon voluntary, partial relationships, entered into as a contract for some specific, instrumental purpose.

The community/association distinction has many parallels in sociology as part of the study of social change. These unit ideas, as Nisbet (1967) has called this kind of formulation, include Sir Henry Maine's (1931) distinction between status and contract societies, and more importantly, Durkheim's (1933) mechanical and organic solidarity. These correspond to Tönnies's ideas to the extent that mechanical solidarity, like community, is based upon resemblances, its 'conscience collective', where 'conscience' has a meaning corresponding to both conscience and consciousness in English, is highly religious, transcendentally superior to human interests and beyond discussion, attracting supreme value to the interests of society as a whole. Organic solidarity, like associational order, is based upon differences, and its secular 'conscience collective' attaches importance to equality of opportunity, the work ethic and social justice, and is open to discussion (Lukes, 1973).

Resemblances are also to be found in Max Weber's analysis of forms of authority (1948). Like Tönnies's community, Weber's traditional authority is based upon an almost unexamined acceptance of the status quo. The rationality that forms part of Tönnies's association is found in the idea of bureaucratic authority, in which power receives social approval or legitimacy on the basis of its acceptance on a rational basis. From many points of view Weber's ideal-type bureaucracy comes very close to Tönnies's association, based as it is upon the distribution of tasks as official duties, carried out by technically qualified, specialist staff, whose actions and decisions are governed by formally established rules and regulations, whose offices are linked in a hierarchy of authority, and who have an impersonal orientation to their clients.

Whereas the secondary headteachers' acceptance of the idea of the school as a community is well documented, the technical college principal's acceptance of the college as an association is not quite so easily established. This is partly because 'community tends to be a God word. In many circumstances, when it is mentioned, we are expected to abase ourselves before it, rather than define it' (Butterworth and Weir, 1970). The term association has none of this moral approbation, and consequently is in less general usage. Nevertheless, when college principals in interview use phrases such as, 'we are in business – the education business', or when a head of department says 'my job is to sell courses', the idea of the college that is being expressed is that of an association, even if the term is not actually being used. Beryl Tipton (1973), in a study of Jones Technical College, reports that former schoolteachers who came to teach there complained of the lack of 'community feeling'. The college as an association represents the organisational form in which the principles of voluntarism of attendance and consumerism of provision may be expressed. When students register they are entering into a contract to which they owe obligations, mainly in relation to fulfilling the requirements of the course, and from which they obtain certain rights in terms of access to college facilities. Pupils have no contract. They have obligations, which are expected to be expressed as loyalties, but few rights. Rights may be taken away from them, such as being able to dress as they choose, and later returned as privileges.

It has already been suggested that the ideology of the school as a community originated with the reforms of the public schools in the nineteenth century, and was accepted and institutionalised in the emerging system of maintained grammar schools following the 1902 Education Act, together with related ideas about the content, nature and purpose of education, and the traditional idea of the sixth form (chapter 2). The original purposes served by the ideology of the public school as a community were basically those of social control. The setting up of new schools as 'communities' in country areas was partly to isolate their delinquent pupils from the temptations of town life, and later in the century to prepare them for their destinies as army officers and civil servants, often in the remote parts of the Empire. 'The educational community [was made] a symbol for other communities which would later claim the individual's loyalty' (Wilkinson, 1963).

These and other related notions are part of the contemporary idea of the maintained secondary school as a community. Head-teachers expect both pupils and teachers to express loyalty to the school: 'Don't let the school down.' These loyalties may endure and be expressed in the membership of former pupils' associations. The concept of the pupil as a member of the community implies conformity and acceptance of the school's moral order and prevailing authority structure. Community implies consensus. The teacher's position as a member of the community is expressed in the diffuseness of his role, which in turn is related to the wide scope of interest he is expected to have in his pupils. This is integral to the idea of pastoral care, which is sometimes called community care.

The integration of pastoral care with the community ideology also links it with one of the principal ideologies of modern education: that of child-centredness or paedeocentricity, which is related to a contemporary concept of childhood which stresses the individuality and intrinsic worth of children. The care of children is accomplished within the school community.

Many school rituals are also felt to propagate and be justified by the ideology of community. Although headteachers held that the school assembly had both religious and administrative or communication purposes, these were considered less important to what were felt to be its community fostering purposes, expressed in phrases such as 'communal value', 'brings everyone together', 'development of corporate attitudes', 'pulls school

153

together', and most explicitly, 'develops a sense of community' (King, 1973a, 1973b).

Although headteachers sometimes attributed utilitarian purposes to the wearing of school uniform, 'suitable clothing for school', their recognition of its symbolic value was often quite explicit: 'The wearing of the school uniform demonstrates respect for the things the school stands for.' One of the things symbolised was the idea of the pupil as a member of the school community: 'Uniform promotes unity and community.' The wearing of uniform is considered to help in defining the child as a pupil: 'Distinguishes home from school.' It is not only an attempt to make latent the identity of the child within the family, but also the social and economic inequalities that exist between the families: 'Removes social differences.' The purpose of uniform as a way of preventing competition in dress is part of this, but is also sometimes an attempt to reduce commitment to the role of being a teenager. Many schools forbid the wearing of badges indicating allegiance to political organisations or sports activities, such as speedway or football (King, 1973a, 1973 b). Commitment to communities cannot be partial.

The importance of the idea of the school as a community is shown when its realisation is thought to be threatened. A familiar criticism of the large all-through comprehensive school is that the pupils will feel lost in a big, impersonal organisation. The response to the implied threat to the pupil's sense of community has been to create smaller organisational units as a basis of pastoral care. They are based either on a reformed house system, often stripped of its traditional intra-school competitions, or a year group system. These smaller communities have their own surrogate headteachers; heads of House or Year Group (King, 1973a).

The idea of community implies consensus and so it is precarious where there is conspicuous conflict in a school. In boys' secondary modern schools, where the prescription of the allegiance-forming uniform is lowest, and where the teachers' definition of conflict is shown in the widespread use of caning, headteachers were less likely to refer to the school as a community, but to substitute a custodial ideology drawing upon ideas emphasising containment and firm discipline with strong military connotations. In one such school pupils were actually marched from class to class (King, 1973a).

Another element in the English notion of the school is that it must be concerned not only with instruction but also with 'character development' (Baron, 1955). This analysis of the duality of the educational process has many parallels. Durkheim (1961) contrasted specialist education with moral education. Weber (1948), in his discussion of the education of the Chinese literatae, made the distinction between specialist or expert education and education for cultivation. More recently Basil Bernstein (1966, et al. 1966) has made the distinction between the instrumental and expressive cultures of the school, where the former refers to 'the acquisition of specific skills', and the latter to, 'conduct, character and manner'.

This dichotomous model of the nature of education not only exists in the analyses made by sociologists, but also in the general consciousness and in the thinking of teachers and headteachers. Clyde Kluckholn (1964) has perceptively pointed out that common speech makes a distinction between two connotations of the word 'good', either in the sense of being skilful and accomplished, or in being morally and socially amenable. Colin Lacey (1970) has shown how teachers use 'good' in connection with a pupil's work and behaviour. A similar distinction is made when headteachers refer to academic and social education (King, 1973a).

The expressive component of English education is based upon the concept of the school as a community. The behaviour and disposition expected of a pupil is justified in terms of his membership of the school community. Schools are transcendental organisations in that attempts are made to create for present purposes situations which are believed to have future consequences. Pupil behaviour is regulated so that the school can be run smoothly and this experience is supposed to be a preparation for later life. Thus lateness rules are not only an attempt to bring learning groups together efficiently but also to internalise the importance of punctuality (King, 1973a). This collapsing of means and ends is expressed in the phrase 'the school as a microcosm of society'.

Among secondary school headteachers there is a tendency to place greater value upon the expressive activities of the school rather than the instrumental. In the Schools Council Enquiry (Morton-Williams and Finch, 1968) they placed a higher importance on the objectives of character and moral development than did teachers, parents or pupils, but gave the lowest importance to examination achievement, getting a job and learning things of direct use in jobs. They tended to evaluate school work on an intrinsic basis, and as Bernstein (1966) has pointed out, the notion that learning has intrinsic worth is part of the expressive order of the school.

In contrast the technical college celebrates the idea of useful, practical knowledge; an extrinsic evaluation. This is illustrated in the distinction made in operation of the Industrial Training Act (1964) between training, the acquisition of vocational skills and knowledge, and education, the non-vocational 'liberal' content of a course. In the college the instrumental has pride of place over the expressive; its students are mainly young adults whose general socialisation is felt to be complete and whose favourable orientation is assumed from their voluntary attendance. 'It is adult in its outlook and its standards of discipline and behaviour are governed automatically by the requirements of its members. Students attend college to gain new knowledge to get the academic requirements of G.C.E. examinations boards or the intricate technical requirements of the institutes' (brochure, North College).

It was Weber's view that bureaucracy was the predominant form of organisation in modern society. The general acceptance of this among sociologists is indicated in Etzioni's (1964) suggestion that 'bureaucracy' and 'organisation' are virtually synonymous. However, in non-sociological circles the term bureaucracy has pejorative connotations expressed in phrases such as 'red tape' and 'the bureaucratic machine', so that although technically both schools and colleges have bureaucratic features it is rare to hear the term used by headteachers or principals. But when they talk of administration, office work or even doing the timetable, they are referring to bureaucratic processes. In the college these processes are accepted, even rejoiced in. There is often a pride in their efficiency. The image of the principal is that of the top administrator (Wheeler, 1966). Beryl Tipton (1972) found that involvement with administration was regarded by college lecturers as the main route to promotion. In contrast to the diffuseness of the teacher's role, that of the lecturer in the more explicitly bureaucratic college is relatively specific, in that each has a contract defining hours of work often with the possibility of overtime.

Although the phrase 'teachers as managers' has some recent currency, Bernbaum (1971) has reported the reluctance with which headteachers view their administrative chores, preferring to think of themselves as educators and leaders. Administration in schools is given importance when it is thought to be a solution to a problem, often that of size (Easthope, 1973), usually connected with what is called a communications problem. Whereas college principals refer to the multiplicity of their committees with some pride (Easton, 1969), those in schools are regarded as substitutes for the more desirable informal staff communications, thought only possible in small schools. Size is a problem for those who run schools because it is considered to make the community idea harder to realise and because it seems to demand more paper work and more meetings. Increasing size is an important goal of those who run colleges; as one principal in interview put it, 'The bigger the better.'

The more bureaucratic disposition of college staff is shown in Tipton's (1973) observations of their strong career orientation. However, among secondary school teachers Grace (1972) has shown that the most important source of conflict is that between pursuit of career, often involving a move, and loyalty to their present school.

In his treatments of the education of the Chinese literatae and the system of higher education in America, Weber (1948) used two salient images to represent educational ideals: those of 'cultivated man' and 'specialist man'. The gentlemanly ideal of the nineteenth century public schools is an excellent example of a cultivated man image (Wilkinson, 1963), which persists in some maintained schools today: 'The School Rule. Every boy must behave as a gentleman on all occasions' (from a boys' grammar school, King, 1973a). Cultivation as an outcome of education represents an emphasis on the expressive, and in English education is thought to be achieved through the experience of the school as a community. This observation also holds with reference to ideas about university education.

The image of the specialist man, implicit in the operation of the technical college, represents an emphasis on the instrumental over the expressive. This analysis is given some further coherence in that Weber considered that the education of specialist man would be associated with bureaucratic control. That of cultivated man would be associated with the exercise of traditional authority. Although the idea of ritual does not figure in Weber's treatment, it is often considered that it draws extensively upon tradition as a source of legitimacy (Bernstein, 1966).

The place of older pupils, particularly the sixth form, in the

157

idea of the school as a community illustrates its strong moral and expressive connotations. Older pupils, particularly when chosen as prefects, are expected to act as role-models or moral exemplars for younger pupils. Prefects are usually chosen on the basis of judgments of their commitment to expressive activities, including games and school clubs, rather than their instrumental performance in passing exams (King, 1969a, 1973a). The conspicuous age-stratification of schools, where sixth formers occupy the highest stratum among the pupils, expresses not only the structure of learning in accord with developmental ideologies (see King, 1973a), but also the distribution of moral worth. As a result of socialisation and/or selection the common moral order of the school is assumed to be held most strongly, and so older pupils may be trusted with some authority and rewarded with privileges. Pupils 'grow up' in school.

Although the sixth form unit and the sixth form college represent changes in the concept of the sixth form, they preserve much of the idea of the school as a community. Although the physical separation of the sixth form in Newstyle School made their use as role-models rather difficult, they were heavily involved with younger pupils in voluntary activities, and the sixth form unit itself was referred to by senior staff as 'a little community on its own' (see chapter 3). Sixth form colleges are also commonly referred to as communities: 'The value to the student of active cooperation in the life of the community cannot be too strongly emphasised' (prospectus, Richard Taunton College, Southampton, 1973; see also Carter, 1970). Table 10.1 summarises the principal ideas in this section.

Ideology and identity

The title of Baron's paper, 'The English Notion of the School', implies that the community ideology at the heart of his analysis is held consensually by the general population; that is a part of English culture, shared by all. This may be true, but it is unlikely that many people hold the ideology in any well-formulated or explicitly pronounced way. This is because the idea has become institutionalised, it receives the legitimacy of tradition, and so is largely unconsidered, regarded as being the natural order of things, something taken for granted. In a more limited way a similar analysis could be made with respect to

Table 10.1 *Ideologies of organisational form – secondary school and technical college*

	School	College
'Ideology'	Explicitly 'the school as a community'	Implicitly 'the college as an association'
Asserting groups	Headteachers, teachers	Principals, lecturers
Consonant identity	Headteacher as leader	Principal as entrepreneur
Public image	Widespread and reasonably clear	Diffuse and out-of-date
Assumed significant relationships	Enduring, affective, diffuse, wide scope of interest	Temporary, affectively neutral, contractual, partial, narrow scope of interest
Expected sentiments	Pride, feeling of belonging, loyalty, and duty	Sentiments private
Asserting groups	Stress on privileges	Stress on rights
	Strong control of pupil culture	Little control of student culture
Time orientation	Transcendental	Strongly present and future
		'New better than old'
Instrumental/expressive distinction	Expressive emphasis	Instrumental emphasis
	'Character development'	'Useful skills'
	Knowledge intrinsically valuable	Knowledge extrinsically valued
Organisational control	Administration and management tolerated or regretted. Bureaucracy an unfortunate necessity	Administration and management celebrated. Efficient bureaucracy admired
	Much ritual	Little ritual
	Increasing size a problem	Increasing size a goal
	Strong age-stratification	Little age-stratification
'Consonant ideologies'	Paedeocentricity-development	Voluntarism and consumerism
'Institutional reference'	Public school archetype, universities	Work organisations
'Theoretical linkages'		
Tönnies	Gemeinschaft	Gesellschaft
Weber	Traditional legitimacy	Rational legitimacy
	Cultivated man image	Specialist man image
Durkheim	Mechanical solidarity	Organic solidarity

the ideology of the technical college as an association, although the general population's experience of these colleges is not as widespread as for school. Beryl Tipton (1972) has suggested that the technical college has an indistinct public image, and this is supported by the findings of an enquiry commission by the National Advisory Council on Education for Industry and Commerce (1964) which showed persistent ignorance and misunderstanding among young people, parents, schools, industry and the general public. The 'night school' image remains.

However, for some groups these ideologies are more explicit, in a certain sense more real, because their acceptance creates some order and meaning in their lives, and helps them to realise their identities. These groups are mainly those which have power in schools and colleges; teachers and lecturers, but especially headteachers and principals. The identities of those who have power in educational organisations are bound up in the ideas they hold about the nature of the organisation and about the nature of education itself.

Baron (1955) has suggested that it is part of the English notion of the school that each school community should possess individuality and a measure of independence. This is used to legitimise the considerable autonomy of headteachers; power to achieve this end. The individuality and independence of the school is realised through the individuality and independence of the headteacher. The concept of the school as a community is bound up with that of the headteacher as its leader. This romantic notion has its origins with what Norwood called the 'autocrats of autocrats', the headmasters of the reformed Victorian public schools. This fusion of the idea of the school with the identity of its headteacher has been expressed as a case of 'L'école c'est moi' (King, 1973a). Headteachers are often judged by the success of their school; its failure is their failure.

Headteachers of maintained schools have the legal responsibility for the school's organisation and discipline, and as such possess bureaucratic authority (King, 1968). However, the headteacher's expression of his authority makes use of ritual which implies the receipt of traditional or moral legitimacy. In educational matters the headteacher 'knows best', and this knowing has a revelatory quality. The position of headteacher as a moral exemplar was often, in the early days of the maintained secondary schools, related to his being a clergyman. Even today it is common for

160

him to be involved in religious education, but its most powerful expression is in the school assembly.

Edmund Leach in his study of the Kachin reached the conclusion: 'ritual serves to express the individual's status as a social person in the structure system in which he finds himself for the time being'. In the school assembly the most high, the most conspicuously separated and the most active participant, holds the most powerful position in the school – the headteacher (King, 1973a). This symbolism is admitted by headteachers to the extent that they refer to the assembly as an opportunity for 'the pupils to get to know me'. The communication aspect of the school assembly is part of this. When a headteacher makes an announcement to the whole school the fact that he is making it to everyone is part of the message. Sometimes this secular business is carried out by the deputy head, so emphasising the sacredness of the headteacher's position.

There is a fusion between the religious, communal and authority presentation purposes of the school assembly. The school community is the body of worshippers, worship sanctifies the community, and the idea of the school as a community is legitimised by these connections. The authority of the headteacher is fused with the authority of religion. Disrespectful behaviour in assembly is an offence to both the school and to the faith, to the headteacher and to God.

The school assembly is not only a daily reminder to the pupils of authority relationships, but also an assurance to the headteacher that he retains his power. All authority has a tenuous quality. The school assembly is a test of the allegiance of the collectivity of the pupils. The school uniform is that of the individual pupil. Its observance becomes a quickly applied test of the acceptance of prevailing authority. Only those whose allegiance is reasonably assured may be exempt from this test; sixth formers may have the privilege of not wearing uniform.

The ideology of community is used to legitimise these ritual aspects of the school and the authority relationships they symbolise. Because of the strong normative element in the idea, the mixing, even confusion, of the what is with the what should be, and the sacred quality of the associated ritual, it is difficult to challenge it without provoking the associated strong emotions. The implication of consensus among the members of the school is used to obtain and justify the compliance of the pupils to the

161

authority of the teachers, and that of both to the authority of the headteacher.

The transcendental nature of the school as a community is also shown in the way that what is considered good for the pupil is also good for the school. Good behaviour enhances the school's reputation. When headteachers use phrases such as 'the school expects' they may pose in the reification the view of the school as a superordinate impersonal entity, a resemblance to Durkheim's mechanical solidarity. However, they also express an idea of the school which constrains the weak and supports the powerful.

The idea of the association does not have the emotional content of that of community, its moral approbation or diffuseness. Associations are more affectively neutral, and may be judged by the extent to which they fulfil the contracts entered into. The principal of the technical college does not seek moral approval. Whereas the moral order of the school collapses time by implying continuity from the past into the present and the future – eternal values, the time orientation of the college is strongly to the present and future – new is better than old. The principal's and head of department's identity as administrators is confirmed in the overt acceptance of bureaucratic paperwork, committees, administration and planning (see Charlton et al., 1971; Bratchell, 1968). Their related identities as entrepreneurs are confirmed in these ways and in their encounters with clients, representatives of local industry and potential students. Their authority rests with their ability to deliver the goods. To the extent that they are businessmen, the college is business-like.

The social control of mature voluntary students is not seen as a problem. The partial relationship between student and lecturer has little expressive content. Outside the instructional context the students can behave much as they like. Beryl Tipton (1973) has described how many college lecturers put emphasis on their technical expertise rather than on being a teacher. This identity is maintained in learning situations where the actual physical arrangements replicate industrial situations, as in model offices, kitchens and workshops.

The day-to-day experience of school or college serves to confirm the identities of those who control them. Both experience and identity are given meaning by the ideology that unites them. This fusion of identity and ideology is not only confirmed in present experience but also in the past. The ideology of the college as an association enables those staff recruited from industry to integrate their different careers by stressing the resemblances between the college and work organisations. As the more successful pupils of schools encapsulating the community idea, teachers and headteachers attended either colleges of education, which William Taylor has shown to be organised around the same idea, or universities idealised as communities of scholars.

> ... the pattern of community life envisaged has a close affinity with that which has long obtained in Houses in Independent Schools and in Colleges within Universities where pastoral care for the individual is paramount and education has a distinctly personal flavour ('The Sixth Form of the Future', Headmasters' Association, 1968, p. 76).

Thus both groups can place their own institution and their own identities in relation to other institutions with similar ideologies. It is the legitimacy of the members of these institutions that is sought, partly on the basis of ideological resemblance.

The idea of educational organisations as communities is very strong in England. For those who hold it, it is thought to be natural and the best; the technical college model receives less approbation – a second class model for a second chance institution. However, the community ideology has not always existed in this country and is not necessarily accepted in other countries. In the USA the idea of the school as belonging to the community is expressed in the nostalgic image of what Margaret Mead (1951) calls 'the little red school house'.

Ideologies and interest groups

Each form of post-sixteen education has an associated ideology which is used to justify and defend it. These ideologies are held and propagated by individuals and, more particularly, groups associated with the different organisational forms.

The secondary school with integral sixth form represents the traditional form of organisation, and until recently was unchallenged. The ideology of the school as a community for the whole secondary age range was institutionalised. However, when the legitimacy of an institution is questioned its ideology is made explicit, it becomes what Vaughan and Archer (1971) call a defensive ideology. The defensive ideology of the all-through school is asserted by individual headteachers of such schools, for example Murphy (1972), but mainly by various teachers' associations. These include the Assistant Masters' Association (1974) the Headmasters' Association (1968, 1969), the National Association of Headteachers (1973) and the National Union of Teachers. 'The union is among the strong supporters of the 11–19 secondary school' (NUT, 1969).

Why do these particular groups defend the status quo? 'Why?' questions are always difficult to answer, and any attempt to do so involves some sort of theory. Two related theoretical lines are followed here, both derived from Weber (1948). In his conflict model of society he posed a situation in which there was a continuous struggle between groups in maintaining and defending their interests. He proposed a threefold typology of groups: classes, which exist in the economic order; status groups, which exist within the social order and are concerned with social honour and a shared way of life; and parties, which 'live in the house of power'. Educational associations have some of the characteristics of all three types, in that their members share a similar position in the economic order in terms of remuneration and conditions of work, in that they may share views about their place in society, and may seek power to implement their ideas. For Weber sociology was concerned with the understanding of social action, where action refers to 'all human behaviour when and in so far as the acting individual attaches subjective meaning to it'. Thus the question why any group seeks to defend or change the existing order is answered by understanding the meanings the group assigns to actions which relate its members' interests.

It has already been suggested that ideologies are bound up in the identities of those that hold them. In asserting the ideology of the all-through school these groups are defending the ideas they have about themselves. In the justification of their actions, educational interest groups characteristically claim that they not only serve group interests but also those of children. 'Its guiding principle is, and will continue to be, what is in the best interests of the educational service, the children and the teaching profession' (NUT, 1972). This drawing upon the prevailing paedeocentricity of the educational process implies legitimacy for the other interests that are served, and also prevents competing groups for imputing one another's motives. What is required is what Berger (1961) calls an unmasking process to reveal covert intentions. This

kind of analysis is clearly open to the charge of cynicism. However, it does not deny that groups or individuals may pursue
causes for idealistic or altruistic motives. For some the acceptance
of their ideas is the main interest served, but it is rare to find
that it is the only interest. (The reader might legitimately ask
what interests of the author are served in the writing of this
book? In a simple exercise in what Gouldner (1971) calls reflexive
sociology it may be said to confirm my identity as a university
teacher, which is bound up in the ideology of the university as
concerned with the disinterested pursuit of knowledge. (University
teachers have an interest in being disinterested.) Additional
interests are some modest royalties and the possibility of enhanced
career chances, although previous experience does not confirm
this.)

It is of some significance that the groups supporting the idea
of the all-through school tend to have a male membership and
to represent headteachers. Although the NUT has more women
members than men, several studies including those of Roy (1968)
and Manzer (1970) have shown the latter to be the more active
members, and that headteachers are over-represented on its
committees. The propagation of the all-through school not only
confirms the identities of the headteachers of such schools but
also seems to present the best opportunities for high status,
remuneration and power. The career patterns of headteachers
consist of moves to larger rather than smaller schools; they are
'promoted' to larger schools. Headteachers' salaries are regulated
by the size of the school and the proportion of older pupils.
Leaving aside the considerations of power and status, it is not
suggested that the motives of headteachers are purely mercenary,
but they must be aware of the relationships between school size
and remuneration, and it is not unknown for their associations to
bargain for higher salaries. To some extent this implicit acceptance
of the large school is at variance with the concern about the
difficulties of establishing the community idea in such schools,
but this may be mitigated by the headteachers celebrating the
larger range of opportunities and provision which may be offered
(King, 1973a).

For some headteachers the promotion of the traditional idea
of the school may also confirm their links with its high status
public school archetype. The Headmasters' Conference, the
principal boys' public school protective association, has a few
maintained school headteachers among its invited members. The

HMC and HMA have acted jointly in matters of mutual concern (1970).

A survey by Hilsum and Start (1974) has confirmed the conventional wisdom that men teachers are more ambitious than women. The all-through school is thought to provide wider opportunities for high scale posts.

In advocating the all-through school the NUT not only serves what appear to be the interests of its members in terms of career opportunities, but also the continued existence of the union itself. Bucher and Strauss (1961) have suggested that major professional associations present a 'spurious unity' to the public, which conceals a loose amalgamation of 'segments'. The NUT draws its members from men and women with different qualifications and from different kinds of school, representing a variety of different, even conflicting, interests. The history of the union has been marked by attempts to prevent factionalism and maintain an internal coalition. The NUT response has been to pursue policies which will not lead to the breakaway of factions, such as gave rise to the National Association of Schoolmasters (Tropp, 1957; Manzer, 1970); hence their fear of a 'split profession' should the all-through school be replaced by some form of separate post-sixteen provision (NUT, 1966).

It is interesting to note that the exclusively women teachers' associations do not give unqualified support to the all-through school. The recently founded Union of Women Teachers has no formulated policy about the form of post-sixteen education (private correspondence from the General Secretary, 1974). The Association of Assistant Mistresses is not favourably disposed to the use of technical colleges for 16–19 year olds, but feels the sixth form college is 'right in some areas' (private correspondence with the Secretary, 1974). The all-male NAS takes a similar view although having a more favourable disposition towards the further education college (private communication with Assistant Secretary, 1974). This pragmatic view may reflect the more modest career ambitions of NAS members, who unlike the AMA members, are probably more likely to be non-graduates.

The ideology of the sixth form college is a variant of that of the school as a community: the sixth form as a separate community. 'Our many extra-curricular activities also help to draw us all closer together as a community. Certainly no one can say that Luton Sixth Form College is a soulless A level factory' (Carter, 1970). No professional association has given total or unqualified support to this form of post-sixteen education. Most of the justifications of their use have been made by local education authority officers (see David, 1972). In most cases these have been made public after the colleges have been introduced or when the plan for their introduction has been accepted. To this extent their accounts of the schemes represent what Hopper (1968) calls ideologies of legitimisation, which seek wider social approval for actions already taken. Their theme is not 'what we should do' but 'why we did it'. The interests that are served are those of the smooth and successful implementation of their plans and a confirmation of their identities as planners.

Until recently the ideology of the technical college as an association existed in a different social domain to that of the school. Colleges were second chance institutions concerned with 'training' rather than 'education'. However, when colleges and schools began to compete for the same scarce resources – young people between sixteen and nineteen – the interest groups were in conflict and their ideologies were unfurled.

The case for the full-time education of young people in colleges of further education has been made by a number of associations representing groups within technical education. These include the Association of Principals of Technical Institutions (1969), the Association of Teachers in Technical Institutions (1969, 1972), and the Association for Colleges of Further and Higher Education (formerly the Association of Technical Institutions, 1969). Individual ideologues include principals of colleges, such as D. E. Mumford (1970), who are sometimes officers of these associations.

These groups and individuals assert the right of young people to choose to attend colleges as an alternative to school, and in some cases they wish to see a unified system of education for the 16–19 age range, in which colleges would play an important part. The recent expansion of the numbers of such students is seen by these groups to confirm the ideology of the college and the value of the principles of voluntarism and consumerism expressed in it, and also to confirm their associated identities. Granted the existence of a genuine desire to help young people and to further their education and careers, what group interests are served by the pursuit of policies to maintain or increase this aspect of college work?

The recent history of the technical education system has been marked by two related trends: greater standardisation of pro-

167

cesses and greater centralisation of control. 'Nothing in FE is ever uniform' (Bristow, 1970). This diversity is celebrated in further education circles, where it is taken to indicate the adaptive flexibility of the colleges to local demands; an adaptability made possible though the considerable autonomy expressed through the principal as entrepreneur. Concerns about increasing educational costs, about the plethora and diversity of courses, and some doubts about the system's ability to deliver the educational goods, have been expressed in a series of central government actions all of which have reduced this autonomy and clipped the entrepreneurial wings.

The most important of these actions has been the implementation of the Industrial Training Act (see chapter 7). The Act recommended that the activities of the various Training Boards should relate to the existing provision of further education, but the Engineering Board set up an entirely new part-time course, devised by the City and Guilds of London Institute and the Regional Examining Unions. Furthermore, some of the boards, including that of the construction industry, have set up their own institutions, separate from those of further education, in which to conduct their courses (ITA 'Year Book', 1969). In some cases the distinction between 'education' and 'training' has been forced open with the colleges providing only the former and industry providing the latter through firms. Although, in interview, college principals and heads of department often welcomed the ITA as an expression of the central government's concern about technical education, they sometimes expressed fears of recessions and of the reduction in their old autonomy. They found their entrepreneurial activities in setting up courses were curtailed, and that their colleges were now inspected by the boards' training officers for their suitability.

Three other actions may also be seen as a reduction of this autonomy by means of centralisation of control and standardisation of process. The Pilkington report (1966) made recommendations about minimum class sizes in noting that both the plant and staff of the colleges could be used more efficiently. The Haslegrave report (1969) made suggestions to regularise courses for technicians and workers in business on the grounds of effectiveness and economic efficiency, which have led to the setting up of the central Technicians Education Council and the Business Education Council, with powers to plan and administer examinations and courses of a national character, so replacing those generated by individual colleges. Finally, the Hunt report (1970) recommended that the college year be expanded from its present largely academic dimensions to the forty-eight working week year of industry.

In these circumstances the opportunity to receive a regular, perhaps guaranteed supply of students for O and A level courses becomes doubly desirable in helping with planning and staff stability and in giving a measure of independence from the ITBs. In addition the content and nature of these courses do not have to be negotiated through the increasing number of central committees since they are laid down by the university examining boards.

Although the adaptive flexibility of the college is a matter of pride it is also a source of anxiety. This is shown in the great numbers mystery found in colleges. In a school it is acceptable to ask how many pupils there are on the roll, and the answer is usually prompt and accurate. But in colleges student numbers are known to only a few, often just the heads of department. In some colleges the principals are unable or unwilling to give a total. This mystery is partly due to the changing population of the college, where even full-time courses may last only a few months and part-time students may be on day-release or block-release. However, student numbers have a currency in the struggle for resources within the college and with the Regional Advisory Council and other bodies outside. They are used to justify claims for departmental finance, extra staff and promotions, to legitimise the existence of courses and to argue for new ones. Student numbers are an index of consumer satisfaction, and therefore an index of success.

A further benefit of the erstwhile sixth form type of student is that they are full-time students. Whilst part-time students are welcomed as a contribution to the numbers war, several studies, including that of Ethel Venables (1967), show that they are associated with problems for the staff. Hancock and Wakeford (1965) have contrasted the quick integration of the full-time student into the life of the college with that of the part-timer: '... more identified with his home and job. For him College life is marginal.' As one head of department put it: 'They are a different race to the full-timers.'

In the debate about the form of post-sixteen education the confrontation has been mainly between the ideologies of the all-through school and the colleges of further education. In their oblique criticisms of the colleges, the assertive new inheritors, the school ideologues indicate their view that the college is not a community, and therefore, in their opinion, not a valid educational organisation. The headteacher of a comprehensive school has written that it is a mistake to put young people in a college, 'where they need only attend lectures'. 'Education needs to concentrate principally with the problem of living together in a community as well as the liquidation of ignorance' (Hill, 1972). Some principals of colleges have responded to this sort of criticism by protesting that their colleges do have activities beyond the liquidation of ignorance (Moore, 1972, p. 1):

> In spite of rumours to the contrary there is a real concern in the colleges for all aspects of student welfare which schools refer to as pastoral care. Apart from student union sports clubs and associations there are often specialist student welfare officers to support the work of course tutors and other staff.

This represents an interesting modification of the traditional associational ideology, but it is made compatible by posing that activities and pastoral care are provided as a result of student demand.

The expansion of A level studies has led to a stronger orientation towards higher education as a source of legitimacy (Moore, 1972, p. 1):

> Obviously Further Education colleges will have to promote their more recent role among the universities and polytechnics, but one hopes that those responsible for admissions will not automatically assume that the products of the Further Education 'stable' are later starters or non-runners.

Interest groups differ in their power to implement their ideas. The power to decide the form of post-sixteen education rests mainly at the level of the local education authorities and at the Department of Education and Science. The former have the duty to provide such education, and the latter the power to approve or disapprove any changes in the form of that provision. It is in the nature of the powerful to resist research. Cabinet papers are kept from the public for thirty years. Only intimations of the inside workings of the DES are available, as in the published interviews with two former Secretaries of State, Anthony Crosland and Edward Boyle (1971). Kogan and Van der Eyken (1973), as a result of interviews with three recently retired chief education officers, concluded: 'Chief education officers are powerful men. The quality of the service is in their hands.' This conclusion is confirmed by Rene Saran (1973) who in her studies of secondary school reorganisation broadly agreed with the view expressed by David Donnison (et al., 1965) that 'providers of a service will usually initiate change and must always carry it through'. This is clearly most true of Miriam David's (1973) 'educator' type of chief education officer who may have both the ideas and the authority to implement them. As the studies of reorganisation in Croydon, Exeter and Barnstaple have shown (chapter 9), they present their ideas, often as memoranda to the appropriate committees for approval, but may choose to present them more widely after the effective decision has been taken. This rather draconian analysis can be modified by admitting that these powerful officers do not always receive the approval of their education committees, as the failure to introduce sixth form colleges in Croydon shows (Urwin, 1965).

Teachers' and lecturers' unions and associations, individual headteachers and principals, do not have the power to change fundamentally the form of their organisations. Kogan and Van der Eyken have written, 'the main axis of authority in education lies between the chief education officer of an LEA and the heads of schools and colleges', but although these heads have considerable autonomy in relation to the internal activities of their organisation, they cannot change its basic definition in terms of age range, sex composition or its governing regulations.

These groups and individuals can only seek to bring pressure in the furthering of their interests. Coates (1972) has described the ways in which teachers' unions may do this, including informal, regular access to the officials of the DES, formal deputations and memoranda, through membership of central ad hoc committees and the Schools Council, by giving evidence to Central Advisory Committees, and through their sponsored Members of Parliament. Most of the documents referred to in this book were generated at this central, national level. These techniques may have been used in relation to the form of post-sixteen education, but the available evidence suggests that most pressure is applied at the local level. This follows Eckstein's (1960) proposition that the structure of pressure groups is similar to that

171

of the organisations they seek to influence. Thus in Croydon, Exeter and North Devon, memoranda, letters to the press, delegations, petitions and rallies were all used at a local level, as well as representations through membership of education committees and working parties. Some of these can be documented, but there is no record of telephone calls and talks on the golf course or over drinks in the club.

The mixed and changing forms of post-sixteen education indicate that the struggle between the interest groups is not resolved. A hint that the DES could take on a more decisive part than that set out in circulars 10/65 and 4/74 is given in two publications by the Labour Party (1973a, 1973b), both proposing a single sector of comprehensive education for 16–18 year olds. There is in British education a power above that of headteachers, principals and chief education officers, and unlike theirs it has a more conspicuously democratic basis.

Chapter 11

Organisation and experience

The interest groups in the field of post-sixteen education consider that its different organisational forms give rise to different experiences for students – that, for example, they will or will not feel cared for or constrained. This assumption of a connection between organisation and experience is put to the empirical test. Both the assumption and the results of testing it may be explained by attempting to understand the meanings assigned by those in the situation to their own and others' actions.

The organisational structures of school and college

This discussion concentrates on the organisation of student learning and behaviour and therefore does not deal with what is usually called administration or with teacher-teacher relationships. Organisational structures may be studied by answering questions framed around those useful Anglo-Saxon interrogative adverbs. Who is educated, when, how, where, in what way and by whom? Although these structures may be studied using some of the most objective methods available, they must be regarded as the social creations of the investigator, and they may not necessarily coincide with the ideas of those who run the schools and colleges concerned. The organisation of the school or college is an expression of their ideology. One reason for the discrepancies is that ideologies are a blend of what is thought to be and what ought to be, so that a certain degree of difference between an

idea and its expression in action is acceptable. Ideologies legitimise intentions as well as realisations. Furthermore the structure
of a school or college may be experienced through an ideology.
A headmaster's experience of the school as a community is
monitored through the ideology of the school as a community.
Ideologies are spectacles worn to view the social world, although
they are not all rose-tinted.

Teachers in schools and colleges of further education are
strongly contrasted in terms of their social characteristics. School
teachers, especially those of sixth formers, are more socially
homogeneous, for, although of different sexes, they are mostly
full-time and all received higher education either in a college
of education or, more commonly, in a university. In contrast
(Tipton, 1973, p. ix):

> The college's staff is almost a microcosm of the country's
> social divisions featuring, as it does, all the following:
> graduates and non-graduates, industrially experienced and
> non-experienced, craftsmen, white collar workers, managers,
> scientists, social scientists and artists, men and women, and
> the relatively young through to the relatively old.

To this may be added the large proportion of part-time college
staff, which Cantor and Roberts (1972) estimate provides nearly
one-third of the teaching. These differences strongly reflect both
the adaptive flexibility of the colleges and what Tipton (1973)
calls their 'multi-purpose educational function'.

The structure of relationships between teacher and taught are
also strongly contrasted. From the descriptions already made
(chapter 7) it is clear that colleges tend to use tighter forms of
control over the formal learning process. Some of this standardisation, such as the prescription of class contact hours and the precise
amount of homework, arises from conditions imposed by internal
examining bodies such as the City and Guilds, but a similar
organisation is used in relation to O and A level courses where
no such external imperative exists.

In contrast, schools are associated with the use of more control
over pupil behaviour, the expressive over the instrumental, as is
shown in Table 11.1, and including the rituals of school assembly
and uniform. Colleges do have rituals but they are not those of
membership but celebrations of success, prize-givings and sometimes formal departmental dinners. Termly departmental or even

college assemblies do occur, but they are administrative and devoid of obvious symbols. The strength of feeling in colleges against this kind of school-associated activity is shown in the reply of a vice-principal to a question about whether the college had an open day: 'Over my dead body. This isn't a school!' However, Pro-Tertiary College did have an open day as part of its recruitment campaign.

In contrast to the teacher in the school, it is claimed that 'teachers [in further education] have no sanctions in the form of punishments, with which to enforce their authority' (Russell, 1972). However, there is the sanction of expulsion, which is rarely used, and almost always reported to be for chronic failure to meet course requirements. The only actions of students which provoke anything like indignation are using the staff car park (parking is the colleges' emotional equivalent of the uniform in schools, according to several informants), and the suspicion of drug possession or taking, the one thing that involved immediate reference to the principal in all the colleges.

Observations of student-lecturer relationships in the colleges showed considerable departmental differences. In general studies departments, especially in A level courses, these were very similar to those observed in sixth forms, although the modes of address used by lecturers included titles, Mr and Miss, as well as first names. Lecturers (often referred to as teachers by students) were usually called by their title and surname, although an occasional 'sir' was used, to the disapproval of some lecturers. In vocational departments the relationships were strongly convergent with those found in the related industry. A fair amount of apprentice-type horse play was tolerated, and the modes of address included 'lads' and 'chief'. The teacher-taught relationship was often in a role-play situation, in which the former may act as head waiter to the latter's waiter in the college restaurant, one of a number of work simulations.

These broad differences in the control of student activities reveal the different emphases upon the instrumental and the expressive in schools and colleges. Although the lower emphasis on the expressive is shown in the colleges' looser control of general behaviour, models of appropriate behaviour are strongly transmitted on vocational courses. Student secretaries are not only expected to master the skills of shorthand and typing but also to learn how to behave as a secretary. This not only involves appropriate presentation in terms of dress (a subject of much staff-

Table 11.1 *Control of student behaviour in schools and colleges*

	Schools and sixth form colleges						Further education colleges					
	T	N	C	Co	O	S	P	N	E	S	W	Co
Smoking prohibited		x				x						
Limited to certain places	x		x	x	x		x	x	x	x	x	x
Limited to certain times	x		x							x		x
Permission needed to go out lunch time	x		x									
Permission needed other times	x		x	x		x		x				
Permission required to use motor vehicle	x	x	x	x	x	x				x		
Uniform compulsory			x									
Jeans prohibited	x		x	x		x	D	D	D	D		
Boys must wear jackets	x		x			x		D				
Boys must wear ties	x		x	x		x		x				
Control of boys' hair style or length	x	x	x		x	x	D	D	D	D	D	D
Style or colour restrictions on girls' clothes	x		x	x				D	D			
Trousers prohibited for girls	x		x	x				D	D			
Makeup prohibited or controlled			x	x								
Restrictions on jewellery			x	x		x						
Daily compulsory assembly	x		x	x	x							
Compulsory assembly each term							x	x	D	x	x	x
Compulsory attendance of prize-givings			x	x	x	x						
Voluntary attendance of prize-givings						x	D	D	D		D	D
Games compulsory			x	x	x			D	x			
Parents' evenings	x		x	x	x	x	D	x	x		x	x
Reports sent to parents	x	x	x	x	x	x	x	x	x		x	x

Legend: x = incidence of feature; D = incidence in some departments
Schools: T = St Trad's; N = Newstyle; C = Central; Co = Cooperative;
O = Open; S = Selective
Colleges: P = Pro-Tertiary; N = North; E = East; S = South; W = West;
Co = Cooperative

student conflict) but also in subtleties of demeanour: 'You won't make your boss feel very happy on a Monday morning with a face like that.' In some departments, especially catering, these expressive prescriptions were readily accepted by students, but they were sometimes resisted and students wished to behave as 'students' and not in their putative work-roles, a source of concern among some of their lecturers. The general contrast between the school and the college is of that between a unitary expressive order or a single model of behaviour and a multiplicity of expressive orders or models of behaviour.

Table 11.2 *Students' facilities in schools and colleges*

	Schools and sixth form colleges						Further education colleges					
	T	N	C	Co	O	S	N	E	S	W	P	Co
Number of hours refectory open each day	1	1	1	1	1	1	6.5	5.5	8.5	6	5	2
Meals need not be ordered							x	x	x	x	x	x
Snacks available in refectory							x	x	x	x	x	x
Coffee bar				x			x					
Food vending machines	x		x		x		x	x			x	x
Student shops		x						x	x	x		x
Telephone							x					
Unlimited record playing in common room(s)		x	x		x		x	x	x	x	x	x
Eating allowed in common room(s)		x	x	x	x	x		x		x	x	x
Parking available	x		x	x	x	x				x		
Cigarettes sold on premises							x	x				

Legend: As Table 11.1.

The provision of facilities is also an aspect of student control (Table 11.2). The rules in relation to smoking and playing records represent a tighter control of student culture in school, as part of the stronger expressive emphasis.

The structure of pastoral care (tutorial care in colleges) was based upon the tutorial system in all twelve institutions. In the colleges the tutor always taught all the members of the group and apart from short daily meetings the group also met for a longer period each week. This happened in four schools, but in two the course tutor did not teach all the group members. One school and one college had a counsellor, but the colleges had longer lists of institutional advisers including welfare and careers officers. This stronger formal provision of care in colleges represents the bureaucratic tendency to distribute named offices and to specify duties. The conspicuous display of advisory facilities in colleges is part of the idea of supplying what the students regard as their needs. In schools the provision of help is based more upon a presumption of the 'needs' of sixth formers by those supplying it.

The students' experience of school and college

One of the purposes in organising schools and colleges in particular ways is to bring about particular kinds of experience for the pupils or students. The surveys of sixth formers and college students may be used to compare the experience of different kinds of organisational structures. In making this analysis, and some of those in previous chapters, the basic units used were the responses to questions made by all the students in each of the twelve institutions. There are a number of reasons for doing this. Although each individual has a unique experience of education, this experience becomes social on the basis of the extent to which it is shared with others. Individual schools and colleges represent the situation in which the experiences occur and the social units in which their meanings may be shared. The extent to which a meaning is shared is indicated in the percentage response to a particular question. In this comparison of schools and colleges it would not be acceptable simply to compare the responses of all the students in colleges with all the students in schools. These aggregates do not represent the social units to which the responses refer – a particular college or school – and may also give rise to false conclusions because of an aggregative fallacy (see Robinson, 1950; Swift, 1970; King and Easthope, 1973).

This is illustrated in Table 11.3. This shows that a larger proportion of school students agreed there are unnecessary restrictions in school than did college students with respect to college. The difference between the percentages, 45.7 per cent and 31.6 per cent respectively, is statistically significant at the

Table 11.3 *The aggregative fallacy – students' agreement
to there being unnecessary restrictions* (%)

Technical colleges

North (n = 539)	East (n = 205)	South (n = 164)	West (n = 126)	Cooperative (n = 120)	Pro-Tertiary (n = 617)	All (n = 1,771)
31.9	35.6	29.3	57.1	36.7	24.4	31.6

Schools and sixth form colleges

St Trad's (n = 179)	Newstyle (n = 122)	Central (n = 41)	Cooperative (n = 94)	Open (n = 171)	Selective (n = 313)	All (n = 920)
71.5	27.0	29.3	54.3	13.5	55.3	45.7

0.1 per cent level. It might be concluded that schools are evaluated as being more restrictive than technical colleges, but this would be fallacious. When the percentages for individual schools and colleges are inspected (Table 11.3), a considerable overlap is seen between the types of organisation, Open sixth form college having the lowest value and West technical college having the second highest. The total number of sixth formers (920) and total number of college students (1,771) are false aggregates in that they do not represent the social units in which the question was posed and to which the answers referred. This kind of analysis ignores the possibility of variation between organisations of the same type, a possibility posed by those who run the schools or colleges when they express their belief in the individuality of their institutions.

When a survey is carried out on a sample of students from different institutions their responses to questions do not necessarily indicate anything about the particular institution they attend. For example, in the survey carried out by Sharp (1970), 38 per cent of sixth formers reported that life in school had been very happy for them, compared with 45 per cent of students in colleges referring to college life. These results may be interpreted as showing that college students are happier than sixth formers, but they may not be interpreted as showing that schools and colleges are organised in such a way as to contribute to this difference. This could only be concluded if the percentage responses of the sixth formers from each of the 154 schools surveyed were all lower than the percentage responses of students from each of the 131 colleges. To reach conclusions about organisations it is necessary to build organisational aggregrates into the analysis.

For these reasons the comparison of the students' experience of school and college are only held to indicate a difference attributable to the organisation of these two contrasted forms when the percentage response to a question is higher or lower in each college compared with each school. (In a few cases an overlap of one is reported.) This permits the more concise reporting of data for all school sixth formers and all college students without committing an aggregative fallacy in their interpretation.

Table 11.4 therefore shows differences in the students' experience that may be cautiously associated with their attending different types of organisation. The experience of colleges is marked by the greater dissatisfaction in relation to the control of work – where most organisational emphasis is placed.

Table 11.4   *Students' experience of school and college* (%)

	Schools and sixth form colleges (n = 920)	Further education colleges (n = 1,771)
(a) Agree know some staff well	60.2	43.6
(b) Agree a real sense of belonging	30.5	21.9
(c) Agree too little private study	18.4	57.3
(d) Disagree you have to look after yourself	18.7	8.8
(e) Disagree decide how much work you do	11.7	22.8
(f) Disagree a good preparation for going to work	41.1	24.6
(g) Most friends in school or college	76.9	65.4
(h) Some friends of opposite sex in school or college	93.2	81.6
(i) Some friends made before entering sixth or college	90.4	73.5

All differences significant at the 0.1 per cent level by chi square.

In each college proportionally more students wanted more private study and felt less control over their own studies than did sixth formers in each of the schools and sixth form colleges. However, not surprisingly, the colleges were all the more highly valued as a good preparation for work than the schools were.

In many ways the absence of consistent differences between schools and colleges is just as important and interesting. There is no tendency for the school or college to be associated with the experience of a strong emphasis on exams, non-examination subjects as a waste of time, of the staff only being interested in those who do well, or being a good preparation for future education. The variation in the levels of student response in these and other questions partly supports the expectation that the organisation of different schools and colleges gives rise to different levels of student satisfaction.

The particular satisfactions of schools are those concerned with pastoral care and what can be called community feelings, which mirror the intentions of the organisation of schools. In each school, sixth formers showed higher levels of disagreement with the proposition that they had to look after themselves than students in each college did. With one exception sixth formers showed higher levels of agreement about knowing staff well and

181

feeling a real sense of belonging. (In retrospect the inclusion of 'real' in the question 'There is a real sense of belonging' was a mistake, although the phrase was actually used by a student in interview. Its exclusion would probably have raised the levels of agreement above a minority percentage in the schools.) The one exception was Cooperative School which had the lowest levels of agreement to these two propositions for special reasons suggested in chapter 8. Clearly, strong community feelings are not inevitable in school.

It should be noted that there were no consistent differences between schools and colleges in the levels of satisfaction with respect to staff interest in their welfare, to there being unnecessary restrictions or in being treated as an adult. The claims that either school or college has a monopoly of student satisfaction in these respects are not substantiated. The highest levels of satisfaction in terms of the absence of unnecessary restrictions and of being treated as adults were actually found in Open Sixth Form College.

There were different patterns of friendship in the schools and colleges (Table 11.4). Sixth formers in each school-based institution reported a larger proportion of friends in the institution, more friends made before entering the sixth form or sixth form college, and more friends of the opposite sex, than students in each college did. All of these results could be seen as aspects of the school as a community.

The difference in the rate of friendships between the sexes may reflect different patterns of sex-specialisation. In both schools and colleges this is found in the provision of toilets and other facilities. In schools sex differences may be symbolised in the ceremonials of assembly when boys and girls stand separately, even when they are prefects (King, 1973a). Whereas in schools the formal differences between the sexes with respect to the organisation of learning are not strong at sixth form level (although girls do choose to do Arts A levels more often than boys, King, 1973a), in colleges courses do have stronger sex connotations, especially secretarial, pre-nursing, hairdressing, engineering and construction. Indeed one college had only just dropped the generic title of Women's Subjects for hairdressing, cookery and child care, a concession to sexist sensitivities. People tend to make friends with those they meet most frequently (see King and Easthope, 1973). The fewer friendships between the sexes in the colleges may be explained by the fewer opportunities they have to meet.

Although the pattern of friendships was different for schools and colleges the experience of friendliness did not vary consistently. There were no differences in their desire to keep their social lives separate or in their experience of the ease of making friends.

These results show that to a limited extent the experiences of schools and colleges are those expected by school and college ideologues. However, what could be called community sentiments are not an exclusively school experience, and what could be called consumer satisfactions, not an exclusively college experience.

Sex differences and the students' experience of school and college

In chapter 7 it was shown that there were differences in boys' and girls' experience of technical colleges. In all six colleges the girls felt less often than the boys that they knew the staff well, that they were treated as adults and there was a sense of community, but felt more often they had to look after themselves. It could be said that girls found colleges less of a community than did boys.

Table 11.5 compares the experiences of boys and girls in sixth forms and sixth form colleges. It could be said that girls find school more a community than do boys, in that in every institution they felt more often that the staff were interested in their personal welfare, and less often that there were unnecessary restrictions. They also had less reservations about non-examination subjects. However, like girls in college, they found school a better preparation for work than did boys.

Table 11.6 compares the experience of girls in sixth forms and sixth form colleges with those in technical colleges. In every one of the school-based organisations there was a more common experience of staff being interested in their personal welfare, and in all six colleges there was a more common experience of having to look after yourself. There were no consistent or significant differences in boys' experience of schools and colleges.

From these comparisons it may be tentatively concluded that, overall, girls have a more satisfactory experience of schools than do boys, but a less satisfactory experience of technical colleges. Whilst there are no overall differences in the satisfactions of boys in schools compared with those in colleges, girls have a more satisfactory experience of schools than colleges.

Table 11.5 *Sex differences and students' experience of schools and sixth form colleges* (%)

	Girls (n = 441)	Boys (n = 479)	Significance (%) (chi square)
Agree staff interested in welfare	59.4	51.6	1
Agree unnecessary restrictions	35.4	54.9	0.1
Agree good preparation for future work	37.6	24.8	0.1
Agree non-exam subjects take up valuable time	33.5	43.8	0.1

Table 11.6 *Girls' experience of schools and sixth form colleges compared with that of colleges of further education* (%)

	Schools and sixth form colleges (n = 441)	Further education colleges (n = 981)	Significance (%) (chi square)
Agree staff interested in welfare	59.4	46.8	0.1
Agree you look after yourself	66.2	80.4	0.1

Despite the incidence of courses more or less exclusively for girls and the high proportion of girls among full-time students, it has been suggested that technical colleges have a strongly male ambiance (see chapter 7). The phenomenon of the higher levels of female satisfaction in schools has many parallels in other studies showing girls more involved in different aspects of school or receiving more favourable teacher ratings. At the primary level these include Douglas (1964) and Kellmer-Pringle (1967), and at the secondary level King (1973a). These may suggest a more feminine ambiance in mixed schools (all the studies, including those reported here, were based on mixed schools), and that girls are in some way more responsive to community sentiments. They may find the authority relationships associated with the school as a community more acceptable than do boys. This suggestion finds some support in the work of Easthope (1973) who found that the larger the secondary school and the more bureaucratic the school, the lower were the teachers' feelings of belonging to the school. However, the 'effects' of increasing size and bureaucracy on the reduction of these feelings were greater for women than for men.

These sex differences in the experience of the same school or college have a double significance. They first of all provide examples of the unintended, and possibly unrecognised, consequences of social action. Neither the schools nor the colleges were purposefully organised in such a way to give rise to either greater male or female satisfaction. Second, they show that the experience of an organisation is not directly determined by the structure of the organisation but varies from one social group to another. This is also shown in the way in which the experience of college varies with the students' previous experience of school (chapter 7). The belief that organisational structure determines experience assumes more power for teachers and lecturers than they actually have. Organisational rules clearly regulate student behaviour but they do not necessarily regulate the meanings the students assign either to the behaviour or to the rules. These meanings are at least partially derived from previous experiences and relate to their other identities as young men and women. The structural determinism of those who run schools and colleges suggests that they define the student; but the student also defines the school or college.

It is therefore difficult to identify particular aspects of the formal organisation which may be associated with favourable student responses. Sometimes the meanings that are assigned to organisational elements are quite local and even ephemeral. For example, students at Cooperative College were incensed at a new rule which required them to produce a note if they had been absent for more than three days. Students compare college rules with the staff claim that they are treated as adults, and sometimes define them as unnecessary restrictions. Sixth formers are often contemptuous of minor restorations of rights, granted as privileges. However, on the basis of informal interviews and unsolicited student comment alone, it can be suggested that two organisational elements that some students in most schools and colleges use as a test of being treated as adults and of not finding unnecessary restrictions are being able to smoke and being allowed out of the building without permission during non-lesson time.

Table 11.7 *Tertiary College students' opinions and those of school and college students* (% agreement)

	Schools and sixth form colleges		Tertiary College		Further education colleges	
	Mean	(Range)	%	(Rank/13)	Mean	(Range)
Keep social life separate	38	(25–57)	37	(4)	52	(46–63)
Staff interested in welfare	55	(47–67)	48	(8)	46	(32–50)
Unnecessary restrictions	46	(14–72)	16	(2)	32	(24–57)
Know some staff well	60	(57–71)	44	(9)	44	(36–64)
Easy to make friends	77	(47–93)	67	(10)	71	(64–82)
Treated as adults	50	(28–74)	65	(3)	55	(40–63)
Staff only interested in those who do well	14	(7–26)	17	(8)	15	(11–21)
Non-exam subjects take up time	39	(29–50)	36	(10)	48	(42–58)
Have to look after yourself	65	(50–78)	77	(5)	78	(72–80)
An emphasis on exams	83	(71–95)	62	(13)	77	(72–80)
Sense of belonging	31	(4–44)	24	(9)	22	(18–28)
Decide how much work to do	85	(82–88)	73	(7)	69	(48–78)
Enough private study	70	(59–78)	53	(7)	34	(21–46)
Enough individual help	49	(37–61)	57	(3)	49	(45–54)

The students' experience of Tertiary College

Tertiary College was organised in such a way as to attempt to provide students with an experience which incorporated what was thought to be the best of that of school, in terms of supportive relationships, and the best of that of technical college, in terms of relevance and purposefulness in learning. It has already been shown that a comparison of the experience of students before and after its reorganisation provides evidence to suggest these aims had been fulfilled, at least in part (chapter 9). Table 11.7 compares the experience of Tertiary College students with those in six school-based institutions and in the six technical colleges. (It is important to note that the Tertiary College was surveyed two years after the others.) The experience of Tertiary College was rather school-like in terms of its importance for the students' social life and favourable attitudes to non-examination studies, which was probably linked to the feeling of a low emphasis on examinations. It was college-like in terms of relationships with staff, low feelings of restraint, looking after yourself, in feelings of belonging and autonomy in work. Satisfaction with private study provision was midway between schools and colleges, and there was high satisfaction with the amount of individual help.

If the reduction in the differences in satisfaction between the sexes are added to these comparisons (see chapter 9) it can be suggested that Tertiary College had combined some of the elements of what are thought to be the typical experiences of both school and technical college, had achieved some détente in the generation of feelings of both security and freedom, and therefore represents something of a social hybrid of the community and the association.

Chapter 12

Policy and practice

British education has become structurally more diverse. Until recently children transferred schools at seven and eleven; now they may do so at any age between seven and fourteen. Educational labels are more deceptive than ever. 'College' and 'school' are applied at all age levels, 'comprehensive' may be applied to last year's secondary modern, 'grammar' may actually be part of the name of a comprehensive school. In post-sixteen education there is often confusion about the meanings of sixth form unit, sixth form centre, sixth form college, secondary college, further education college, technical college, tertiary college, and comprehensive college.

The structural diversity behind this confused nomenclature has come about largely because of the increasing acceptance of the ideology of comprehensive education. Central pressure, strong from Labour, weak from the Conservatives, on local education authorities for the abolition of selection in secondary education has been justified mainly in meritocratic terms: providing all children with equal opportunities for educational success. However, the organisational form in which this may be realised has not been closely prescribed. The ideologies of school and college have been given secondary importance. The studies of Croydon (chapter 5), of Exeter and North Devon (chapter 9), of Gateshead and Darlington (Batley et al., 1970) show that the sequence of events begins with the local education authority officials who, prompted to a greater or lesser extent by the activities of the DES and local pressure groups, draw up plans for reorganisation, including the provision for the education of the over-sixteens. In the local context, interest groups attempt to change, modify or endorse the plans. These plans, possibly modified, are then submitted, unofficially and eventually officially, to the DES for approval. It is the decisions made by the officials of local education authorities and the DES that have effectively created the diversity, if not the confusion.

The actions of the DES officials in this respect may be interpreted as suggesting that they consider the different forms of post-sixteen education are all, potentially, equally good ways of achieving comprehensive education. The common tag of plans being suited to particular areas either supports this or represents the expediency of general educational reform over a favoured organisational form. However, both nationally and locally the notion of the equal effectiveness of all forms of education is not accepted by many educational interest groups. Their preference for a particular form has been explained in the terms of the way in which this serves group interests, and confirms the members' identities (chapter 10). What may be asked is, Do they have advantages for others as well, particularly the students and pupils concerned? The answers are often presumed by interest groups in their own favour, but what is presumed is not always confirmed by investigation. Policies should be judged by their practice as well as their intentions. This requires the attempt at an objective viewpoint made without the aid of the ideological spectacles of any immediate interest group.

The supposed advantages are often classified as being economic, social and educational. They are, however, closely related and they are all, in a sense, social, in that they represent meanings shared by particular groups. Different groups give each kind of supposed advantage a different emphasis. When a teachers' group dismisses economic arguments, dubs the social arguments as political, and asserts the importance of the educational, they are making a claim for their educational expertise which it is hoped will pre-empt criticism. In the context of trying to influence policy, all the arguments are political.

It is no longer acceptable to justify educational expenditure as an economic investment (chapter 4). This represents a change of view on the part of many sociologists, economists and policy makers. The only reasonably substantiated connection between education and economic growth is in the operation of a threshold in terms of basic universal literacy (Collins, 1971). The economic

189

advantages of different forms of post-sixteen education are therefore to be judged on the basis of expenditure; a best buy judgment. Their supposed advantages in this respect have usually been made without detailed or sophisticated calculations; at least, these are not disclosed when decisions are publicly justified. Sometimes the calculations are wrong, and a scheme proves to be more expensive than expected, as in Exeter (chapter 9).

A particular aspect of the economics of provision is the utilisation of specialist teachers as a scarce educational resource. This scarcity could be considered to be created by the operation of centrally generated policies. These are the use of teacher quotas and the tight control of the members entering teacher education. Their relaxation would involve more public expenditure. This would not necessarily cure the condition but would alleviate it. However, this could affect the distribution of teachers as freer mobility may result in an imbalance by age, experience and qualifications, between the desired suburban, middle class areas and the working class areas of the inner cities, as in the USA (Herriott and St John, 1966). However, the policies that have allowed colleges of education to prepare students for degrees should increase the proportion of graduate teachers, so alleviating what is thought to be a problem.

There are two related aspects of the supposed 'educational' advantages of the various forms of post-sixteen education. The first concerns the extent to which each can provide opportunities for educational success, and the second, the degree of choice of courses or subjects available to the students. There is clear evidence that young people want these as well (chapter 2).

From the discussion of short-course comprehensives in chapter 6, it is clear that it is extremely difficult to measure the academic success of a school. In the popular judgment a 'good school', in this respect, is one that has a large proportion of pupils with many examination passes and high grades. This is a process-output model; the educational process is judged by the examination product. However, the kind of pupil recruited by a school relates to the level of examination success, and so the model becomes an input-process-output one. The machine is not only being judged by the kind of sausages it produces, but also by the quality of the sausage meat fed into it. This crude factory model of the school is not adequate for the understanding of the nature of the educational process. If, however, its limitations are accepted it can be used, as in chapter 6, to show that simple propositions about the academic viability of the different forms of education are difficult to substantiate because of the large number of variables involved. The 'good school' remains largely a subjective judgment.

Course or examination provision and academic success are linked at least to the extent that, if a course is not provided, then no one can pass an examination in that subject, but beyond this, more courses do not necessarily mean more passes (chapter 6). The wide provision of courses is therefore to be justified mainly in terms of the choice offered to students. The celebration of choice that occurs in some schools reflects a kind of further education consumerism, and its operation may have a number of consequences. First, there has been the emergence of a substantial proportion of A level students following mixed science and arts courses (chapter 3). This is welcomed in some quarters as a move against premature specialisation, but it should also be recognised as the emergence of what Bernstein (1971) calls 'mixed' or 'impure' combinations of subjects, which has implications for the status of the older 'pure' combinations. It has been thought that the principles common to chemistry, physics and mathematics demand that they should be studied together in the sixth form. It must be posed that chemistry means something different to pupils when it can be studied with economics or French. This greater autonomy of students means less power for teachers to define the nature of the subjects they teach. The widening of choice is associated with the admittance of new subjects into the academic pantheon, which reduces the élite status of the older established subjects. The availability and popularity of the social sciences may have contributed to the so-called swing from science (chapter 3).

There are also two related aspects to the supposed social advantages of the different forms of post-sixteen education, both of which may be also called educational. The prime emphasis in comprehensive reorganisation has been meritocratic; the egalitarian ideology has been relatively less important. Providing opportunities to succeed in the existing social order has been considered more important than changing that social order. However, forms of post-sixteen education have been considered to have egalitarian qualities. This equality may refer to individual organisations in the total system, to groups within an organisation, and most commonly to relationships between students in a particular organisation. The supposed process is another example of the way in which time is transcended in educational thinking. A more egalitarian society will be achieved in the future, through the present experience of being educated with others from different social backgrounds. The social mix of the school is baked as the cake of society.

In operational terms the 'now' of the proposition is measured by friendship groupings. The more mixed the social origins of a group's members, the more social divisions are thought to be broken down in school, and ultimately (although this is never tested) in life after school. Pupils choose friends from those that they come into contact with most frequently and from those that they define as being rather like themselves. Thus they choose friends largely within the school they attend and from within their own teaching group. However, social class of origin does not seem to be an important factor in pupils' friendship choice (King and Easthope, 1973). The implication is, the more mixed the social composition of the institution, the more mixed may be the friendship groups, and, if the connection is accepted, the outcome may be greater egalitarianism.

But the pie need not only be in the sky. People spend a large proportion of their lives in education, and if schools and colleges had mixed social compositions there may exist a large egalitarian sector of society. The separation of school and society is a false one; schools are society for millions of children and young people. What could also exist now is more equality between educational institutions; equality of provision is probably a pre-condition of equality of status.

The second aspect of the supposed social advantages of the different forms of post-sixteen education is in terms of student satisfaction, not only with reference to the provision of courses but also with their general experience of school or college. This interest is a new one. If young people are considered to be more mature and responsible their opinions should be considered more closely. The choice for those who run schools and colleges is between the intrinsic worth of activities or rules, and the desire to satisfy those who must follow or obey them. This represents a shift of power in the teacher-taught relationship. This student power is higher when their attendance is voluntary. If student satisfaction becomes a criterion in the organisation of schools and colleges, the relationship between the teacher and the taught becomes more equal, so that another kind of equality may be attained.

A great deal of lip service is paid to taking account of young people's opinions about their own education, but those who run schools and colleges are not always aware of them. They view their institutions through the ideologies of school as a community or of college consumerism, and their intention to secure student satisfaction becomes a signal of supposed satisfaction. When the powerful intend something to happen, to them, it happens. Students express their opinions in an authority relationship in which they monitor what they say through their perceptions of the expectations of their superiors. The notion of loyalty to the school may prevent dissatisfactions being displayed, particularly if they are judged to reveal undesirable character traits with implications for suitability in future jobs or continued education. Studies of school councils by King (1973a) and Chapman (1971) show that although such things as school rules and uniform may be discussed, decisions about them are rarer, and the one aspect of school life that is never discussed is relationships with individual teachers. Students and sixth formers do constitute interest groups but despite the existence of the Schools Action Union and the National Union of School Students they have less effective means of expressing their interests than other groups. At the institutional level, students' unions in colleges appear to be more effective in this respect than do councils in schools.

The surveys already reported do give some indication of student opinion and experience. However, there are problems of interpreting them in terms of policy. The experience of a school or a college is not directly determined by its organisation but varies from one social group to another within the same organisation (chapter 11). Boys and girls may define situations in different ways related to their sexual identities. Students from different types of school may have different experiences of the same college (chapter 7). Situations are not just experienced in the here and now but also in relation to experiences in the past and elsewhere. The assessment that must be made is therefore not simply which form of post-sixteen education is associated with high levels of student satisfaction, but, which is associated with high levels of satisfaction among both boys and girls. This assumes that the provision is co-educational, a neglected aspect of egalitarianism.

In the sections that follow, each of the forms of post-sixteen education is examined in terms of the following criteria, bearing in mind the reservations already made about them: How

193

G

economically can they be provided? Which makes best use of scarce resources? What degree of student choice is possible in relation to subjects and courses? How egalitarian are they? In what ways are they associated with student satisfaction?

The integral sixth form

Given the high costs of building, the economic expenditure judgments are against the all-through school with integral sixth form. This is based upon two common assumptions: that such schools must be large and that they require new buildings. Split site arrangements using existing buildings are not favoured, partly because this denies the concept of the school as a unified community. It has been suggested that some local authorities pose the use of split sites as being the only way of reorganising secondary education in their area but claim this to be unacceptable and therefore a reason for delaying going comprehensive on economic and 'educational' grounds rather than for political or ideological reasons (Burgess, 1972). Some commentators, including Elizabeth Halsall (1971), have argued that the all-through school need not be large, and so not require new buildings. The main adjustment would be in the number of subjects available to pupils in the sixth form. For headteachers such as Murphy (1973) the economic arguments against the all-through school are not sufficient. The form of schooling is more important than money.

If the calculations of Egner (1960) and Taylor (1971) are accepted then the all-through school appears to be an inefficient utilisation of scarce specialist teachers. The reply made by the HMA (1968) and others is that these teachers prefer to teach to all age levels. However, a survey by Bernbaum (1968) showed that young graduates have a very strong preference for sixth form work, and that some are attracted to the college of further education because of its age range.

The protagonists of the all-through school face a number of dilemmas. Feelings of community are thought to be more difficult to generate in large schools. Consequently structural innovations are made to split the school into smaller units for pupil care and control. The studies of King (1973a) and Ross et al. (1972) suggest that these have been reasonably successful, but Easthope (1973) has shown there to be a problem for teachers.

194

Those in larger schools showed less sense of community, in terms of feelings of belonging and satisfaction with social relationships. There is an irony in his further findings. Headteachers see the problem of size as being one of communications as far as staff are concerned. In response they often institute elaborate committee structures and introduce bulky staff handbooks. The more these bureaucratic devices were used the lower were the teachers' levels of satisfaction. It seems that the 'problem' of the large school is more for teachers than for pupils. For many head-teachers the wide range of courses made possible in such schools is a compensation for any problems of size (King, 1973a).

Some, but not all, headteachers of all-through comprehensive schools make their acceptance of an egalitarian ideology quite explicit (King, 1973a). On the basis of the previous discussion it could be suggested that schools which recruit pupils on the basis of banding maximise the possibility of friendships between the social classes. Allocation by banding involves the equal distribution of children of different imputed ability between schools in a given area. Because of the relationship between social class and measured intelligence, the social composition of each school would be more mixed than it would have been had there been a zoning form of allocation. Because of the residential segregation of the social classes, neighbourhood schools would have a narrower class range. On a similar reasoning it would be expected that the less selective the entry into the sixth form and the greater the number of levels of courses provided, the more social mixing may occur.

The extent to which the all-through school is associated with sixth form satisfactions is difficult to estimate. The surveys of St Trad's and Newstyle (chapters 2 and 3) show there are considerable variations from one school to another. One thing that is clear is that mixed schools are associated with higher levels of satisfaction among girls than boys (chapter 11). This would obviously present a dilemma if student satisfaction were to be made the principal criterion in deciding organisational form. This does not point to a policy of keeping girls in school and sending boys to technical colleges where as a group they are more satisfied than girls (chapter 7). The result would be single sex institutions, and the work of Dale (1969) strongly suggests that both sexes are more contented in mixed schools. (There are no single sex technical colleges.)

Older pupils of both sexes in mixed schools tend to show a

lower acceptance of the rituals of assembly and uniform, than do younger pupils in the same school (King, 1973a). The evidence suggests they put up with these irritations in order to take the opportunities to compete for success through the examination system. If the argument is that such practices are intrinsically worthwhile then it does not matter that some pupils dislike them. Another view expressed by one headteacher in interview was: 'They've got to have something to complain about.'

The comparisons of St Trad's and Newstyle suggest that when these and other pupil-defined 'unnecessary restrictions' are removed, the levels of their satisfaction tend to be higher. The dilemma posed here has already been pointed out in chapter 3. When sixth formers' privileges extend to such things as the relaxation of control over clothing and appearance they are less easily used as role-models or agents of social control. To prevent dissatisfaction among non-sixth formers who continue to be chaffed by what the older ones among them also define as unnecessary restrictions, the liberated sixth formers are kept out of sight in a separate unit. The price of student satisfaction in the all-through school is the sacrifice of part of the traditional idea of the sixth form.

Sixth form centres

There would appear to be economic advantages in the use of sixth form centres, in terms of the utilisation of existing buildings and scarce specialist teachers. On this basis they probably present a wider choice of courses for students than could be made if each school in the consortium had its own small sixth form. They do, however, present a new choice for some students: to leave school or transfer to a different school. The evidence suggests there is little in the fear that the prospect of entering a strange institution reduces the numbers staying on (chapter 6). This is also partly confirmed in the evidence showing that those who do transfer settle into the sixth form almost as quickly as those from within the school, and have as satisfactory experience, including the levels of their voluntary participation (chapter 4).

As with all-through schools the egalitarian qualities of such arrangements would relate to the selectivity of the sixth form centre and the extent of its course provision. However, a special element also exists. Some evidence exists to confirm the fear that such arrangements may be associated with the perpetuation of disparities of esteem, between short-course and long-course sixth form centre schools, particularly as the former tend to be created from modern schools and the latter from grammar schools (chapter 6). Inequalities of esteem between schools means inequalities of esteem between pupils. Such arrangements are potentially anti-egalitarian.

Sixth form colleges

Sixth form colleges seem to have economic advantages in terms of the way they may use existing buildings and in the concentration of specialist teachers to teach only older pupils. The concentration of older pupils also permits the provision of a wide range of subjects and courses. This provision is linked to the degree to which the college shows egalitarian qualities. In the open entry colleges the range of courses may be wider than in selective colleges, and so may increase the range of contacts between students.

The variations in sixth formers' satisfactions seem to be mirrored in sixth form colleges. The comparison of Open College with Selective College suggests that the former's looser control of students' behaviour is associated with their greater satisfaction (chapter 5). The pattern of higher satisfaction among girls seems to be reduced in the colleges. However, given the variation between individual schools and colleges it is not possible to say whether either type has higher levels of general student satisfaction. From the students' point of view the colleges are by no means transit camps or A level factories.

For some the economic advantages of the sixth form colleges do not outweigh the 'decapitation' of sixth forms that is entailed. The idea of the integral sixth form is less sacred to sixth formers than to their teachers (chapter 2). A minority in both schools and colleges felt that there were only gains for the sixth formers in being part of the same school with younger pupils (chapter 5).

The corollary of the sixth form college or any form of separate sixth form provision is the short-course comprehensive. The economic advantages of the colleges are permitted by the existence of such schools. The research reported in chapter 6 shows that most of the fears about the academic viability of such schools, in terms of provision of courses and examination success, are not substantiated in at least one local education authority. In the absence of sixth formers such schools are still able to carry out most of the activities considered desirable in English education. Today's fifth formers can become yesterday's sixth.

The distribution of graduate teachers across the sixth form college with short-course school system may be seen more as a concern of the National Union of Teachers than of teachers (chapter 10). The fear of the split profession is the fear of the split union. This, however, seems unlikely in that the educational system is already strongly age-stratified and, given the increasing number of ages of transfer, is becoming more so. If short-course schools are associated with technical colleges as centres of post-sixteen education, as in Exeter and North Devon, then the teachers' unions may lose members to the ATTI. But the ATTI and the NUT are closely associated bodies; a relationship that may be strained by their different views on post-sixteen education.

Technical colleges

This discussion concerns the place of technical colleges existing together with school-based forms of post-sixteen education. If a visit is made to a college during the day it is common to find it looking half empty. The movement of day-release, block-release and part-time students, and the high proportion of evening students, accounts for this under-utilisation of plant. One economic advantage in using the colleges to cope with the expansion of academic full-time education is therefore clear. There may also be the same sort of advantages associated with any kind of separate post-sixteen education, in concentrating specialist teachers, but there is the possibility in some areas of the uneconomic duplication of courses by colleges and schools.

The choices available to college students are potentially wider than those in any school-based form, in that they can provide courses other than O and A level, including vocational courses leading to OND, RSA and other awards. It is possible that they provide more opportunities for social studies. Certainly a larger proportion of college students take examinations in these subjects (Smith, 1974). The diversity of their courses makes the concern about the sixth form curriculum, centred around the 'problem' of specialisation versus breadth of studies, and ability-related courses, look rather narrow and parochial. One disadvantage of colleges compared with schools is that the stronger control of class numbers (chapter 10) may mean that subjects with a minority appeal may not be provided. A case of economy reducing choice.

Colleges that have a large proportion of students following O and A level courses have social compositions more mixed than that of many schools, recruiting as they do across the age range (a few community schools do admit some adults: see Rogers 1974), from different kinds of school and from different work backgrounds. They are therefore, by the criteria discussed before, more egalitarian than many schools. However, their place in a mixed system of post-sixteen education is not very egalitarian, because they often receive either ill-defined or inferior status compared with schools with sixth forms; second chance and second best.

The satisfactions of college students must be considered against the background, for some, of an unsatisfactory school experience. The fact that some of them have chosen to leave schools with integral sixth forms is better seen as a dismissal of what they have left rather than approval of where they go to. This reservation made, it can be suggested that technical colleges do not have the monopoly of student satisfaction with regard to the way they are treated, and there are indications of a certain distance in the relationships with staff, felt particularly by girls. The tighter control of work is also associated with some dissatisfactions.

School-college cooperation

The different kinds of school-college cooperation appear to have economic advantages in terms of utilisation of plant and teacher resources, and advantages in providing a wider choice of courses for students. However, disparity of esteem may be perpetuated when the college partner is used (often most willingly) to help out a school with its 'problem' of low status non-examinees, by providing them with some kind of quasi-vocational course. In a consortium type of cooperation, the schools and colleges appear to be equal partners, but, as the study of the Nossex Consortium suggests, schemes that aim to present students with a choice of courses in different institutions may in fact be presenting them with a choice of different organisations, in which the colleges are the more favoured (chapter 8). This is an interesting inversion of the usual status difference.

Tertiary colleges

Tertiary colleges as centres for all post-sixteen education probably have the economic advantages of any form of separate education for this age group and those of technical colleges, upon which all of the existing examples are based. The choices of course they provide could be as wide as any other kind of institution. Since they provide education for virtually all over sixteen, they are the most egalitarian form. The study of one college (one of the only two in existence at the time) shows that despite its technical college origins students showed satisfaction in relation to both the control of their behaviour and their work. The pattern of higher levels of satisfaction among boys, common in technical colleges, was not strong (chapter 9).

Policy and practice in post-sixteen education

Policy decisions about the form of post-sixteen education are made by members of education committees, education officers and officials of the DES. Other groups attempt to influence their decisions in ways which would lead to policies reflecting their ideologies and interests. Presumptions are made about the practice of such policies before they are implemented, and assumptions made afterwards. Ideologies allow us to see what we want to see, so that the differences between policy and practice are not always apparent. If they are, then it is not in the interests of those with responsibility to make them public. This chapter has attempted to review the practices behind the policies, to sort out the intentions from the outcomes. It is not to be expected that the various interest groups will necessarily approve or agree with this kind of analysis, or its results. Such an exercise is at least a critique if not a criticism. Made explicit, it suggests that contemporary post-sixteen education falls short on student satisfaction and is far from egalitarian; two characteristics claimed for each of its different forms.

Social analysis is a search for understanding and explanation. It may also be used as a basis for further social action. If student satisfaction and egalitarianism are desirable states of affairs then the analysis points to the creation of a national system of open access tertiary colleges, perhaps better called comprehensive colleges. Such a system would also have economic advantages and present students with a wide choice of courses and subjects. As had been argued already, student satisfaction and course choice are bound up in egalitarianism. There are not sufficient colleges of further education for conversion purposes so that sixth form colleges and units would also be involved. If a technical college and an integral sixth form were in the same area, an analogy between the unacceptable existence of modern with grammar schools would be made, and reorganisation plans drawn up. There seem to be none of the supposed disadvantages in the operation of existing tertiary colleges under further education regulations. As the ATTI (1972) has realised, a new set for 16–19 year olds might cut off the adult population that attend existing technical colleges, and, in the context of this discussion, reduce the new colleges' egalitarianism.

Such a policy would mean the end of the integral sixth form in the maintained sector of education and a reduction in the expressive component in the education of young people. If they are now more mature they have less to learn about acceptable behaviour. Its death would not be universally mourned. In the survey by Smith (1974) the majority of sixth formers would have preferred to have been in sixth form colleges or colleges of further education. Those who did would mourn not only the death of a cherished idea, but among teachers and headteachers the transfiguration of their identities and a slump in their interests. The technical college as a second chance institution would also be lost to young people, a matter of regret among some of its products teaching in the colleges.

A system of comprehensive colleges might lead to a healing of British education where what Hopkinson (1970) calls the classical and vocational traditions are brought together in one institution. This would mean a reduction in domination of the public school as a model for educational practice. Maintained comprehensive education would be structurally different, no longer inviting comparisons which lead to its being placed bottom of the status rankings below public schools, direct grant and grammar schools. There are refugees from these schools in most technical colleges. Exeter College attracts students from local independent and direct grant schools. Like the primary school the comprehensive college could be acknowledged as the better system when private and public education are compared; by being different and not a pale imitation. The spirit of Dr Arnold may rest in some head-teachers' studies but it would be wrong to accuse all teachers of a conscious educational snobbery. Ideas outlive their originators, have different meanings assigned to them as they are passed from generation to generation. The sixth form was invented to solve a problem of order. It succeeded and took on new meanings, so that this upper class expedient eventually became the zenith of secondary education. Those who pushed the maintained secondary school in the wake of the public school are dead and unknown to those who continue to steer in that direction. Some of the passengers are swimming towards boats taking a different course. 'The educational systems of most European countries have grown up in the image of outmoded social class systems' (Floud, 1961). The emergence of a new form of education might help to confirm that the image was indeed outmoded.

The corollary, a system of comprehensive schools for 11 or 12–16 year olds, may develop its own methods and ideologies of teaching, as have primary schools. Such schools could be relatively small, perhaps preserving the feeling of community so important to teachers, and providing a setting for the propagation of an expressive order, which it could be argued is appropriate for younger children with much to learn about what is considered to be appropriate behaviour.

It is fashionable among sociologists of education to point to the neglect of the study of what is taught and learnt – the sociology of educational knowledge. This neglect has been real, but it would be unfortunate if, in correcting it, a neglect were made of institutions. As Eggleston (1973) has pointed out, where you are taught is bound up with what you are taught. In British society the assessment of being educated is made though a knowledge of which institutions a person has attended as much as through what he manifests as learning, because the two are strongly related. Comprehensive colleges may modify this, in that many different courses would be provided in the same institution. A consequence may be that what counts as valid educational knowledge may be differently defined. The invidious and dubious distinctions between education and training may be reviewed. Equality among the courses goes with equality among the students, and poses the possibility of more equal honour among occupations.

Policy and practice

In a selective, hierarchical system, education is a privilege, where some children get more than others or receive what is thought to be a better, exclusive education. This is the spirit of the traditional sixth form. In an egalitarian, comprehensive system, education is a right. The forerunners of a national system of comprehensive colleges already exist. Those who support the public education of all young people outside the sixth form tradition are not usually those who make official decisions about the form of education. In this the students are the avant-garde. The decision makers, like generals, take the rear.

Bibliography

ALEXANDER, W. (1969), 'Towards a New Education Act', Councils and Education Press.

ARMYTAGE, W. H. G. (1970), 'Four Hundred Years of English Education', second edition, Cambridge University Press.

ASSISTANT MASTERS' ASSOCIATION (1965), 'Sixth Form Colleges', AMA.

ASSISTANT MASTERS' ASSOCIATION (1974), 'Sixth Form College System', AMA.

ASSOCIATION OF PRINCIPALS OF TECHNICAL INSTITUTIONS, ASSOCIATION OF COLLEGES FOR FURTHER AND HIGHER EDUCATION (1972), 'Joint Evidence to Education and Arts Sub-Committee of House of Commons Expenditure Committee', APTI, ACFHE.

ASSOCIATION OF TEACHERS IN TECHNICAL INSTITUTIONS (1972), 'The Education of the 16–19 Age Group', ATTI.

ASSOCIATION OF TECHNICAL INSTITUTIONS, ASSOCIATION OF PRINCIPALS OF TECHNICAL INSTITUTIONS, ASSOCIATION OF TEACHERS IN TECHNICAL INSTITUTIONS (1969), '16–19 – An F. E. View', ATI, APTI, ATTI.

BAILEY, F. D. (1972), Luton, in T. David (ed.), (1972).

BANKS, O. (1955), 'Parity and Prestige in English Secondary Education', Routledge & Kegan Paul.

BARON, G. (1955), The English Notion of the School, unpublished paper, University of London Institute of Education.

BATLEY, R., O'BRIEN, O. and PARRISH, H. (1970), 'Going Comprehensive', Routledge & Kegan Paul.

BEETHAM, D. (1968), 'Immigrant School Leavers and the Youth Employment Service in Birmingham', Institute of Race Relations.

BELL, C. and NEWBY, H. (1971), 'Community Studies', Allen & Unwin.
BENN, C. (1969), The Separate Sixth Form, 'Comprehensive Education', 11.
BENN, C. (1971), Short Course Comprehensives, 'Comprehensive Education', 18.
BENN, C. (1972), 'Comprehensive Reorganisation Survey', Comprehensive Schools Committee.
BENN, C. and SIMON, B., (1972), 'Half Way There', Second Edition, Penguin.
BERGER, B. (1961), 'An Invitation to Sociology', Penguin.
BERNBAUM, G. (1967), Educational Expansion and the Teacher's Role, 'Universities Quarterly Review', 21.
BERNBAUM, G. (1971), Heads See Themselves as Leaders, 'Times Educational Supplement', 1 August.
BERNSTEIN, B. (1966), Sources of Consensus and Disaffection in Secondary Education, 'Journal of the Association of Assistant Mistresses', 17.
BERNSTEIN, B. (1971), On the Classification and Framing of Educational Knowlege, in M. F. D. Young (ed.) (1971).
BERNSTEIN, B., ELVIN, H. L. and PETERS, K. S. (1966), Ritual in Education, 'Philosophical Transactions of the Royal Society of London', series B, no. 779, vol. 251.
BEYNON, E. G. (1966), Sixth Form Colleges, 'Times Educational Supplement', 19 August.
BISHOP, T. J. H. and WILKINSON, R. (1967), 'Winchester and the Public School Elite', Faber.
BRATCHELL, D. F. (1968), 'The Aims and Organisation of Further Education', Pergamon.
BRIGGS, A. (1965), 'Victorian People', Penguin.
BRIGHT, J. (1972), Stoke-on-Trent's A Level Academy, 'Comprehensive Education', 21.
BRISTOW, A. (1970), 'Inside Colleges of Further Education', HMSO.
BROWNING, D. P. J. (1972), Open Access Sixth Form Colleges in Southampton, 'Comprehensive Education', 22.
BUCHER, R. and STRAUSS, A. L. (1961), Professions in Process, 'American Journal of Sociology', 66.
BURGESS, T. (1972), 'A Guide to English Schools', third edition, Penguin.
BUTTERWORTH, E. and WEIR, D. (1970), 'The Sociology of Modern Britain', Fontana.
BYRNE, D. and WILLIAMSON, W. (1972a), The Myth of the Restricted Code, 'Working Papers in Sociology', Department of Sociology and Social Administration, University of Durham.
BYRNE, D. and WILLIAMSON, W. (1972b), Some Intra-Regional

Bibliography

Variations in Educational Provision, 'Sociology', 6.

BYRNE, D., WILLIAMSON, W. and FLETCHER, B. G. (1973), Models of Educational Attainment, 'Urban Education', 8.

CANTOR, L. M. and ROBERTS, I. F. (1972), 'Further Education in England and Wales', second edition, Routledge & Kegan Paul.

CARTER, D. (1970), Reflections on a Sixth Form College, 'Journal of the Incorporated Association of Assistant Masters', 65.

CASE, P. and ROSS, J. M. (1965), Why do children leave school early?, 'New Society', 162.

CENTRAL ADVISORY COMMITTEE REPORT (1954), 'Early Leaving', HMSO.

CENTRAL ADVISORY COMMITTEE REPORT (1963), 'Half Our Future' (Newsom report), HMSO.

CENTRAL ADVISORY COMMITTEE REPORT (1967), 'Children and their Primary Schools' (Plowden report), HMSO.

CENTRAL ADVISORY COMMITTEE REPORT (1969, 1970), '15–19' (Crowther report), HMSO.

CENTRE FOR EDUCATIONAL RESEARCH AND INNOVATION (1973), Devon, United Kingdom, in 'Case Studies of Educational Innovation, II. At the Regional Level', OECD.

CHAPMAN, J. (1971), School Councils: in Theory and Practice, 'Journal of Moral Education', 1.

CHARLTON, D., GENT, W. and SCAMMELS, B. (1971), 'The Administration of Technical Colleges', Manchester University Press. CITY AND COUNTY OF EXETER (1972), 'Exeter College – Report of the Committee of Enquiry', City and County of Exeter.

COATES, R. D. (1972), 'Teachers' Unions and Interest Group Politics', Cambridge University Press.

COLEMAN, J. S. (1961), 'The Adolescent Society', Free Press.

COLEMAN, J. S. (1966), 'Equality of Educational Opportunity', National Center for Educational Studies, Washington.

COLLINS, R. (1971), Functional and Conflict Theories of Educational Stratification, 'American Sociological Review', 36.

COOK, B. C. (1970), School or College? A Further Contribution, 'Vocational Aspects of Education', 22.

CORBETT, A. (1969), Sixth Form Colleges, 'Comprehensive Education', 11.

COTGROVE, S. (1958), 'Technical Education and Social Change', Allen & Unwin.

COTGROVE, S. (1962), Education and Occupation, 'British Journal of Sociology', 13.

CROSLAND, A. and BOYLE, E. (1971), 'The Politics of Education', Penguin.

D'AETH, R. (1973), 'Youth and the Changing Secondary School', UNESCO.

206

Bibliography

DAINTON, F. (Chairman) (1968), 'Enquiry into the Flow of Candidates in Science and Technology into Higher Education', HMSO.
DALE, R. R. (1969), 'Mixed or Single-Sex School', Routledge & Kegan Paul.
DALTON, J. J. (1969), Reorganisation of Secondary Education, 'Comprehensive Education', 11.
DAVID, M. (1971), Your CEO. Is He a Pioneer or a Prisoner?, 'Education', 137.
DAVID, M. (1973), Approaches to Organisational Change in LEA's, 'Educational Administration Bulletin', 1.
DAVID, T. (ed.) (1972), 'The Sixth Form College in Practice', Councils and Education Press.
DAVIES, B. (1968), 'Social Needs and Resources in Local Services', Joseph.
DAVIES, H. A. (1965), 'Culture and the Grammar School', Routledge & Kegan Paul.
DAVIES, T. I. (1971), The Minimum Size of School, 'Trends in Education', 23.
DAVIS, R. (1967), 'The Grammar School', Penguin.
DEPARTMENT OF EDUCATION AND SCIENCE (1961-74), 'Statistics of Education', HMSO.
DEPARTMENT OF EDUCATION AND SCIENCE (1965), Circular 10/65.
DEPARTMENT OF EDUCATION AND SCIENCE (1970), Circular 10/70.
DEPARTMENT OF EDUCATION AND SCIENCE (1974), Circular 4/74.
DONNISON, D. V. et al. (1965), 'Social Policy and Administration', Allen & Unwin.
DOUGLAS, J. W. B. (1964), 'The Home and the School', MacGibbon & Kee.
DURKHEIM, E. (1933), 'The Division of Labour in Society', Free Press.
DURKHEIM, E. (1961), 'Moral Education', Free Press.
DUROJAIYE, S. M. (1971), Social Context of Immigrant Pupils Learning English, 'Educational Research', 13.
EASTHOPE, G. (1973), 'Power Bureaucracy and Community and their Relation to Size in Secondary Schools', unpublished PhD thesis, University of Exeter.
EASTON, W. A. G. (1969), Analysis of a College, 'Technical Journal', 7.
ECKSTEIN, H. (1960), 'Pressure Group Politics', Stanford University Press.
EDMONDS, J. V. (1972), Scunthorpe, in T. David (ed.) (1972).
EDWARDS, A. D. (1970a), 'The Changing Sixth Form in the Twentieth Century', Routledge & Kegan Paul.

Bibliography

EDWARDS, A. D. (1970b), Exeter's Sixth Form Solution, 'New Society', 16, 3 July.

EGGLESTON, S. J. (1967), Some Environmental Correlates of Extended Secondary Education in England, 'Comparative Education', 3.

EGGLESTON, S. J. (1973), Decision Making in the School Curriculum: A Conflict Model, 'Sociology', 7.

EGNER, W. E. (1968), Sixth Form Dilemma, 'Education', 132.

ELKIN, F. and WESTLEY, W. A. (1955), The Myth of Adolescent Culture, 'American Sociological Review', 20.

EPPEL, E. M. and EPPEL, M. (1966), 'Adolescents and Morality', Routledge & Kegan Paul.

EPPERSON, D. C. (1964), A Reassessment of Indices of Parental Influence in 'The Adolescent Society', 'American Sociological Review', 29.

ETZIONI, A. (1964), 'Modern Organisations', Prentice-Hall.

EXETER EXPRESS AND ECHO (1972), City College Cuts its Name to Upgrade its Appeal, 4 February.

FLEMING, Lord (Chairman) (1944), 'Report of the Committee on Public Schools', Board of Education.

FLOUD, J. E. (1961), Social Class Factors in Educational Achievement, in A. H. Halsey (ed.), 'Ability and Opportunity', OECD.

FLOUD, J. E. and HALSEY, A. H. (1956), English Secondary Schools and the Supply of Labour, in 'The Yearbook of Education, 1956', Evans.

FLOUD, J. E. and HALSEY, A. H. (1957), Intelligence Tests, Social Class and Selection for Secondary Schools, 'British Journal of Sociology', 8.

FLOUD, J. E. (ed.), HALSEY, A. H. and MARTIN, F. M. (1957), 'Social Class and Educational Opportunity', Heinemann.

FORD, J. (1969), 'Social Class and the Comprehensive School', Routledge & Kegan Paul.

FOWLER, G. (1973), Technical Education, in R. E. Bell et al. (eds), Education in Great Britain and Ireland', Routledge & Kegan Paul.

FROST, D. (1973), Killing Rugby at its Roots, 'Guardian', 28 March.

FURTHER EDUCATION REGULATIONS SI (1969), no. 403, HMSO.

GAWTHORPE, R. D. (1972), Hampshire, in T. David (ed.) (1972).

GERTH, H. and MILLS, C. W. (1948), 'From Max Weber: Essays in Sociology', Routledge & Kegan Paul.

GLASS, D. V. (ed.) (1954), 'Social Mobility in Britain', Routledge & Kegan Paul.

GOLDTHORPE, J. et al. (1967), The Affluent Worker and the Thesis of Embourgeoisement, 'Sociology', 1.

GOULDNER, A. W. (1963), Anti-Minotaur: the Myth of Value-free

Bibliography

Sociology, in M. Stein and A. Vidich (eds), 'Sociology on Trial', Prentice-Hall.

GOULDNER, A. W. (1971), 'The Coming Crisis of Western Sociology', Heinemann.

GRACE, G. R. (1972), 'Role Conflict and the Teacher', Routledge & Kegan Paul.

GRIFFITHS, A. (1971), 'Secondary School Reorganisation in England and Wales', Routledge & Kegan Paul.

GUNN, S. E. (1972), The Small Comprehensive School Debate, 'Trends in Education', 26.

HALSALL, E. (1971), The Small Comprehensive School, 'Trends in Education', 22.

HALSALL, E. (1973), 'The Comprehensive School – Guidelines for the Reorganisation of Secondary Education', Pergamon.

HANCOCK, A. and WAKEFORD, J. (1965), The Young Technicians, 'New Society', 120.

HASLEGRAVE, H. L. (Chairman) (1969), 'Report of the Committee on Technician Courses and Examinations', National Advisory Council on Education for Industry and Commerce, HMSO.

HEADMASTERS' ASSOCIATION (1968), 'The Sixth Form of the Future', HMA.

HEADMASTERS' ASSOCIATION (1969), 'Sixth Forms and Colleges of Further Education', HMA.

HEADMASTERS' ASSOCIATION and HEADMASTERS' CONFERENCE (1970), 'Our Schools and the Preparation of Teachers', HMA, HMC.

HERRIOTT, R. E. and ST JOHN, N. H. (1966), 'Social Class and the Urban School', Wiley.

HILL, W. S. (1972), letter to 'Times Educational Supplement', 10 November.

HILSUM, S. and START, K. B. (1974), 'Promotion and Careers in Teaching', NFER.

HOLLINGSHEAD, A. B. (1948), 'Elmstowns' Youth', Wiley.

HOPKINSON, D. (1970), The 16–18 Question, 'Trends in Education', 20.

HOPPER, E. (1968), A Typology for the Classification of Educational Systems, 'Sociology', 2.

HUNT, J. (Chairman) (1970), 'Report of an Enquiry into the Pattern and Organization of the College Year', Committee on the more Effective Use of Technical College Resources, HMSO.

INDUSTRIAL TRAINING AUTHORITY (1969), 'Year Book', ITA.

INNER LONDON EDUCATION AUTHORITY (1968), 'Sixth Form Opportunities in Inner London', ILEA.

INSTITUTE OF MUNICIPAL TREASURERS AND ACCOUNTANTS (1972), 'Education Statistics', IMTA.

Bibliography

JACKSON, B. (1963), 'Streaming – An Education System in Miniature', Routledge & Kegan Paul.

JACKSON, B. and MARSDEN, D. (1962), 'Education and the Working Class', Routledge & Kegan Paul.

JAHODA, M. and WARREN, N. (1965), The Myths of Youth, 'Sociology of Education', 38.

JAMES, E. (1951), 'Education and Leadership', Harrap.

JENCKS, C. et al. (1973), 'Inequality', Basic Books.

JENNINGS, A. (1974), The Role of the Schools Council in the Reform of the Sixth Form Examinations, 'Secondary Education', 4.

JONES, H. R. (1972), 'The Exeter Scheme of Secondary Re-Organisation', Institute of Education, University of Exeter.

KANDEL, D. B. and LESSER, G. S. (1972), 'Youth in Two Worlds', Jossey-Bass.

KELLMER-PRINGLE, M. et al. (1967), '11,000 Seven Year Olds', Longmans.

KELSALL, K. (1963), Getting on at the Grammar, 'Times Educational Supplement', 15 March.

KING, R. A. (1968), The Headteacher and his Authority, in J. B. Allen (ed.) 'Headship in the 1970's', Blackwell.

KING, R. A. (1969), 'Values and Involvement in a Grammar School', Routledge & Kegan Paul.

KING, R. A. (1971), Unequal Access in Education – Sex and Social Class, 'Social and Economic Administration', 5.

KING, R. A. (1973a), 'School Organisation and Pupil Involvement', Routledge & Kegan Paul.

KING, R. A. (1973b), School Rituals, 'New Society', 562.

KING, R. A. (1974a), Short Course Neighbourhood Comprehensive Schools – An LEA Case Study, 'Educational Review', 26.

KING, R. A. (1974b), Social Class, Educational Attainment and Provision – An LEA Case Study, 'Policy and Politics', 3.

KING, R. A. and EASTHOPE, G. (1973), Social Class and Friendship Choice in School, 'Research in Education', 4.

KING, R. A. and FRY, J. D. (1972), School Magazines, 'English in Education', 6.

KING, R. W. (1969), 'The English Sixth Form College', Pergamon.

KLUCKHOLN, C. (1964), 'Mirror for Man', Premier.

KOGAN, M. and VAN DER EYKEN, W. (1973), 'County Hall: The Role of the Chief Education Officer', Penguin.

LABOUR PARTY (1973a), 'Higher and Further Education: Report of a Labour Party Study Group', Labour Party.

LABOUR PARTY (1973b), Programme for Britain, 'Labour Weekly Supplement', Special Issue.

LACEY, C. (1970), 'Hightown Grammar', Manchester University Press.

LAMBERT, R. (1966), 'New Wine in Old Bottles', Evans.

Bibliography

LAWRENCE, P. (1973), The Forgotten Sixth Form, 'New Society', 26, 6 December.

LEACH, E. (1964), 'The Political System of Highland Burma', Athlone.

LENNARD, A. G. K. (1972), Southampton, in T. David (ed.) (1972).

LINEHAM, P. (1974), The All-in College, 'Comprehensive Education', 27.

LITTLE, A. et al. (1971), Do Small Classes Help?, 'New Society', 18.

LITTLE, A. and WESTERGAARD, J. (1964), Educational Opportunity and Social Selection, 'British Journal of Sociology', 13.

LITTLE, A. H. (1972), Stoke-on-Trent, in T. David (ed.) (1972).

LONDON AND HOME COUNTIES REGIONAL ADVISORY COUNCIL FOR TECHNOLOGICAL EDUCATION (1972), 'The Full-Time Education of the 16–19 Age Group'.

LUKES, S. (1973), 'Emile Durkheim – His Life and Work', Allen Lane.

LYNCH, J. (1972a), Sixth Form Colleges, 'Comprehensive Education', 20.

LYNCH, J. (1972b), Sixth Form College Planning, 'Comprehensive Education', 21.

McGRATH, K. (1973), State Sixth Form Colleges, 'Where?', 82.

MACK, E. C. (1938), 'Public Schools and British Opinion 1780–1860', Methuen.

MAINE, H. S. (1931), 'Ancient Law', Oxford University Press.

MANZER, R. A. (1970), 'Teachers and Politics – The Role of the NUT', Manchester University Press.

MARSDEN, D. (1969), Which Comprehensive Principle?, 'Comprehensive Education', 13.

MAYS, J. B., QUINE, W. and PICKETT, K. (1968), 'School of Tomorrow', Longmans.

MEAD, M. (1951), 'The School in American Culture', Harvard University Press.

MEAD, M. (1958), Adolescence in Primitive and Modern Society, in E. E. Maccoby et al. (ed.), 'Readings in Social Psychology', Methuen.

MERFIELD, P. H. (1969), letter to 'Times Educational Supplement', 5 September.

MERFIED, P. H. (1973), The Exeter Scheme, 'Forum', 15.

MIDWINTER, E. (1973), The Key to those LEA League Tables, 'Where?', 'Information on Education', 77.

MILLER, D. (1964), Sixth Form Colleges, 'New Education', December, vol. 1, no. 1.

MITCHELL, G. D. (1964), Education, Ideology and Social Change in England, in G. K. Zollschan and W. Hirsch (eds), 'Explorations in Social Change', Routledge & Kegan Paul.

MO, T. (1972), Barnstaple Strides away from its Slums, 'Times Educational Supplement', 29 December.

MONKS, T. G. (1968), 'Comprehensive Education in England and Wales', NFER.

MOORE, D. (1972), Why Teenagers Do A levels at the Tech, 'Times Higher Education Supplement', 21 April.

MORTON-WILLIAMS, R. and FINCH, S. (1968), 'Young School Leavers', Schools Council Enquiry 1, HMSO.

MORTON-WILLIAMS, R., RAVEN, J. and RITCHIE, J. (1970), Sixth Form Pupils and Teachers, 'Schools Council Sixth Form Survey Volume 1', Books for Schools.

MUMFORD, D. E. (1965), '16–19, School or College?' ATI.

MUMFORD, D. E. (1970), 'Comprehensive Reorganisation and the Junior College', ACFHE.

MUMFORD, D. E. (1972), Unified 16–19, 'Comprehensive Education', 20.

MURDOCK, G. and McCRON, D. (1973), Scoobies, Skins and Contemporary Pop, 'New Society', 23, 29 March.

MURDOCK, G. and PHELPS, G. (1972), Youth Culture and the School Revisited, 'British Journal of Sociology', 23.

MURPHY, J. (1972), The Sixth Form in a Comprehensive School, 'Secondary Education', 3.

MUSGRAVE, P. W. (1964), 'The Sociology of Education', first edition, Methuen.

MUSGRAVE, P. W. (1967), 'Technical Change, the Labour Force and Education', Oxford University Press.

MUSGROVE, F. (1964), 'Youth and the Social Order', Routledge & Kegan Paul.

NATIONAL ADVISORY COUNCIL ON EDUCATION FOR INDUSTRY AND COMMERCE (1964), 'The Public Relations of Further Education', HMSO.

NATIONAL ASSOCIATION OF HEADTEACHERS (1973), 'Over 16's at School', NAHT.

NATIONAL UNION OF TEACHERS (1962), 'The State of Our Schools', NUT.

NATIONAL UNION OF TEACHERS (1966), 'Secondary Reorganisations and Sixth Form Colleges', NUT.

NATIONAL UNION OF TEACHERS (1969), 'Into the 70's: A Policy for a New Education Act', NUT.

NATIONAL UNION OF TEACHERS (1972), 'What is Mrs. Thatcher up to?', NUT.

NISBET, R. (1967), 'The Sociological Tradition', Heinemann.

NISSEL, M. (ed.) (1974), 'Social Trends No. 5', HMSO.

NORWOOD, C. and HOPE, A. H. (1909), 'The Higher Education of Boys in England', Murray.

O'CONNOR, M. (1967), The Sixth Form: Where Do We Go From Here?, 'New Education', 10.

OWEN, J. G. (1970), A 16–19 Solution, 'Education', 135, 27 March.

Bibliography

OWEN, J. G. (1972), Devon, in T. David (ed.) (1972).
PARSONS, T. (1943), Age and Sex in the Social Structure of the United States, 'American Sociological Review', 7.
PAYNE, S. (1969), Devon Storm over Integration Plan, 'Times Educational Supplement', 17 January.
PEDLEY, R. (1956), 'Comprehensive Education', Gollancz.
PEDLEY, R. (1973), School or College?, 'Education and Training', 15.
PETERSON, A. D. C. (1973), 'The Future of the Sixth Form', Routledge & Kegan Paul.
PHILLIPS, C. (1972), The Sixth Form Colleges: A Survey, 'Secondary Education', 3.
PILKINGTON, J. (Chairman) (1966), 'Report on the Size of Classes and Approval of Further Education Courses', Committee on Technical College Resources, HMSO.
PRIME MINISTER'S COMMITTEE (1963), 'Higher Education' (Robbins Report), HMSO.
PRUST, A. (1970), The Thomas Rotherham College, in E. Halsall (ed.) 'Becoming Comprehensive: Case Histories', Pergamon.
PUBLIC SCHOOLS' COMMISSION (1968), 'First Report', HMSO.
PUBLIC SCHOOLS' COMMISSION (1970), 'Second Report', HMSO.
PUGH, D. S. et al. (1968), Dimensions of Organisational Structure, 'Administrative Science Quarterly', 8.
REE, H. A. (1956), 'The Essential Grammar School', Harrap.
REPORT OF THE COMMITTEE ON THE AGE OF MAJORITY (1967) (Latey report), HMSO.
ROBINSON, W. S. (1950), Ecological Correlations and the Behaviour of Individuals, 'American Sociological Review', 15.
RODERICK, G. W. and STEPHENS, M. D. (1972), 'Scientific and Technical Education in Nineteenth Century England', David & Charles.
ROGERS, T. (1974), The Community Upper School, 'Comprehensive Education', 27.
ROLFE, J. (1969), 6th Form CFE?, 'Technical Education', 11.
ROSS, J. M. et al. (1972), 'A Critical Appraisal of Comprehensive Education', NFER.
ROY, W. (1968), 'The Teachers' Union', Schoolmaster Publishing.
RUFFLE, W. O. (1973), 14–18 Upper School, 'Forum', 15.
RUSSELL, G. J. (1972), 'Teaching in Further Education', Pitman.
SAMUELSON, B. (Chairman) (1884), 'Report of the Royal Commission on Technical Instruction', HMSO.
SARAN, R. (1973), 'Policy Making in Secondary Education', Clarendon.
SCHOOLS COUNCIL (1972), '16–19 Growth and Response 1. Curricular Bases', Working Paper 45, Evans/Methuen.
SHARP, P. (1970), 'Students in Full-time Courses in Colleges of Further Education', Books for Schools, Schools Council.

Bibliography

SHIELD, G. W. (1964), The First Sixth Form College, 'Education', 822.

SHIELD, G. W. (1970), Mexborough Grammar School Yorkshire, in E. Halsall (ed.), 'Becoming Comprehensive: Case Histories', Pergamon.

SIMON, B. (1969), Egalitarianism Versus Education, 'Comprehensive Education', 14.

SMITH, D. (1974), 'The Times Educational Supplement 16+ Enquiry', Times Newspapers.

STEVENS, F. (1960), 'The Living Tradition', Hutchinson.

SUGARMAN, B. N. (1967), Involvement in Youth Culture, 'British Journal of Sociology', 18.

SWANN, M. (Chairman) (1968), 'The Flow into Employment of Scientists, Engineers and Technologists', HMSO.

SWIFT, D. F. (1970), Recent Research in the Sociology of Education, 'Report of the Joint DES/ACTDE Conference on the Sociology of Education in Colleges of Education', Department of Education and Science.

SWINHOE, K. (1967), Factors Affecting Career Choices Among Fulltime Students in a College of Commerce, 'Vocational Aspect of Education', 19.

TAYLOR, E. (1965), Some Thoughts on the Sixth Form College Idea, 'Conference', 2.

TAYLOR, J. H. (1973), Newcastle upon Tyne: Asian Pupils Do Better than Whites, 'British Journal of Sociology', 24.

TAYLOR, L. C. (1971), 'Resources for Learning', Penguin.

TAYLOR, P. H. et al. (1974), 'The English Sixth Form', Routledge & Kegan Paul.

TAYLOR, W. (1969), 'Society and the Education of Teachers', Faber.

THOMAS, R. H. (1972), Sixth Form and Further Education Share a Site, 'Comprehensive Education', 21.

TIMES EDUCATIONAL SUPPLEMENT (1965), Editorial, 19 February.

TIMES EDUCATIONAL SUPPLEMENT (1972), Editorial, 12 May.

TIPTON, B. F. A. (1972), Some Organisational Characteristics of a Technical College, 'Research in Education', 7.

TIPTON, B. F. A. (1973) 'Conflict and Change in a Technical College', Hutchinson.

TÖNNIES, F. (1955), 'Community and Association', Harper Row.

TOOMEY, D. M. (1970), Home Centred Working Class Parents, 'Sociology', 3.

TROW, M. (1960), The Campus Viewed as Culture, in H. T. Sprague (ed.), 'Research on College Students', University of California.

TRUSTAM, S. F. (1967), School or College? The Consumer's Viewpoint, 'Vocational Aspect of Education', 19.

Bibliography

URWIN, K. (1965), Formulating a Policy for Secondary Education in Croydon, in Donnison et al. (1965).

VALE, M. L. (1972), Sixth Form College, 'Secondary Education', 3.

VALE, M. L. (1973), Sixth Form College, 'Forum', 15.

VAUGHAN, M. and ARCHER, M. S. (1971), 'Social Conflict and Educational Change', Cambridge University Press.

VENABLES, E. (1967), 'The Young Worker at College', Faber.

VENESS, T. (1962), 'School Leavers', Methuen.

WALLER, W. (1932), 'The Sociology of Teaching', Wiley.

WEINBERG, I. (1967), 'The English Public Schools', Atherton.

WHEELER, G. E. (1966), The Management of Colleges, 'Technical Journal', 4.

WHITE PAPER (1966), 'A Plan for Polytechnics and Other Colleges', Command 3006, HMSO.

WHITE PAPER (1972), 'Education: A Framework for Expansion', Command 5174, HMSO.

WHITEHOUSE, B. C. (1962), Relations between Schools and Technical Colleges, 'Forum', 1.

WILCOCK, H. R. (1969), The Witney Model, 'Further Education', 1.

WILCOCK, H. R. (1973), School and F. E. Links, 'Forum', 15.

WILKINSON, R. H. (1963), The Gentleman Ideal and the Maintenance of Political Elite, 'Sociology of Education', 37.

WISEMAN, S. (1964), 'Education and Environment', Manchester University Press.

WOODHALL, M. and BLAUG, M. (1968), Productivity Trends in British Secondary Education, 1950–63, 'Sociology of Education', 41.

WOODWARD, R. (1970), 'Physical Education in the Sixth Form College', University of Exeter Institute of Education.

YOUNG, M. and WILLMOTT, P. (1957), 'Family and Kinship in East London', Routledge & Kegan Paul.

YOUNG, M. F. D. (ed.) (1971), Introduction to 'Knowledge and Control', Macmillan.

ZWEIG, F. (1961), 'The Worker in an Affluent Society', Heinemann.

Index

Aggregative fallacy, 178–80
Alexander, W., 126, 127
All through school, see Sixth form, integral
Armytage, W. H. G., 98
Arnold, Thomas, 25, 28, 30, 31, 34, 38, 202
Assistant Masters' Association, 70, 71, 129, 131, 164, 166
Assistant Mistresses' Association, 166
Association, 151; the college as a, 10, 151–2, 159, 187
Association of Colleges for Further and Higher Education, 167
Association of Principals of Technical Institutions, 127, 167
Association of Teachers in Technical Institutions, 167, 201
Association of Technical Institutions, 127, 128, 167, 198
Atlantic College, 63

Bailey, F. D., 71
Banks, O., 17, 26, 41
Barnstaple, see North Devon College
Baron, G., 150, 155, 158, 160
Batley, R. et al., 188

Beetham, D., 43
Bell, C. and Newby, H., 151
Benn, C., 55, 58, 60, 66, 68, 70, 81, 82, 83, 88; and Simon, B., 58, 60, 67, 68, 69, 82, 83, 85, 88, 89, 127
Berger, B., 164
Bernbaum, G., 156, 194
Bernstein, B., 48, 155, 156, 191
Beynon, E. G., 70
Birkbeck, George, 98
Bishop, T. J. H. and Wilkinson, R., 40
Bratchell, D. F., 162
Briggs, A., 25
Bright, J., 68
Browning, D. P. J., 67, 68, 69
Bucher, R. and Strauss, A. L., 166
Bulge, the, 12–13
Bureaucracy, 152, 156–7, 159
Burgess, T., 194
Butterworth, E. and Weir, D., 152
Byrne, D. and Williamson, W., 84, 89, 90, 91; and Fletcher, B., 130

Cantor, L. M. and Roberts, I. F., 174

Index

Carlson, R. O., 135, 137
Carter, D., 72, 158, 166
Case, P. and Ross, J. M., 14
Central Sixth Form Centre, 60–2, 76
Centre for Educational Research and Innovation, 135
Chapman, J., 193
Charlton, D. et al., 162
Chief education officer(s), 139, 171, 172
Circulars: 10/65, 19, 130, 131; 10/70, 19; 4/74, 19
Coates, R. D., 171
Coleman, J. S., 44, 45, 90, 95
Colleges of further education, see Technical colleges
Collins, R., 56, 189
Community, 151–52; the school as a, 10, 25, 150–5, 159, 187
Comprehensive colleges, see Tertiary colleges
Comprehensive schools, 17–20; all-through, see Sixth form, integral
Conservative party, 19, 21, 130, 131, 132, 133, 188
Consumerism, see Ideology
Cook, B. C., 101
Cooperative College, 102, 111, 118–25, 185
Cooperative School, 60, 76, 118–25, 182
Corbett, A, 72, 81
Cotgrove, S., 99, 100
Crosland, A. and Boyle, E., 171
Crowther Report, 14, 17, 26, 28, 30, 49, 55, 56, 101
Croydon, 18, 63–6, 72, 130, 140, 171, 172, 188
Curriculum, 47–8, 191, 202

D'Aeth, R., 54
Dainton Report, 48
Dale, R. R., 195
Dalton, J. J., 71

David, M., 139, 171
Davies, B., 167
Davies, H. A., 15, 41, 42, 47, 50, 69
Davies, T. I., 59
Davis, R., 67
Department of Education and Science, 18, 116, 131, 136, 137, 140, 170, 171, 172, 188–9
Developmentalism, see Ideology
Direct grant schools, 21, 130, 132, 201
Donnison, D. V. et al., 63, 171
Douglas, J. W. B., 17, 184
Durkheim, Emile, 151, 155, 159, 162
Durojaiye, S. M., 43

Early leaving, see Trend, the
Early Leaving Report, 13, 15, 16, 17
East College, 102–14
Easthope, G., 157, 184, 194
Easton, W. A. G., 157
Eckstein, H., 171
Economy and education, 19, 55–7, 100, 189
Edmonds, J. V., 67, 82
Edwards, A. D., 18, 25, 26, 34, 70, 131
Egalitarianism, see Ideology
Eggleston, S. J., 90, 91, 202
Egner, W. E., 58, 194
Elkin, F. and Westley, W. A., 45
Eppel, E. M. and Eppel, M., 45
Epperson, D. C., 45
Etzioni, A., 156
Exeter College, 19, 81, 126, 127, 128, 130–5, 171, 172, 188, 201

Fleming Report, 21
Floud, J. E., 202; and Halsey, A. H., 17, 56; et al., 43, 95
Ford, B., 49
Ford, J., 9
Fowler, G., 98, 99

218

Index

Frost, D., 72
Further education colleges, see Technical colleges
Further Education Regulations, 129, 201

Gawthorpe, R. D., 67, 71
Glass, D. V., 16
Goldthorpe, J. et al., 16
Gouldner, A. W., 9, 165
Grace, G. R., 157
Grammar school(s), 20, 25-6, 201; ex-pupils in college, 101, 107-11
Griffiths, A., 18
Gunn, S. E., 59

Halsall, E., 89, 194
Hancock, A. and Wakeford, J., 169
Haslegrave Report, 168
Headmasters' Association, 59, 60, 70, 71, 72, 81, 82, 116, 117, 129, 163, 164, 194
Headmasters' Conference, 21, 165
Headteachers, 151, 152, 158-63, 164, 165, 195, 201
Herriott, R. E. and St John, N. H., 94, 95, 190
Hill, W. S., 170
Hilsum, S. and Start, K. B., 166
Hodgkinson, Thomas, 98
Hollingshead, A. B., 45
Hopkinson, D., 201
Hopper, E., 167
House system, 25, 42, 75
Hunt Report, 169

Identity, 10, 150, 158-63
Ideology, 10, 150-72, 173, 200; consumerism and voluntarism, 98-101, 159, 193; developmental, 158, 159; egalitarian, 191-2, 195, 196, 199, 200, 201, 203; meritocratic, 69, 191; of the college, 10, 150, 152-72; of the school, 10, 25, 150, 152-72, 193; paedeocentric, 153, 159
Immigrants, 43
Independent schools, 20-2; ex-pupils in college, 101, 107-11
Industrial Training Act, 59, 67, 71
Inner London Education Authority, 59, 67, 71
Institute of Municipal Treasurers and Accountants, 84, 130, 135
Interest groups, 10, 163-72, 189

Jackson, B., 26; and Marsden, D., 18, 41, 43
Jahoda, M. and Warren, N., 45
James, E., 59
Jencks, C. et al., 93
Jennings, A., 49
Jones, F. I., 66
Jones, H. R., 130

Kandel, D. B. and Lesser, G. S., 45
Kelsall, K., 16
King, R. A., 15, 16, 17, 18, 26, 28, 31, 32, 33, 34, 35, 41, 42, 43, 69, 83, 85, 88, 89, 135, 151, 154, 155, 157, 158, 160, 161, 165, 182, 184, 193, 194, 195, 196; and Easthope, G., 178, 182, 192; and Fry, J. D., 88
King, R. W., 64, 66, 70
Kluckholn, C., 155

Labour Party, 22, 132, 172, 188
Lacey, C., 155
Lambert, R., 25
Latey Report, 46
Lawrence, P., 101
Leach, E., 161
Lennard, A. G. K., 67, 68, 69
Lineham, P., 138
Little, A. et al., 90, 95; and Westergaard, J., 40
Little, A. H., 67, 68, 69, 70, 71

219

Index

Lukes, S., 152
Luton, 67
Lynch, J., 68

McGrath, K., 68
Mack, E. C., 24, 31
Maine, H. S., 151
Manzer, R. A., 165, 166
Marsden, D., 68, 69, 127
Mays, J. B. et al., 85
Mead, M., 44, 163
Merfield, P. H., 127, 128, 129, 133, 134, 135
Mexborough, 59, 67
Midwinter, E., 130
Miller, D., 72
Mitchell, G. D., 26
Mo, T., 129
Monks, T. G., 19, 59, 67, 84
Moore, D., 101, 128, 170
Morant, Robert, 26
Morton-Williams, R. et al., 16, 21, 22, 27, 28, 29, 30, 42, 46, 47, 48, 49, 50, 54, 70, 71; and Finch, S., 16, 155
Mumford, D. E., 126, 127
Murdock, D. E. and McCron, D., 46; and Phelps, G., 45
Murphy, J., 72, 129, 164, 194
Musgrave, P. W., 56, 100
Musgrove, F., 44, 45

National Association of Head-teachers, 164
National Association of School-masters, 70, 166
National Union of School Students, 193
National Union of Teachers, 70, 71, 72, 81, 82, 95, 129, 164, 165, 166, 198
Newstyle Sixth Form Unit, 51–4, 60, 76, 158, 195, 196
Nisbet, R., 151
Nissel, M., 17, 56, 57
Non-examination studies, 49

North College, 102–14
North Devon College, 19, 81, 126, 127, 128, 129, 135–40, 172
Nossex Consortium, 199
Norwood, Cyril, 160
Numbers mystery, 169

O'Connor, M., 70, 116
Open Sixth Form College, 72–80, 180, 182, 197
Organisation, of schools and colleges, 150–63, 173–8, 185, 193
Owen, J. G., 127

Paedeocentricity, see Ideology
Parsons, T., 44
Pastoral care, 103, 135, 142, 153, 177
Payne, S., 140
Pedley, R., 128
Peterson, A. D. C., 49, 58, 59, 60, 61, 70, 71
Phillips, C., 67, 68
Pilkington Report, 168
Plowden Report, 131
Policy, 11, 188, 200–3
Prefects, 25, 26, 30–4, 37, 75, 158
Principals, 99, 158–63, 167, 169
Pro-Tertiary College, 102–14, 141–9, 175
Provision, educational, 88–97, 191
Prust, A., 68
Public schools, 21, 24–6, 40, 75, 202
Public Schools Commission, 21
Pugh, D. S. et al., 105

Rée, H. A., 59
Resources, educational, 55–8, 70, 190
Ritual, 32, 153–4, 157, 159, 174, 196
Robbins Report, 17, 23, 40, 48, 56, 57

Index

Robinson, W. S., 178
Roderick, G. W. and Stephens, M. D., 100
Rogers, T., 199
Rolfe, J., 127
Ross, J. M. et al., 194
Rotherham, 68
Roy, W., 165
Ruffle, W. O., 72, 129
Russell, G. J., 175

St Trad's, 34–9, 51–3, 60, 76, 195, 196
Samuelson Report, 100
Saran, R., 171
School: assembly, 153, 161, 196; councils, 193; ideology of, 10, 25, 150, 152–72; college co-operation, 115–25, 199–200; students' retrospective experience of, 108–11, 193; uniform, 15, 26, 36, 50, 51, 154, 161, 196
Schools' Action Union, 193
Schools Council, 118, 171
Science, swing from, 48, 191
Scunthorpe, 67, 82
Secondary modern, 20; ex-pupils in colleges, 101, 107–11, 148
Selective Sixth Form College, 72–80, 197
Sex differences, 198; in colleges, 106–13; in integral sixth forms, 78–80, 183–5, 195; in sixth form colleges, 75, 78–80, 199; in Tertiary College, 146–7, 200
Sharp, P., 101, 115, 180
Shield, G. W., 58, 59, 60, 61, 67
Short-course comprehensives, 18, 81–8, 190, 202
Simon, B., 69
Sixth form, 24–54, 203; centres, 9, 18, 55, 58–62, 67, 188, 196–7; colleges, 9, 10, 18, 63–80, 158, 165, 197–8; idea of, 24–7; integral, 9, 18, 19, 24–39, 51–4, 76–80, 194–6; units, 9, 49–54, 67, 158, 188
Sixth formers, experience, 34–9, 51–4, 60–2, 72–80, 178–85, 193, 195–6, 197; opinions, 10, 28–30, 193; origins, 40–3
Smiles, Samuel, 99, 100
Smith, D., 129, 198, 201
Social class: and attainment, 89–90, 161; and friends, 192; and provision, 88–97
Social solidarity, 151–2
South College, 102–14
Southampton, 67, 68, 72, 158
Stevens, F., 24, 38, 41, 44
Stoke-on-Trent, 67, 68
Students' Unions, 111–14, 193
Sugarman, B. N., 45
Swann Report, 48
Swift, D. F., 178
Swinhoe, K., 101

Taylor, E., 70, 71, 72, 81
Taylor, J. H., 43
Taylor, L. C., 58, 194
Taylor, P. H. et al., 26
Taylor, W., 163
Teacher(s), opinions, 27–8, 49–50; supply, 57–8, 190
Technical colleges, 9, 10, 22, 98–114, 198–9; organisation, 173–8; tradition, 98–101
Technical college students, 10; experience, 102–11, 178–85, 193, 199; origins, 22, 101–2; part-time, 169
Tertiary College, 10, 141–9, 186–7
Tertiary colleges, 10, 91, 126–49, 200, 201, 202, 203
Thomas, R. H., 72, 116
'Times Educational Supplement', 70, 101
Tipton, B. F., 99, 152, 156, 157, 160, 162, 174
Tönnies, F., 151, 159
Toomey, D. M., 16

221

Trend, the, 13–17
Trow, M., 46, 47
Trustram, S. F., 101

Union of Women Teachers, 166
Universities, 38, 48, 49, 128, 159, 163, 170
Urwin, K., 63–6, 70, 130, 140, 171

Vale, M. L., 67, 68, 69, 71
Vaughan, M. and Archer, M. S., 163
Venables, E., 169
Veness, T., 45
Voluntarism, see Ideology

Waller, W., 44
Weber, Max, 9, 152, 155, 156, 157, 159, 164

Weinberg, I., 25
West College, 102–14, 180
Whitehouse, B. C., 115, 116
White Paper: of 1966, 22, 98, 100; of 1972, 56
Wilcock, H. R., 117, 118
Wilkinson, R. H., 153, 157
Wiseman, S., 89
Witney Model, 116–18
Woodhall, M. and Blaug, M., 56
Woodward, R., 72
Working class pupils, 19, 40–3, 47, 50

Young, M. and Willmott, P., 16
Young, M. F. D., 9
Youth: culture, 44–6; social position, 44, 46–7, 71, 201

Zweig, F., 16